FLYING MINNOWS

FLYING MINNOWS

BY
ROGER VEE

The Naval & Military Press Ltd

Published by

The Naval & Military Press Ltd
Unit 5 Riverside, Brambleside
Bellbrook Industrial Estate
Uckfield, East Sussex
TN22 1QQ England

Tel: +44 (0)1825 749494

www.naval-military-press.com
www.nmarchive.com

In reprinting in facsimile from the original, any imperfections are inevitably reproduced and the quality may fall short of modern type and cartographic standards.

TO
MY BROTHER

CONTENTS

Part I

CHAPTER		PAGE
I	IN WHICH I JOIN THE ROYAL FLYING CORPS	17
II	FIRST FLYING EXPERIENCES AT CAMP MOHAWK	23
III	WE PROCEED TO CAMP BORDEN	44
IV	WE ARRIVE IN ENGLAND	60
V	THE LAST LAP, IN SCOTLAND	90

Part II

VI	FRANCE AT LAST	99
VII	OVER THE LINES	118
VIII	MARCH 21ST, 1918	129
IX	MORE GROUND-STRAFING	154
X	THE LAST BID FOR VICTORY	186
XI	A RECONNAISSANCE AND AN O-PIP	192
XII	CASUALTY CLEARING STATIONS, HOSPITALS, AND A NEW SQUADRON	209
XIII	DOG-FIGHTS AND RUNNING FIGHTS	232
XIV	CLOUD FLYING AND LOW RECONNAISSANCES	255
XV	THE LAST DAYS BEFORE THE ARMISTICE	274
XVI	APRÈS LA GUERRE	290
	APPENDIX: EXTRACTS FROM THE R.A.F. COMMUNIQUÉS	307

LIST OF ILLUSTRATIONS

facing page

"... IT ALL LOOKED VERY DESOLATE ..." . 106

BRISTOL FIGHTER NO. 22 AT BERTANGLES . . 152

THE RAID ON HAUBOURDIN AERODROME ON AUGUST
16TH, 1918 238

THE RAID ON LOMME AERODROME, AUGUST 17TH, 1918 . 242

"FAR BELOW ... THE LITTLE FIELDS ... LIKE A PATCH-
WORK QUILT" 246

THE AMMUNITION TRAIN AT ENGHIEN, SHOWING TRUCK
ON WHICH DIRECT HIT WAS OBTAINED, BLOWN OFF
THE LINE 276

THE DIRECT HIT ON AMMUNITION TRAIN AT ENGHIEN,
ANOTHER VIEW FROM A DIFFERENT ANGLE AND
FROM A LOWER ALTITUDE 280

A RAID ON MARCQ AERODROME (CANVAS HANGARS) OUT-
SIDE ENGHIEN 286

WHEN 2ND-LIEUT. DAWSON GLIDED DOWN INTO THE
MIST 292

TRAIN WRECKAGE AT ENGHIEN, PHOTOGRAPHED AFTER
THE ARMISTICE 292

THREE BRISTOL FIGHTERS OF "A" FLIGHT TAKING OFF IN
FORMATION 298

"WE WOULD FREQUENTLY MAKE THE FIELD IN WHICH
IT STOOD A RESTING-PERCH" 302

ANOTHER VIEW OF THE MOUND AT WATERLOO   302

A FOKKER-BIPLANE AT NIVELLES . 306

PART I

THE BALLAD OF A BRISTOL

There's a good half-dozen buses
On which I've done a whack,
From the R.E.8 to the three-ton weight
Of the lumbering old Big Ack ;
On a rotary-engined Avro
I've attempted several tricks,
And I'm quite a dab at steering a Crab
(Better known as a D.H.6).

And many a first-rate joy-ride
Have I had on 'em, last and first,
And many a strut have I had go phut,
And many a wheel-tyre burst ;
But none of 'em knows the secret
Of making my heart rejoice
Like a well-rigged Bristol Fighter
With a two-six-four Rolls Royce.

She leans at her place on the tarmac
Like a tiger crouched for a spring,
From the arching spine of her fuselage line
To the ample spread of her wing.
With her tyres like sinews tautened
And her tail-skid's jaunty twist,
Her grey-cowled snout juts grimly out
Like a tight-clenched boxer's fist.

Is there a sweeter music,
A more contenting sound,
Than the purring clop of her broad-curved prop
As it gently ticks around ?
Open her out crescendo
To a deep-toned swelling roar,
Till she quivers and rocks as she strains at the chocks
And clamours amain to soar.

Whisk 'em away, my hearties,
Taxi her into the wind,
Then away we skim on a spinning rim
With the tail well up behind ;
Hold her down to a hundred,
Then up in a climbing turn,
And off we sweep in a speckless sky
Till we catch our breath in the air Alp-high ;
I wouldn't exchange my seat, not I,
For a thousand pounds to burn.

                              H.T.B.

PREFACE

THIS is no tale of heroes. It is the plain narrative of the experiences of an undistinguished pilot, and of some of his brother officers of the Royal Air Force, during the war. It tells, too, something of their everyday life in the topsy-turvy days. Occasionally one of the great flying men flares into these pages, and out again, leaving the rest of us looking paler than ever. But the deeds of these Aces have been recorded elsewhere. Little has been written about the smaller fry.

The names of the persons appearing in this book are the only fictitious things about it.[1]

My thanks are due to the Air Ministry for permission to publish :

(1) Details of the system of signals used in artillery observation work.

(2) The extracts from the Royal Air Force official *communiqués*.

(3) The seven official aerial photographs appearing in this book.

The verses entitled " The Ballad of a Bristol " were written by Harold Tetley Burt, who after the War became Associate Professor of Philosophy at Manchester University. He died in February, 1923. The verses appeared in *The Aeroplane* shortly after the Armistice, and I am indebted to the Editor, Mr. C. G. Grey, and also to the

[1] Whenever the actual names of persons are used, they are indicated, on their first appearance in the book, by an asterisk.

parents of the late Mr. H. T. Burt, for permission to reproduce the verses here.

For some of the information regarding the late Capt. A. W. Beauchamp-Proctor, V.C., I am indebted to Mr. A. Carter, of the University of Cape Town, of which institution Capt. Beauchamp-Proctor was a former student.

And above all, for help in the launching of this book I wish to thank Mr. C. G. Grey, that good friend of aces and flying minnows.

CHAPTER I

IN WHICH I JOIN THE ROYAL FLYING CORPS

(i)

IN May, 1917, I was nearing the end of a course of study at the Johns Hopkins University, Baltimore, in the United States of America.

Some months previous to this I had determined to enlist as soon as the academic year came to an end, but for some time had been undecided whether to join the gunners, the infantry or the Flying Corps.

One day I happened to pick up a book on flying experiences, by Gustav Hamel, and was so enthralled by his description of the life of an airman that I decided definitely to throw in my lot with the Royal Flying Corps, if they would have me.

Not long before this they had begun training pilots in Canada. This simplified, for me, the question of enlisting. The fares to England were almost prohibitive, a single fare at that time being about seventy pounds. Students are an impecunious tribe, and I was no exception to the rule. So it was fortunate for me that I only had to go up to Toronto, the headquarters in Canada of the Royal Flying Corps.

About the middle of May I packed up my books and other belongings and took them to the house of a friend who had offered to look after them for me till the end of the war. Then I said good-bye to the friends I was leaving in that city, in which I had spent three very pleasant years, and boarded the night train for Canada.

After breakfast on my first morning in Toronto I made

my way to the Royal Flying Corps headquarters. The officer who interviewed me asked me particulars as to my nationality, age and so forth. He then asked me for a birth certificate. Of course I told him that, in the nature of the case, it would take me several months to get one, but he insisted that it was essential, as they definitely only took men between the ages of eighteen and twenty-five.

This was an unexpected difficulty. Then I thought of Mr. Tom Ball,* the registrar of the university from which I had just come, and I asked the officer if a certificate from Mr. Ball, as to my age, would do. He smiled but agreed to this. Mr. Ball, of course, would know no more than he did what my age was, but I felt quite certain that he would not let me down. So I left the office rather disconsolately to write the letter.

I put a two-cent stamp on it, posted it, and resigned myself to await the reply. To my dismay the letter was returned to me the following day as being insufficiently stamped. I had not known that there was a special war letter rate in force. Owing to this delay I was at a loose end for about a week in Toronto before the letter arrived. A great many times during this week I was stopped by men in uniform and asked whether I would not enlist.

There were a great many permanently disabled men about the town in hospital blues, most of them minus a leg or an arm. I noticed at least two who had neither arms nor legs. One began to notice, or imagine, reproachful glances from these men. And so, altogether, I was much relieved when, on the 23rd May, the letter at last arrived from Mr. Ball declaring that I had been born on the 24th January, 1894.

I blessed Tom Ball and, armed with his letter, hurried back to H.Q. where, after passing easily the medical examination, I became a cadet in the Royal Flying Corps.

I JOIN THE ROYAL FLYING CORPS

(ii)

Five of us joined on the same day. Of the five, three were Canadians, one an American, Fred Lydell from Philadelphia, and myself a South African.

After the various formalities of signing on, we were taken in a large motor-lorry to the Equipment Depot. Here we were each given a uniform (ordinary private's khaki to begin with), a stout pair of boots, and a kit-bag containing a change of underwear, a spare shirt, a razor, a shaving brush, a toothbrush, and various odds and ends.

One of the three Canadians I noticed particularly while we were at the Depot. He was an undersized little chap with a furtive, cowed air. It struck me at the time that one could hardly imagine a less promising-looking airman. To digress for a moment, I lost sight of him when we left Toronto, as we were sent to different flying camps. Many months later I met a Canadian in London who had joined up at the same time, and asked him if he knew what had happened to the little fellow. He told me that he had been put under a rather caddish instructor who had taken a dislike to him and had sent him up solo before he was ready for it. The result was that he had crashed badly and after a spell in hospital had been released from the Flying Corps. Nothing daunted, the little chap had worked his passage across to England and had joined the Royal Naval Air Service, where, coming under a kindlier instructor, he had developed into a very fine pilot. Of such stuff are heroes made.

From now on, for just over four weeks, we had a fairly strenuous time. Réveillé sounded at six-thirty and we had to be on breakfast parade at seven-fifteen, properly shaved, and with our boots and buttons shining. The cadets in this course (which was Course 5, School of Military Aeronautics) were mostly boys who had just left school, and some of them had nothing to shave. But the eagle eye of Sergeant-Major Griffen always detected the tiniest bit of down on the smoothest chin. Some men are born old-soldiers, and one or two of these among us sometimes tried a " talcum-powder shave " when pressed for time, but it never got past Sergeant-Major Griffen.

This man was an efficient sergeant-major but he had no personality. The sergeant-major of the blood-and-thunder type may put the fear of God into recruits, but he will often command their respect. Nobody respected Griffen. He ruled purely by virtue of his authority as a sergeant-major.

After breakfast we had physical training for forty minutes, and then a wing parade at which we were inspected by our officers. After this we had lectures and drill till 12.30, when we stopped for lunch. At 1.30 we began again, lectures or drill till 5 p.m. We were free then till dinner, at 6.30. After dinner we were nominally free till 10.30 p.m. But each evening we had to copy out, in ink, into large note-books, the notes taken during the day. This usually kept us busy till " lights-out " at 11 p.m.

We had comfortable quarters in East Residence of Toronto University and the food was good. After a few days about thirty of us were moved to Burwash Hall, also of Toronto University. The rooms were large and there were only two men in a room.

The discipline I found very irksome at first. If a man smiled on parade he was given some extra fatigue.

Shortly after I joined there was a room inspection early one morning. My room-mate and I got a severe telling off because our coats were lying on a chair instead of being neatly hung up.

About the middle of June, all the men in our course were marched down to a military tailor in the town and measured for their Flying Corps uniforms. We were very

I JOIN THE ROYAL FLYING CORPS

pleased at the prospect of getting these smart tunics, riding-breeches and forage caps, commonly known as split-ass caps, after the ill-fitting privates' uniforms which had first been issued to us. These new uniforms cost about fifty-five dollars, fifteen of which we ourselves had to pay. This was deducted in weekly instalments from our pay, which at this stage of our training was one dollar ten cents per day.

On Saturdays we were free from lunch-time till 11.30 p.m., and on Sundays, too. On Sunday mornings, after the first parade we were free to do as we liked, provided we remained in barracks. We usually spent Sunday mornings in letter-writing, reading, or talking. We used to discuss with great zest the latest stories from the various flying camps. Most of the cadets thought that this preliminary groundwork of ours would be the most difficult part of the course. The general opinion was that any fool could fly, but that it took brains to get through the theoretical examinations.

Actually this theoretical work was interesting and not difficult. We had instruction on the two main types of machine-guns, the Vickers and the Lewis. The former was the type used by pilots and the latter by observers. We were also given practical demonstrations with these guns. There were lectures also on the Constantinesco Gear, a most ingenious device for interrupting the automatic firing of a Vickers gun so that it fired only in between the blades of a propeller, even when the latter was revolving at full speed. Again, we had to listen to simple discourses on the theory of flight, and on the construction and rigging of aeroplanes. I remember the general scepticism when we were told that the air pressure on the lower surfaces of the wings of an aeroplane was responsible for only one-third of the lifting force, while the remaining two-thirds were due to the suction above the wings. Various types of service aeroplanes were described to us. Then we had several lectures on the internal combustion engine, with particular reference to certain types of aero engines.

We were given some lectures on simple wireless sending and receiving sets, and, with the help of buzzers, were taught to send and receive messages in Morse code. Some time also was spent on map-reading, artillery co-operation and observation, formation of troops, aerial reconnaissance, bomb-dropping, aerial fighting, cross-country flying, and aerial photography.

Of these lectures, easily the most popular were those on aerial fighting. A good many of these were given by an officer observer who had just come back from France. He used to illustrate them by accounts of actual scraps which he had witnessed, told in a delightful, unassuming way. He would describe a fight up to a certain stage only, simply to illustrate his point, but sometimes at the end of the lecture we managed to coax him to tell us the rest of the story.

CHAPTER II

FIRST FLYING EXPERIENCES AT CAMP MOHAWK

(i)

WHEN Course 5 broke up, some of the cadets were posted to Long Branch, a flying camp north of Toronto, and the remainder of us, about twenty, left for Camp Mohawk. The train journey was tedious. It took us five hours to cover the hundred and forty miles. We travelled comfortably in a Pullman observation car, and when we got tired of talking and looking out of the windows one of the fellows produced some dice and we gathered round and " rolled the bones."

Two fellows, Gibbon and Scott, were always on hand if there was any gambling going on, Gibbon because he was a born gambler, and Scott because he was inseparable from Gibbon. Gibbon was a thick-set fellow of average height, with a strong face. When he spoke to you he had a habit of narrowing his eyes, but they never wavered from yours. Scott was tall and slight, but well-built. He was excitable and had a devil-may-care look about him. They were a hard-bitten pair.

We reached Deseronto about three o'clock that afternoon and were taken by motor-lorry to Camp Mohawk.

Captain Barnard was the commanding officer at this camp and we reported at his orderly room on arrival. He had the reputation of having a blazing temper, and this had led to the corruption of his name to Captain Bastard. He was quite civil to us when we arrived and gave us a short address on what he expected from us.

" Here you will have to learn to fly straight, and do

turns, take-offs and landings. The frills like formation flying, cross-country work, aerial gunnery and so forth, you will get at your next camp."

Before dismissing us he asked a very cocksure youngster named Davey, amid smiles from the rest of us, if he was sure he was eighteen.

After a corporal had provided us with glass goggles, we walked over to the hangars and met the Flight Commander, Lt. Cotes, and three of the instructors, Lt. Stuart, Sergeant Martin and Corporal Burman.

It was all new to us and we examined everything eagerly. Most of us had never been on an aerodrome before. The machines were lined up on the tarmac, outside the hangars. These were all Curtiss machines of the J.N.4A. type, commonly called Buffalo Curtisses. They had a wheel control instead of the simple joystick.

Presently the instructors began taking cadets up for short joy-rides. More and more of our fellows went up and my heart sank lower as the time went on and I was still not called. After a while Captain Barnard came out of his office, drawing on his flying gloves as he strolled towards the aerodrome. To my delight he beckoned to me, and without saying a word pointed to a machine. I had seen the other cadets getting into the front cockpits, so did the same. He climbed into the pilot's seat at the back and a mechanic shouted ·

" Switch off, sir, petrol on, suck in."

He repeated this and two mechanics pulled the propeller round a few times. Then the first mechanic took hold of the vertical blade of the propeller with his right hand and the second grasped his left hand. The mechanic shouted :

" Contact ! "

The C.O. repeated this, they gave a sudden heave, and the propeller whirred round as the engine began popping. This operation is known as " swinging the prop." The two mechanics now went to the tail of the machine and

FLYING AT CAMP MOHAWK

lay across it while the C.O. opened the throttle. The engine roared for about fifteen seconds, then Capt. Barnard throttled down and waved his arm. This was a signal for the mechanics to kick the chocks away from in front of the wheels. Now he taxied out a few yards and then opened the throttle fully.

The machine sped across the field, faster and faster, the tail-skid left the ground, and we ran along on the wheels. Then we rose in a long hop, bumped ground again once or twice, and then left it. The earth dropped rapidly away below us, the air rushed past, and my ears were filled with the roaring of the engine.

We climbed, I suppose, to about 3,000 feet. I did not feel the least nervousness and was much interested in the curious appearance of the earth from the air. What struck me most forcibly was the astonishing number of twists and windings in a river below us.

Captain Barnard flew the machine towards Lake Ontario which was several miles away, and when we were over it he shut off the engine and began gliding down. The sudden cessation of the roar was a relief. Presently the bracing-wires began to whine. Down we went, lower and lower, until I began to wonder if anything had happened to the C.O. I had heard that height above water was always deceptive, but it began to look as though at any instant we might splash into the lake. At the last possible moment, so it seemed to me, he opened the throttle, and we roared aloft again. Soon we were over the land and he began doing some sharp turns, banking the machine steeply. After several of these he spiralled down to within a couple of hundred feet of the ground and started for home. Some people in a field waved to us as we passed overhead. At last we came in sight of the hangars again. Captain Barnard flew round behind them, so as to land into the wind, turned, and shut off the engine. We glided down over the hangars and landed very neatly. On the ground he turned the machine and with little jerks at the throttle taxied back to the hangars. When we got near them two mechanics came running out, one to each wing-tip, to help in leaving her in position, facing into the wind. As we climbed out I glanced at my watch. We had been up an hour and a quarter. I was bitterly cold.

" Thank you very much, sir," I said.

" Were you cold ? " he asked.

" No, sir," I replied.

All the machines were down when we got back and I was just in time to join the last group of fellows leaving the aerodrome.

As we walked along, the talk was all about the joy-rides we had had. One youngster, still very excited, was telling of some stunting that Sergeant Martin had done with him.

" Up in the air," he said, " he biffed me on the shoulder and signed to me to hold tight. I clawed on to the seat and the bus shot nose up into the air ! One second the earth was under my back and the next second over my head. I thought he was looping the loop, but when we got down and I asked him, he said, ' You don't catch me looping a Buffalo. That was a half-roll ! ' "

" Did you hear what happened to Peplar ? Pep thought he was at a party and was sick all over the place. How you feeling, old top ? "

" Not too bad," grinned Peplar, who still looked rather washed out.

" What happened, Pep ? "

" Oh, the corporal chap took me up, and began bucking the bus up and down like a gee. Every time we came down I thought my tummy had slipped out, and in the last dive it gave a heave and I shot my lunch. Well, anyway," he chuckled, "a good chunk of it caught him as it flew past. That larned him and he came down at once."

" Hell's bells ! Was he mad with you, Pep ? "

FLYING AT CAMP MOHAWK

"I guess so, but he didn't say anything. He cleared off to wash himself as soon as we landed."

The mess was in a building near the sleeping quarters. The cadets sat at two long tables, while the officers were at a smaller table at the end of the hall.

It had been a tremendous day, and flying was all and more than I had expected of it. When I turned in that night I felt at peace with the wide world.

(ii)

At three o'clock the next morning I heard a confused row, half-mixed with my dreams, going on at one end of the room. Suddenly I heard a cadet called Westlake whisper fiercely:

"It's too God-damned early!"

I sat up in bed and saw a mechanic, with a lantern in his hand, arguing with him. Westlake tried to snuggle down again and the mechanic gave him a final shake and went on to the next bed. Outside it was still pitch-dark, and there was a chilly draught through the room. Several fellows were stirring now and soon we were all hurrying into our clothes. A cadet, Dicky Smith, who had been at Mohawk about a week, had told us that a couple of jugs of milk and some bread and butter and jam were put out in the mess for the fellows on early flying. There was never much butter or jam and this was an incentive to turn out early. Late comers got only milk and dry bread. I remembered reading in Hamel's book about the danger of flying on an empty stomach. It was said to cause dizziness and sometimes fainting in the air.

We had to be on the aerodrome at three-thirty, so after a hurried snack we ran down to the hangars. The dawn was just breaking as we got there.

The early morning and late evening were chosen for instruction purposes as there were remarkably few "air-pockets" at these times. At other times a machine would occasionally bump alarmingly, especially on hot or windy days.

My instructor was Corporal Burman. He took me up that first morning to do "straights." There was dual control in all the machines, and as we climbed in he said:

"Don't you touch the controls till we are well up. I'll tell you when to put your feet on the rudder bar."

"Switch off. Petrol on. Suck in!" shouted the mechanic, and the pilot repeated this.

"Contact!" The pilot ran up the engine for a few minutes to warm her, then the chocks were kicked away from the wheels and we taxied out and took off.

It was delightful flying in the grey morning light. After a while Corporal Burman shut off the engine and shouted to me to put my feet on the rudder bar. I did this and tried desperately to keep her on a straight course, but without much success. She seemed to go where she wanted to with me. After about twenty minutes of this he took control again and landed the machine. I was feeling rather ashamed of myself but he told me I had not done badly.

I felt sure that this was only said to give me confidence.

After a considerable time, during which he was instructing other cadets that morning, he took me up once more, but again I put up a poor performance.

Shortly after this the order to "Fall in" was given, and we marched back to our quarters for a wash and a shave before breakfast.

Every day we attended a few lectures and were given some drill. We also spent some time on the machine-gun range. Each evening there was more flying. And so the days went on.

Davey was shaping rather well. His instructor, Sergeant Martin, thought him very promising and, unfortunately, let him know it. Aggravating at the best

FLYING AT CAMP MOHAWK

of times, young Davey now became positively offensive. He was liberal with hints and advice to all of us. Before long, however, he received an effective damper.

A cadet named Barrett was easily the most promising pilot of us all. Usually cadets were sent up on their first solo after approximately five hours' instruction. Barrett's instructor thought him quite capable of taking a machine up by himself after only one hour and ten minutes' dual work.

He was the first of us to go solo and we watched him anxiously as he climbed into the pilot's seat. After a perfect take-off, he made a gradual circuit of the aerodrome, and shut off his engine to come down. He came gliding in exceptionally slowly and my heart was in my mouth as I watched him, for my one predominant dread was of losing flying speed and stalling the machine. But he got down safely, making a good landing.

Camp Mohawk was a pretty place, right out in the country. A long bay, almost like a river, stretched up from Lake Ontario, and passed close to the camp.

We were all agreed that our flying training here was much pleasanter than the dull routine of Toronto. Of course, the early stages of the flying game were bound to have their uneasy moments, but it was a relief to escape the rigid discipline which had been so irksome during our ground-course.

Most mornings we were on the aerodrome at three-thirty. I was beginning to feel worried as I was making so little progress. It was difficult to hear one another in the machine and Cpl. Burman and I arranged some signals. If he jerked the wheel I was to take control. If he jerked the rudder-bar I was to let go the controls. If I let go the controls I was to put my hands above my head so that he might know.

The signals worked successfully and we did some straights and turns. After breakfast I had to go up again with him, and then things came to a climax with us. It was a hot morning and bumpy. I had never experienced bumps before, and when these bumps jerked the rudder bar I thought it was the signal from Cpl. Burman and put up my hands. This happened three or four times and then he landed the bus. He climbed out, with a face like thunder, and shouted to me :

"What the bloody hell's the matter with you ? I'm sitting without touching the controls and suddenly you let go everything and up go your bloody hands. What the hell did you mean by it ? We could have broken our bloody necks." He was livid with rage. I tried to explain what had happened but he was much too angry to listen to me. Finally, I lost my temper too and we cursed one another up and down. Presently Lt. Stuart came up. He was a tall man, with a chin like a prize-fighter's. He enquired what the row was about, and made each of us give an account of what had happened.

"You may go, Cpl. Burman. In future, Vee, Sgt. Martin and I will be your instructors."

As a result of this incident Cpl. Burman lost his stripes. I was sorry to hear this, but very likely he deserved it.

From now on my progress was more rapid. I was taught for the first time that the correct thing to do was to let the machine fly itself and simply *control* it, not to try to *fly* it all the time.

I often found bits from Hamel's book useful in my training. Thus it was firmly impressed upon my mind that it was fatal to lose flying speed near the ground. Often beginners were afraid of tilting an aeroplane, " banking " it, in a turn. The first time one banked a machine, certainly it looked as though the earth had suddenly slipped drunkenly under one, but actually it was far more dangerous not to do it. For if the machine were not banked it would side-slip outwards in the turn and might get into a flat spin. Even if it did not spin it might lose flying-speed and would then drop like a

FLYING AT CAMP MOHAWK

stone. To continue this digression for a moment (and writing in the light of flying experience gained later), many a life and many a machine might have been saved had instructors drummed this fairly obvious fact into the heads of all new recruits. I think it should have been stressed as the cardinal principle of flying.

An experienced pilot, who was giving us some flying tips in England once, told us that if an engine failed directly after taking off (and this was not an unheard of occurrence) one should *on no account* attempt to turn back into the aerodrome. If necessary, he said, land the machine straight ahead, into a brick wall. The famous pilot, Major McCudden,* V.C., lost his life in trying to turn back into an aerodrome.

This is merely a particular case of the more general principle of keeping up flying speed. For if the engine has failed, it is only too easy to stall the machine in making the turn.

Once at Ayr, Scotland, in the School of Aerial Fighting, Captain Birmingham, M.C., took me up in a white-nosed Bristol Fighter, which had a nasty reputation for "conking" just after getting off the ground. She did it on this occasion too, about five hundred feet up. Captain Birmingham immediately put the nose well down so that she began gliding at more than her minimum flying speed. Then he turned, banking very steeply, and landed back on the aerodrome. With these precautions, it was a perfectly safe proceeding.

This is, of course, by no means the whole story in flying. In my case I was exceptionally slow in learning the gentle art, but I know that the conviction of the truth of this principle saved me from many a crash.

As will also appear from the narrative, however, a knowledge of the principle was, on occasion, a positive handicap in certain parts of the training. For instance, it took me a long time to learn to keep my position in formation flying, simply because of the fear I had of throttling back the engine and stalling the machine. Also at first I used to come gliding down, to land, much too fast, for the same reason. But there is no doubt at all that the benefits far exceeded the disadvantages.

(iii)

Most of my friends were by this time ready for their first solo flights.

It was rather nerve-racking watching a pal taking off alone, for the first time.

Young Davey was an aggravating little fellow in many ways, but we were all fond of him. When he went solo most of us were on the aerodrome watching him. He opened the throttle and sped away over the field, tail up. Just as he was leaving the ground his machine swerved viciously, and Davey could not correct this. He pulled her off the ground, and then she swung right round in a flat spin and crashed badly. Davey was extraordinarily lucky to get off with a scratch over the eye. This was the incident referred to earlier, which ended his cocksureness—for a few days. The next day he was sent up again and this time he was successful.

About this time, too, Cameron, Lydell, Scott, Gibbon and Si Perkins made successful first solo flights.

Westlake was not meant to be a pilot. He never developed the air-sense at all. On his first solo he took off quite well and after a couple of circuits of the aerodrome he brought her down. On landing, he bounced badly, and instead of keeping the nose down, he pulled the wheel into his stomach with the result that the machine, which was still travelling fairly fast, shot straight up into the air and stalled. Then it plunged straight down, hitting the ground with a sickening crump. It was a nasty mess, but, miraculously, Westlake escaped unhurt. He joined the rest of us who were sitting on a wall near

FLYING AT CAMP MOHAWK

the hangar. Presently, Lt. Stuart strolled up, " Not hurt, Westlake ? That's good. All part of the day's work, you know." A few minutes later he beckoned to Westlake and sent him up again. This time he, too, was successful.

My new instructors gave me some more lessons in straight flying and turns, and then put me on to take-offs and landings. Teaching a cadet to take off a machine and to land it must have been very trying work for an instructor.

At last one morning Lt. Stuart got out of the machine in the middle of the aerodrome and said to me :

"Vee, you had better take her up now. I wouldn't send you up if I had not every confidence in you. (The usual formula ! I thought.) You should not have any difficulty about it. Hold her straight while you are taking off, and then climb slowly till you reach a safe height. Then bring her round very slowly to the back of the hangars. You need only make one circuit. Well, off you go ! "

While he was talking, my heart was gradually sinking. By the time he had finished it was in my boots. I hoped he did not notice how my teeth were chattering as I climbed over into the pilot's seat. Things looked strange from the back seat and the nose of the machine seemed so far away—then I opened the throttle. I managed to take off pretty well. I had a horrible feeling that this big thing was running away with me. She swayed a bit as we got into the air, and I kept her straight and we climbed slowly for several minutes. I was thrilled with a sense of great adventure on this first solo flight. After a while, when I thought we had reached a safe height, I made a very gradual turn. It was all very well banking steeply when there was an instructor in the back seat, but not quite so well when one was absolutely alone up in the air. It seemed safer to make a gradual turn with less bank. I flew round to the back of the hangars and then made another gradual turn. When I got her near the hangars I shut off the engine. She seemed to be sinking so rapidly that I was afraid of hitting the hangars and so " gave her the gun " (*i.e.*, opened the throttle), till she was over the hangars.

Now I shut off again and began gliding down, but although the aerodrome was large, I was too high now to land on it, and realising that I was going to overshoot it, gave her the gun once more and made another circuit.

The same thing happened the second time. The third time I shut off some distance from the hangars, and this time got into the aerodrome. But my fear of stalling the machine made me land it too fast and she ran for a long distance on her wheels, finally running into a bush.

This worried me very little. I was delighted to have the first solo safely behind me. It had never before occurred to me how comfortingly solid and secure the earth could feel under one's feet.

The propeller was chipped and one wing slightly scratched. Some mechanics had to go out and get her clear of the bush before they could taxi her back to the hangars.

In the afternoon, Lt. Stuart sent me up again. This time I felt more confident and got off the ground quite well. I made one circuit and then, judging the height over the hangars better, glided down till she touched her wheels on the ground. But she bounced badly and shot off again. I gave her the gun, meaning to go round once more. We had been told to open the throttle gradually, so as not to choke the engine. So I pushed it forward slowly, and was so intent on getting safely off the ground again that I did not notice that I had not opened it fully. The result was that the machine was hardly climbing at all. It was heading straight for a thickly-wooded hill. The hill was some distance off and I thought I should be able to climb over it in time.

FLYING AT CAMP MOHAWK

I was afraid of turning too near the ground. Suddenly realising that the machine was not climbing properly, I thought of the throttle and was horrified to find that it was only three-quarters of the way open. I pushed it right open and awaited results—my eyes switching continuously from the trees ahead to the controls, and back again. My whole mind was occupied with the one question of whether or not I should be able to clear the trees.

They came nearer and nearer, and when I was very close to them I thought I should just get over them. The gap between us was disappearing in a rush and suddenly the undercarriage smashed into one of the topmost branches. The machine turned a half-somersault and crashed upside down through the trees right to the ground. Luckily the belt round my waist held. My first thought was to switch off the engine to prevent fire. I did this, then loosening the belt with some difficulty, crawled out. I felt pretty sick, and putting my hand to my face found it covered with blood. There seemed to be a deep hole below my left eye and at first I thought the eye was gone. By holding my hand over the other eye I could see dimly through the left. Then I crawled away from the bus, but felt rather shaky and lay down. After a while I heard voices near the machine and heard Lt. Cotes say:

" Good God! Where's Vee ? "

So I called out to them and he and Lt. Stuart came running across to me. Between them they helped me up and we started down the hill. As I stumbled along between them I said to Lt. Cotes:

" I'm awfully sorry, sir, about your machine."

" Damn it, Vee, it's all in the game—and your neck's of more consequence than the bus ! "

It was a sporting view to take of the mishap, and was characteristic of this popular officer.

" Hungry Liz," the name of the ambulance which was

always in readiness on the aerodrome, was waiting at the bottom of the hill, and took us to the camp hospital.

After a while some of the fellows came to see me and I asked one of them to hold up a mirror for me. I got a shock on seeing my face, as it had been bashed almost out of recognition against the cowling of the machine.

After a week in hospital, the M.O. suggested that he should give me ten days' leave. This I refused, partly because I really had nowhere to go to, being a stranger in Canada, and partly because I did not want to lag still farther behind the rest of my cadet friends.

So when they discharged me from hospital they gave me a day off, which I spent in camp, and then I was declared fit for duty.

Quite a number of new cadets had arrived from Toronto during my absence. One of these, Melton, told me that six of them had arrived on the aerodrome just in time to see my crash. He said it had put the wind up them badly. Everybody who had seen it had felt sure that I had been killed.

For a few days I was not allowed to fly. Then one day, just as we were starting on an hour's drill, Lt. Cotes came up and called out two cadets to fly. He glanced at me and I think he must have seen my disappointment for he grinned and said:

" All right, Vee, up you go."

Naturally my reason for wanting to fly was that I was already behind the rest of my pals, and if I did not soon make up the difference, they would go on to the next camp and I should be left behind with a lot of new cadets whom I did not know.

I completed this flight successfully, but it was just about midday, when air-pockets were always bad, and I found some of the bumps alarming.

Every day we spent an hour or two on the machine-gun range. It was about a mile and a half from the aerodrome,

FLYING AT CAMP MOHAWK

and whenever we marched there, or back, we always sang. This verse, sung almost in a monotone, was a good one to march to:

> " Do you ever think
> As a hearse goes by
> That it won't be long
> Until you and I
> Go rolling by
> In a nice new shirt
> And then they lay us
> Right under the dirt,
> And the worms crawl out
> And the worms crawl in
> And the worms crawl over
> Your mouth and chin.
> And as for your soul
> No man can tell
> Whether it goes
> To heaven or hell."

Dicky Smith was usually the leader in these songs. He had a great variety and taught us many of them on these marches. Some of them would scarcely bear reproduction but we sang them all with great gusto.

At meal-times we always remained standing until the C.O. had taken his seat. The food was good but there was never much butter on the long table. Each man would stand with his knife in his hand, and directly the C.O. sat down everyone would make a lunge at the nearest butter-dish. The slow fellows, therefore, went without butter. I took rather a dislike to a chap called Leisk. He had joined the Flying Corps because of a deformed foot which would have debarred him from the infantry but was no handicap in an aeroplane. He was tall and extraordinarily quick. Usually he would lift the whole piece of butter from the dish. It was quite too much for him but he never suggested sharing it with anyone, and, of course, as it was fairly won, it was his prize. This small incident made me think him rather a selfish fellow and I never sought his company. Later, in England, he and I were thrown together a good deal at one of the training camps and I found him to be a most likeable chap. Afterwards, in France, he did extraordinarily well, getting an M.C. and later a D.F.C.

We used to have some very jolly concerts in the evenings. One of the older cadets had been a music-hall artist and he was an invaluable man on these occasions. Vernon Castle,* too, was at Mohawk at this time as an instructor, and so our concerts were of a high standard. Shortly after we left Camp Mohawk, Vernon Castle was killed.

(iv)

One afternoon, as I was taking off, the bus swerved badly on the ground. I thought I had better shut off, taxi back, and start again. Instead of easing back the wheel I pulled it too suddenly and the machine, which had already gathered flying speed, shot into the air. I immediately opened the throttle and pushed forward the wheel to get the nose down, so as not to stall the machine. This was a bad start, but there was worse to come. I was flying towards a village, Napanee, not many miles off, when I noticed that a storm seemed to be brewing in the distance. It seemed to be a long way off, behind me, and I did not pay any attention to it but continued on my course until I had circled the village. Now I was flying back, towards the storm, and became rather uneasy when I realised how near it was. The air, too, became very bumpy, and in those days bad bumps were serious matters to us. Soon I was under the heavy black clouds, and it began to rain. Owing to the speed of the machine the rain seemed to shoot horizontally at me, and it stung severely. The bus began to lurch

FLYING AT CAMP MOHAWK

about badly and occasionally it would plunge into, and through, some of the lower-lying clouds. I was peering ahead for sight of the aerodrome but presently it became difficult to see the ground owing to the rain and mist below. After a few unpleasant minutes of this the machine plunged into a dense black cloud. For a second or two I could see nothing at all but the swirling vapour around me. Then, just as suddenly, we shot out of the cloud and to my joy I saw the hangars ahead. So I throttled back and glided down through the rain. It was with a feeling of great relief that I felt the wheels touch the ground. I taxied back to the hangars and as I climbed out, Lt. Cotes came up.

"By Gad! Vee, I was glad to see you come out of that cloud. What the devil did you mean by taking off in that manner? Anyway," he added smiling, "you redeemed it to some extent by not losing your head."

I grinned and saluted. As I turned away he called me back.

"Vee!"

"Sir!"

"You need not report for early flying in the morning."

"Thank you, sir."

"You're a lucky young devil," said Si, gloomily, as we trudged back to the quarters together. "I always take off conventionally and land tamely, and never get let off a *damn* thing."

We had one of our occasional concerts that evening and I enjoyed it more than usually, knowing that our friend with the lantern was not going to call me in the morning.

Up to this time I had only done two and a half hours' solo, and now, to my dismay, I found that I was developing nerves. When told to go up I would feel cold shivers running up my spine, and worse than this was the thought that someone might notice this nervousness. One afternoon I had climbed into a machine, feeling pretty blue. Lt. Cotes came up, carrying a little pup in his arms that some mechanic had brought to the aerodrome.

" Isn't he a jolly little chap ? " he said, pulling his ear.

" Yes, sir," I replied. " I wonder, sir, if I could have a bit of leave. I hate asking for it but I think a few days away from the camp might do me a lot of good."

As usual he was at once sympathetic, but said that it was impossible at present as they were anxious that we should finish our five hours' solo flying so that we could go on to Camp Borden. He promised that he would write to the C.O. there and try to persuade him to give me a few days. As he was leaving the machine, he told me to go up and do eight landings. So I taxied out, took off, made one circuit, and landed. Then I took off again, made another circuit, and landed, and did this eight times.

When I came in I was delighted to find that my nervousness had completely vanished. This one afternoon's landings had fully restored my confidence.

I should like to stress this fact, as it made a vast difference to me. After this, flying became a sheer delight. It is a most glorious feeling to be able to swoop *confidently*, like a bird through the air. When I got in, I went at once in search of Lt. Cotes.

" I don't think it's necessary any more, sir, for you to write that letter."

" Sure, Vee ? All right," and there was a knowing twinkle in his eye.

Shortly after this I had a pleasant, though exciting experience. One morning at 4.30 I took off and flew towards the lake. In the distance I noticed a low-lying fog. In a remarkably short time I was over it. Everywhere in front, below me, lay the white billowy sea. It was a beautiful sight. I flew on for a few minutes and then turned the bus round to go back, but now I discovered that the fog had advanced and was over the

FLYING AT CAMP MOHAWK

aerodrome. I had never before had a forced landing, but realised that I was in for one now. So I flew on and was soon clear of the fog, and began to look for a possible landing-field. Beyond Napanee I saw what appeared to be a very large, perfectly flat field, so shut off and landed the bus as slowly as I dared in this.

It was fortunate that the landing was so slow, for the field was covered with long wheat! Had the machine landed fast it would inevitably have turned up on its nose, and might even have gone right over. As it was, no mishap occurred. Nearby was a farmhouse. I switched off the engine, climbed out, and walking towards the house met the farmer running out to see if anyone had been hurt. He had never before seen an aeroplane at close quarters, and after examining this one most carefully took me back to the house for breakfast.

Early flying makes one ravenous, and I was quite ready for the breakfast to which the farmer and his wife and I sat down. We began with a great basin of fresh strawberries and cream. This was followed by quantities of fried eggs, sizzling on the dish. And when we had waltzed through the lot, the farmer's wife produced some jam of her own making. With it all we had great slices of home-made bread and butter, and huge cups of fragrant coffee.

It was, in very truth, a breakfast fit for a king!

During breakfast we discussed the problem of getting the machine off again when the fog, which was over the farm by this time, had lifted. The wheatfield and an adjoining newly-sown field belonged to a neighbour, and so after breakfast he took me in his Ford car to this man. On the way he boasted about the speed of his car and assured me that it was much faster than my aeroplane. After the glorious breakfast he had given me I could not disillusion him, and so let the boast pass. His neighbour immediately granted me permission to taxi the machine into the newly-sown field, from which I could take off. The kind fellow even suggested cutting a lane through the wheat so that I might take off along that, but I funked it as I knew that if the machine swerved from the lane during the take-off, she would be wrecked. Then we drove to a large house nearby in which there was a telephone. From there I was able to get through to the aerodrome. Lt. Cotes wanted to send out mechanics to help me get off, but I told him that I thought we could manage without them. At about eight o'clock the fog lifted, so after bidding my hostess good-bye I returned, with the farmer and his friend, to the aeroplane. They had to swing the prop. for me and I had to give them detailed instructions for doing this. I made them stand as far as possible from the propeller, for when an engine starts, it does so very suddenly, and if a blade of the propeller caught a man's arm it would smash it to bits. Fortunately the engine started easily. Then, with one of them at each wing-tip, I taxied over into the next field. After thanking them very heartily for their help I opened the throttle and got off easily. Then I turned the machine and flew back over the field. The two tiny little figures were still gazing up at the aeroplane, and after waving to them I turned her nose homewards and was soon back on the aerodrome.

The majority of the cadets in our squadron had completed their five hours' solo by this time, and also the 15 landings which were prescribed for this preliminary flying-course. But they had to remain on at Camp Mohawk until there were sufficient vacancies at Borden. This was fortunate for Westlake and me as we each had still over an hour's solo to put in, and we should otherwise have been left behind.

One Sunday morning, several of us were going off for a swim in the bay, when a mechanic came running down to call Westlake and me for flying.

I felt sorry for Westlake as we trotted along to the aerodrome together. He was cursing softly all the way.

FLYING AT CAMP MOHAWK

He was never happy in a machine, but never hesitated a moment when told to go up. He was a plucky fellow. On reaching the aerodrome we heard that we were all to be sent off to Borden the next day. Westlake and I each put in about half an hour's flying that morning, and in the evening we completed our five hours.

After dinner that night the C.O. made us a short farewell speech, and told us that we should have four days' leave before reporting at Borden. We got Dicky Smith to reply to him.

At 10 o'clock the next morning we left by train for Toronto.

CHAPTER III

WE PROCEED TO CAMP BORDEN

(i)

WE reported at Borden on the 18th of July. The camp was not far from the railway station and we marched down to it on arrival. On the way we passed the mess and our quarters which were in adjoining large wooden buildings.

On the steps of the mess we saw several fellows of Course 4, whom we had known in Toronto. Among them was a great strapping chap called " Big Six." He greeted us cheerily enough but the poor fellow had gone to pieces completely. He was twitching and trembling all the time. His appearance was not reassuring, especially in view of some of the rumours we had heard about Camp Borden. Two days later " Big Six " received his discharge as being totally unfit for flying.

When we reached the Orderly Room, the C.O. of the 81st Squadron, to which we were posted, gave us a short outline of the nature of the work before us, the tests we should have to pass in cross-country and formation flying, the height test and so on. Then he referred to a belief which was universal among cadets at this time, the belief that a spinning nose-dive was always fatal. The name almost explains itself. The machine plunges down nose first, whirling round as it goes. The C.O. told us that one could always get out of a spin by shutting off the engine and putting the controls central. Finally he said:

" I am not going to compel any man to stunt here. You are at liberty to loop a machine if you wish to do so.

WE PROCEED TO CAMP BORDEN

I shall be disappointed if you do not attempt *some* stunting at Borden."

After we had registered we were going off when the Adjutant called me back and told me that a letter had been received from Lt. Cotes suggesting that I should be given a few days' leave. I felt grateful to Lt. Cotes for writing this letter in spite of my having told him that I no longer required the leave. I told the Adjutant that I had just had four days' leave in Toronto and should prefer not to have any more.

However, I noticed that for a few days I was not sent up for any flying.

We had a fairly easy time at Borden. For the first ten days we spent the greater part of each day on the aerodrome. Each cadet had to put in two hours' flying a day, and when not flying, had to be on hand at the hangars. As they did not send me up I only had some drill and machine-gun work each day.

At this camp there were Buffalo Curtisses (J.N.4A. type) and also Canadian Curtisses (J.N.4). The latter machine had the simple joystick control, without the wheel at the top, which the Buffaloes had. Turns would be made, in either machine, by means of the rudder-bar on which the pilot's feet rested. This merely controlled the rudder. To bank a Buffalo Curtiss over to the left, say, in making a left turn, the wheel would be swung over as in making a left turn in a motor-car. But in a Canadian Curtiss the joystick itself would simply be pushed over sideways to the left. In a Buffalo Curtiss the joystick had only a backwards and forward, and not a sideways motion. In both types the backwards or forward motion operated the elevator planes. If the stick were pushed forward the machine would dive, if pulled back it would climb.

On the sixth day, Lt. Hicks took me up for instruction in a Canadian Curtiss. Lt. Hicks had had his left elbow shattered in France, and the forearm was withered in consequence, so he used to wear a leather mitten with a socket in it which fitted over the top of the joystick. With his right hand he operated the throttle and switch. After taking me up twice in a machine he let me go solo. I liked the joystick control from the start and had no difficulty with it.

The Canadian Curtiss had practically no dihedral, that is, the left and right wings did not dip down towards the fuselage, or body, of the machine. They were practically in the same horizontal plane. The Buffalo Curtiss, on the other hand, had a dihedral of five or six degrees. The Canadian Curtisses were easier machines to land.

It was very hot at Borden and usually there was a strong wind blowing, both of these factors causing " bumps " in the air. At night, too, we were much worried by mosquitoes. Our sleeping quarters were enclosed with mosquito-proof wire, but they found their way in somehow by the hundred.

After the first ten days we spent a good deal of time on the machine-gun range, practising with both types of gun. We also did some indoor work with these guns, learning, among other things, the reasons for, and how to cure, stoppages which might occur during firing.

We were divided into groups for this work. I was in a group under Cpl. Turnham, a cheerful little Scotsman whom everybody called Scotty. He had seen service during the Anglo-Boer War and could easily be side-tracked into telling us yarns about that campaign—with one eye always on the door in case an officer came in. One day he was discussing with us the assembling of the lock of the Vickers gun. At one point in this operation the spring has to be pressed home until a click is heard.

With the lock in his hand he had drifted into one of his stories, when the door suddenly opened. Holding up the lock he said in a loud voice, " Did ye no see the click ? " causing smothered laughter from us and a smile from the officer.

WE PROCEED TO CAMP BORDEN 47

We had a number of flying and signalling tests to get through before passing into the School of Aerial Gunnery which was the final course in Canada. In one test a pilot would have to climb to 3,000 feet, shut off his engine, glide down, and touch his wheels in a white circle of 40 yards diameter. This was invaluable practice for forced landings. Sometimes when a cadet came gliding down he would find that he was going to overshoot the mark and would thereupon push the nose down to get into the circle. If he dipped the nose suddenly enough the machine might turn a complete somersault when it touched the ground.

Peplar went out on this test. He was the cadet who had been so sick on his first joy-ride at Camp Mohawk. As Peplar came gliding down we who were watching him could see that he was going to overshoot the circle. As he got nearer he realised this too, but simply dived more steeply. His bracing wires began to whine with the speed.

" It's no use, Pep, you'll have to go up again," remarked one of the fellows, and the rest of us laughed.

But as he shot towards the circle, Peplar suddenly pushed the nose down, and, in an instant, the machine hit the ground and whipped over. The pilot's belt gave way and Peplar was catapulted through the air a distance of forty feet from the crash. He was killed instantly.

Two days later a cadet, Bunny Davis, was gliding down on the same test. He had misjudged the distance and would have landed short of the circle. Evidently with the hope of gliding farther, he held his stick back too long and stalled his machine. It suddenly flopped over and side-slipped into the ground, crumpling up like an eggshell. Death here, too, was instantaneous.

In another test, signals would be flashed in Morse code from some conspicuous place near the hangars. The pilot, flying at 3,000 feet, would have to read these and write them down on a pad tied above his knee. This was not as simple as it might appear to be, for it meant that the cadet had to fly his machine with his eyes, and all his attention, fixed on the signals. It was no easy matter for an inexperienced pilot to keep his machine level, and to fly straight, without watching his controls.

In Artillery observation work a great many abbreviations were used, for instance, "Are you firing?" would be represented by R U F, "Are you receiving my signals?" by B, " Am returning to landing-ground " by C I, " Are you ready to fire? " by K Q, " Continue firing in your own time " by G O, " All available guns open fire " by L L.

The cadets had to be perfectly familiar with all these symbols and, in one test, a series of these letters would be displayed by white ground-strips outside the wireless hut. A cadet, trailing an aerial behind him, would fly in the neighbourhood at 3,000 feet and telegraph down the meaning of each symbol as it was put out.

In another rather interesting test the pilot would conduct a "shoot" with a mock gun-battery in the wireless hut. He would have a celluloid disc with a series of concentric circles y, z, A, B, C, D, etc., drawn on it, also a map of the locality. The gunner would have a corresponding pair. The circles were drawn to a scale representing diameters of 10, 25, 50, 100, 200, 300, etc., yards respectively. On the outer circle would be figures, I, II, III, and so on, arranged like those on a clock face. Before the shoot the pilot would consult the battery commander who would tell him where the " target " was situated. Each of them would stick a pin through the centre of his disc into the target on the map. Then the pilot would take the air, and, flying at about 3,000 feet, would let out his aerial and call the aerodrome with his wireless set to see if his signals were being received. The aerodrome would acknowledge with a ground signal K, meaning " yes." He would then send down T, which meant that the ground signal had been observed. After this he would fly over to the battery and call it. If he

WE PROCEED TO CAMP BORDEN

were pilot 8 of Squadron S calling battery R, he would send

S 8 R B B B

the letter B standing for "Are you receiving my signals?" and being repeated three times. They would acknowledge with K in ground-strips, and he in turn would acknowledge with

S 8 R K T

(Squadron S, pilot 8, calling battery R. I have observed your signal K).

He would then send

S 8 R G G G

(Squadron S, pilot 8, calling battery R. Fire).

He would now watch carefully and might see a puff of smoke appear, say, 300 yards due east of the target, *i.e.*, on circle D on the disc in the direction of the clock face figure III. So he would send

S 8 R D 3 D 3 D 3

and follow this again by

S 8 R G G G.

The next puff might appear 200 yards west-north-west of the target, so he would send

S 8 R C10 C10 C10.

And so the shoot would go on until at last a puff appeared on the target. When this happened he would send

S 8 R O K O K O K

and follow this with

S 8 R C I C I C I

(am returning to landing-ground).

This artillery co-operation work was most interesting. The puffs representing bursts from the guns were very realistic. They were released electrically from the wireless hut.

On the first occasion on which I was sent up to conduct a shoot, I had sent down two corrections to the hut when one of the tappet-rods in my engine worked loose. The cover had been removed from the engine by the mechanic on the ground, for additional cooling, and presently I saw the tappet-rod come right out. I was over a mile from the aerodrome when this happened, and I turned towards it immediately. As the aerial had to be wound in before landing I had no time to send S 8 R C I C I C I, but simply tapped out one C I. The engine was knocking badly and the bus losing height rapidly, but I just managed to crawl in over the hangars. After landing I walked across to the wireless hut. They had quite reasonably ignored the isolated C I (probably at least half a dozen cadets, on other tests, were sending wireless messages at the time) and had wondered why their observation pilot had suddenly gone dumb. The wireless corporal was rather severe with me about this.

The cross-country flying was usually interesting, and if the objective was sufficiently far off, there was always the possibility of getting lost, with a consequent forced landing, to add an element of excitement to the flight.

(ii)

Before we could pass into the School of Aerial Gunnery, we had to complete thirty hours' solo flying. Every available moment, when we were not actually at a lecture or on the range, we spent round the hangars. We saw some bad crashes take place, many of them fatal. "Hungry Liz" was always in readiness, and was kept busy.

WE PROCEED TO CAMP BORDEN

A question which had often been discussed among the cadets at Camp Mohawk was whether or not a machine could be struck by lightning in the air. Some of the men from Course 4, who were still at Borden when we arrived, told us of a disaster that had occurred a short time before. A thunderstorm had come up rather suddenly one afternoon. Before the storm broke all the machines in the neighbourhood of the aerodrome came down, but one which had left an hour before on a cross-country flight, was still missing. The storm was severe. Every flash of lightning was followed immediately by a deafening crash. Everyone on the aerodrome was scanning the skies for the missing airman. A very vivid flash occurred and just after this the aeroplane was seen hurtling out of a black cloud, completely out of control. There seemed little doubt that it had been struck by lightning. When it crashed to the ground it burst into flames.

We saw some mild stunting while waiting outside the hangars. Nobody ever put a Curtiss into a spinning nose dive, although it was a common enough stunt in England. Occasionally a rash fellow would loop, and we frequently saw side-slips, vertical banks and tail-stalls.

The latter stunt, without doubt, gives one the greatest sensation obtainable in the air. While flying horizontally the joystick is pulled back quickly so that the machine rears up vertically. The engine is shut off, and the machine for a thousandth of a second hangs motionless. Then it slides back on its tail and suddenly flops forward sickeningly, dropping like a stone. One's stomach seems to have been left miles above—till the machine gradually gathers flying speed and shoots out horizontally once more.

We had among us a ventriloquist, by name Compton. He had a turn for practical joking and as he used his gift sparingly, he sometimes achieved amusing results. After breakfast one morning a dozen of us were sitting on the grass between the hangars awaiting our turns to fly.

Our Flight-Commander, Captain Wakefield, was strolling up and down the tarmac and would from time to time call out a cadet and send him up. Si Perkins was lying full length on his back, with his eyes shut, occasionally butting into the chatter that was going on round him with some humorous remark. Suddenly his name was called.

"Cadet Perkins!"

"Sir!" said Si, jumping up, walking over to the officer, and saluting smartly.

"Well?" said Captain Wakefield.

"I thought you called me, sir," said Si.

The Captain stared at him, and walked on. Si looked comically crestfallen as he returned to us.

"I could take my solemn oath that he called me," he said, as he sat down again.

"You must have dropped off and dreamt it, Si," someone told him.

After about ten minutes, just as the officer was once more approaching us, Si's name was called again, sharply.

"Cadet Perkins!"

Like a reflex action came Si's response,

"Sir!" and he sprang up. I was sitting next to Si and was as completely taken in as he was, but Lydell, beyond him, tumbled to it and pulled Si back by the seat of his trousers.

"Don't be a damn fool, Si," he whispered urgently, "It's only that guy, Compton."

The officer, who had heard Si's response, stared at him suspiciously, but walked on.

Presently a machine taxied up, and Cameron got out of it.

"It's as bumpy as hell this morning," he said as he joined us.

"Cadet Perkins!"

"You big mutt," said Si, turning on Compton, "if you do that again——"

WE PROCEED TO CAMP BORDEN

"C A D E T P E R K I N S! Are you deaf, man?" roared the officer.

"Sir!" yelled Si, jumping up for the third time. "Yes sir?"

"Take up that machine at once, and don't let me have any more of your damned insolence!"

One by one we completed the various ground and air tests.

At last one afternoon I was sent aloft to finish up my last three and, as we were pressed for time, was told to combine them in one. These were the cross-country flight, the height test and the forced-landings test. I reached my objective, a reservoir some twenty miles off, and then turned homewards. On the way back, according to instructions, I picked out two fields and without actually landing in them, satisfied myself that I could do so. Had we not been rushed for time I should have had to land in them. After this I climbed to 7,000 feet. In the height test we were expected to reach 8,000 feet, but as it was beginning to get dark I had not time to go any higher. On the way down I made up my mind to loop the bus, but before attempting this I tried a tail-stall. When the nose flopped forward after the stall, the rush of air bulged out the cowling round the engine very ominously, so I gave up the idea of looping and glided down to the aerodrome. On reporting to the Flight-Commander, he accepted 7,000 feet for the height test and also signed off the other two.

On the 13th August, we were transferred to the School of Aerial Gunnery.

In this course we did little solo flying. Another pilot would fly a cadet over silhouettes of machines on the ground, and the cadet would fire at these with a Lewis gun. Usually the pilots were young fellows who had just received their commissions. After completing the final course, some men were kept back for this purpose, instead of proceeding overseas. These young officers would take very unnecessary risks, doing vertical banks near the ground and not infrequently spinning into it, as there were bad air-pockets at Borden during the summer months. It was not unusual for there to be four or five casualties during each gunnery course. Things had got to such a pass that orders had come out, strictly forbidding any steep banks near the ground. Ours was the first course to benefit by these orders, and was the first course in which there were no casualties.

In another test a machine would fly up and down near the aerodrome, trailing a white flag a long way behind it. A pilot would take up a cadet in another machine, on the top plane of which a Lewis gun was mounted. The cadet would have to climb out of his cockpit, sit on top of the fuselage in the full blast of the wind, and fire over the top plane at the tow-target.

One day some of us were watching a machine which had gone up for silhouette practice. After one burst from the Lewis gun the machine came down and directly it landed we heard a storm of abuse coming from it, and saw the pilot gesticulating fiercely. We heard later that when the pilot had given the order to fire, the young fool in the front cockpit had closed his eyes and blazed away, shooting clean through one of the longerons of his own machine.

In aerial gunnery practice a ring-sight was always used. The fore-sight was in the form of a ring, and the bead back-sight had to be placed in line with the centre of the ring. If firing in the direction of flight, no allowance would have to be made for the pilot's speed, but the target's speed would have to be corrected for. For instance, if the target machine was flying directly across the line of fire, it would have to be placed on the outer edge of the ring, and flying towards the centre of the ring.

One afternoon I was sent up for some camera-gun practice. A camera was fitted up inside the casing of a

WE PROCEED TO CAMP BORDEN

Lewis gun, and was mounted over the top plane. It was operated by a Bowden control which ended on the joystick. I was ordered to take two end-on pictures and four side-on of any machine which I could get near to in the air. In the Curtiss which I took up, the aileron control-wires were dangerously slack. The wind was blowing away from the hangars over the aerodrome and in order to fly into the wind I had to take off over the hangars. The machine was low when it crossed them and it struck an air-pocket and began side-slipping down towards the hangars. To correct this I pushed the joystick over, as much as was customary, in the opposite direction to the tilt of the machine. Had the aileron wires been taut, this would instantly have righted the bus, but in this case nothing seemed to happen till I rammed the stick hard over. Then the machine suddenly flopped over to the other side. It was a fairly near thing, but realising what the trouble was, and with a bit of luck, I managed to get clear. Once at a safe height I soon got used to the controls. Then I chased a bus till I got the two end-on pictures. After this I set about the side-on views. In the distance a machine was flying towards the aerodrome, so I proceeded to fly at right angles to it, hoping to snap it as it crossed my line of flight. But I was not used to judging distances in the air and suddenly realised that there was every likelihood of a collision. At the last moment I pushed the stick forward and dived and most fortunately the other fellow pulled his back and zoomed.

Collisions in the air are almost always fatal. On one occasion at Borden, a cadet flew into another machine and took its tail off. The machine thereupon turned over on its back and came down into a tree. The pilot escaped unhurt!

We practised some formation flying at Borden. The leader would set the pace by that of the slowest machine and the rest of us would have to throttle down to keep in formation. I was poor at this, chiefly due to my dread of stalling a machine.

Our course in the School of Aerial Gunnery only lasted two weeks. After we had got our cards signed we were allowed to slack it for four days. As we had permission to fly whenever we wanted to, we did a good deal of joy-riding.

At Borden, I saw a good deal of Barrett, the fellow who had learnt to fly so easily at Camp Mohawk. When he had begun his solo flying, he had been extraordinarily confident, but as time went on this confidence gradually left him. One evening he and I were smoking together on the balcony of our sleeping quarters and I was distressed to find how morbid he was becoming. We had been talking "shop" in a desultory way. Then he led the talk round to some recent fatal crashes that had occurred at Borden. I noticed that he was becoming excited and nervous and tried to get the talk back into safer channels. Two or three times he reverted to the subject of these crashes, and then, after a while, lapsed into silence. We smoked on for a bit. After a few minutes, he said, " I don't suppose, Vee, that any of us will come through this. Sooner or later we shall crash like these other chaps did, and it will be all over. Sometimes I wish it would happen and be done with it ! "

I tried to argue the fellow out of it—I reminded him how he had been streets ahead of any of us at the start, and that he had never yet had a crash of any sort, or even scratched a wing. Most of us had already had a crash or even two—but it was of no use, I could feel that it was making no impression on him.

Barrett was rather too highly-strung for the game. His keen imagination pictured horrors which the rest of us duller fellows never dreamt of. I do not know what eventually happened, whether he got the better of his growing nervousness, or went under. In army fashion we had been thrown together for a while and just after

WE PROCEED TO CAMP BORDEN

this were thrown apart again. When most of us left Borden a couple of days later, he was kept behind as an instructor and I never saw him again.

(iii)

On the 31st August, we left Borden for Toronto. Here we were given our commissions (but not our wings) and two hundred and fifty dollars outfit allowance. We also got a lecture on how to behave ourselves. The fellows of one of the previous courses had, on receiving their commissions, painted Toronto red with their outfit allowances. To avoid a recurrence of this the next course had only received their commissions on reaching England, but it had been decided to give the original system another trial.

We were given a fortnight's leave and most of the fellows left at once for their homes. I had some difficulty in getting into an hotel as the Canadian Exhibition had opened that week in Toronto. At last I managed to get a room in a second-rate hotel, and that evening, very proudly, I sewed a pip on each shoulder of my tunic.

I had decided to spend a few days in Toronto, to see the Exhibition. After that I was going on to spend a weekend with Westlake at his home near Ottawa.

A jolly little chap, Babe Sanderson, whom I had met at Borden, lived in Toronto and invited me to his home several times. He and his sister, a delightfully pretty girl, and I, went to see the Exhibition. After tea the Babe suggested going on the Great Wheel. The three of us got into one of the open swing-seats, and when this got to the very top, the wheel stopped to let people in below. The Babe started rocking the seat, declaring that he was going to loop it. Miss Sanderson screamed, the Babe chortled with glee, I cursed him, and the operator on the ground swore at us all.

When at last we got to the bottom this man was still fuming and threatening to have Sanderson arrested. But the Babe's innocent smile, or that of his dainty sister, disarmed him, and he let us off with a caution.

After five days in Toronto I went on to Ottawa and from there to the village where Westlake lived. I spent a very pleasant, restful week-end at his home. His mother, like all mothers at that time, was very worried at all the risks he had to run. To her it had been like a reprieve when he had told her, on his arrival a few days before, that he was not going overseas immediately, but was being kept back as an instructor for a few weeks.

It was curious that Westlake should have been kept back instructing as he was never a good pilot. Even after about forty hours' solo he was still not at home in a machine. I felt sorry for Westlake that he had to stay behind, and I think he felt it, too, though he hid his disappointment from his mother. I told her that it was a feather in his cap to be kept behind, as only the best pilots were made instructors. May I be forgiven. It pleased her to hear this.

On the Monday morning he and I travelled back to Ottawa together and there we parted, he going back to Toronto and I on to Montreal. He was a good chap and I was sorry to say good-bye to him.

On arriving in Montreal I put up at the Queen's Hotel. The first two or three days passed easily enough. I had never been to Montreal before and I wandered about exploring the city. I should have liked to look over McGill University, but the summer vacation was still on, and the place seemed deserted.

In the streets of Montreal I was struck by the large number of young fellows going about in mufti. The amount of French spoken everywhere, too, made it hard to believe that this was a British city.

I did not know anybody in Montreal and was beginning to wonder how on earth I should put in the time before

WE PROCEED TO CAMP BORDEN

our boat sailed, when one day I met an interesting fellow. He stopped me in the street and asked the time. Then we drifted into conversation and, in the end, he invited me to have lunch with him. He was Lt. Keith-Davies of the Canadian Field Artillery, and had returned shortly before from France. He told me that he had become so sick of seeing so many slackers in Montreal that he had determined to speak to the first man that he met in uniform. And so our acquaintanceship began. He was a well-read man and a good talker, and altogether a very welcome companion. He knew Montreal well and we visited all the sights of the city together.

Unfortunately Keith-Davies was called out of town a few days later. During our brief acquaintanceship he had introduced me to several people in Montreal, and had obtained for me visiting-membership of his club, and so the time did not hang as heavily as before.

The sailing date had been postponed twice, but eventually it arrived, and I rejoined my flying comrades on board the s.s. *Missinabi*.

We steamed down the St. Lawrence to Halifax, where we lay for three days. Then at long last we sailed for Liverpool.

CHAPTER IV

WE ARRIVE IN ENGLAND

(i)

THE days on the *Missinabi* were uneventful, but the time never dragged. We saw no submarines during the voyage, but our skipper maintained a zig-zag course all the way across. This may have accounted for the fact that it took us fourteen days to reach Liverpool.

We kept fit by turning out on deck each morning before breakfast for physical-training. During the day we played deck games, and at night poker or bridge.

I have seldom seen such heavy gambling as went on during that voyage. When we had played poker in Canada we had always fixed a reasonable limit. Now it was played without any limit and, as though that were not enough, four jokers were used, determined by the dealer. At the beginning of a round the dealer would say, for instance, "Fives are wild this trip." This would mean that each of the four fives in the pack was a joker. It was not unusual to see a man, holding a single pair in his hand, bid five pounds on it, and another, holding perhaps threes, throw in simply because he could not afford to risk seeing him.

In Toronto I had taken out a draft for forty pounds on a bank in London, and had about twenty pounds in cash with me. Ten of these I was prepared to lose at poker, and did so within two days of sailing. After this, for the rest of the voyage, I played bridge. All the gambling on board was done in English money as the Canadians wanted to get used to the English coinage before the end of the voyage.

WE ARRIVE IN ENGLAND

At dawn on the 15th day we reached Liverpool. Then for an hour or two there was a great scurrying and bustle on board. Valises were rolled and strapped, and then unrolled again to have pyjamas and other forgotten articles crammed into them, officers in charge of men hurried to and fro shouting orders, and overhead cranes were rattling and groaning as they swung great nets containing officers' valises and men's kit-bags and other baggage ashore.

Before very long the ship and the wharf looked deserted. The men had all been marched off, taking their kit-bags with them, and lorries had removed the heavier baggage. The Flying Corps officers were the last to leave the boat as they had only themselves to look after, and when we went ashore the landing officer was wiping his steaming brow. We were told to report to Colonel Weeks, near the railway station, at twelve o'clock sharp, to receive our warrants for London. Then we set off in various groups to see the town.

It was the first time most of these fellows had set foot on English soil and, in any case, they would have welcomed a change after being cooped up for fourteen days on board. The morning slipped past and it was noon before we realised it. It was half past twelve before we reached the office, to find a peppery little colonel positively bristling with rage. Some of our fellows were there already, but others came straggling in even later.

We had missed the train and had to wait till the late afternoon for another.

The next day in London, on reporting at the Hotel Cecil, commonly called "Bolo House," we were given ten days' leave.

Sanderson and I went across to Belfast, Ireland, where I had relatives. Scott went up to Aberdeen to visit an uncle whom he had never seen before, and he took Gibbon with him.

(ii)

When we reported back in London we were posted off to various aerodromes in England.

I was sent to Shawbury, in Shropshire, and was glad to find that Gibbon, Scott and some of the others were going there, too. On the way up Scott was amusing about his visit to Aberdeen. He had thoroughly enjoyed the trip, and his uncle, and thought he had discovered the origin of the stories about the niggardliness of Scotch people. His uncle had treated him and Gibbon right royally, and had taken them to dinners and theatres every night, and for motor drives whenever he could get away from his office during the day. Yet he had described to them with great relish how, after receiving tuppence short change from a tram conductor, he had tracked the man all over the city till he had eventually run him to earth and got the tuppence back from him.

After dinner, on our first evening at Shawbury, a young fellow with whom I was chatting looked across at the newcomers and asked me:

"I say—er—who is that *wild*-looking fellow over there?"

Without looking up, I answered:

"That's Scott," and then, glancing round I added, "and that chap, paging magazines over there, is his pal, Gibbon. Two of the very best."

We had a jolly time at Shawbury. Our C.O. was a good chap who never indulged in "hot air." On dud days, and there were many of these, flying was "washed out," and we were free to do as we pleased. Most of these we spent playing cards, and occasionally we went in by tender to Market Drayton, or walked into Shrewsbury. I got to know Leisk well here, and found that my first impressions of him at Camp Mohawk had been quite wrong. In the evenings the four of us often went for

WE ARRIVE IN ENGLAND

long walks together. Leisk's deformed foot did not hamper him much, though he walked with a limp.

My room was next to the one shared by Gibbon and Scott. Gibbon was five or six years older than Scott, and as I got to know them better I realised that he was much the steadier character of the two. He was always at hand to check Scott's impulsive outbursts. Scott cared neither for man nor devil, but could always be brought to heel by Gibbon.

I told Gibbon once about the difficulty I had had about a birth certificate when I enlisted, and he grinned and said he was twenty-nine when he joined, but had faked his own birth certificate.

We were put on Avros to begin with. They were fitted with 90-h.p. Monosoupape engines. It took me some time to get used to these rotary engines, and to the extremely sensitive " balanced " rudder. But they were remarkably stable machines and easy to land.

Captain Musgrave gave me over three hours' dual instruction before allowing me to go solo. We used ' phones in these machines, so that it was no longer necessary to shut off the engine and yell to one another.

He gave me some interesting forced-landing demonstrations. He would suddenly switch off his engine and look about for a landing field. He invariably got down into one safely, but simply ran his wheels along it and took off again. Sometimes if we were too near a field to glide into it, he would bank the machine over and lose height rapidly by side-slipping. He made me do some of this, too and many a time later I blessed him for giving me this useful practice.

On my second solo on Avros I began stunting. It was a glorious morning when I took off. In England when the days are good they are very, very good, and when they are bad they are horrid. This was one of those sunny days, with just a touch of autumn in the air, when even a timid fellow is inspired to take risks.

I was cruising along at eighty miles an hour. The country below, cut up into green fields by little hedges, looked very beautiful. Gulping down the last remnants of funk I pushed the stick forward till the speed rose to ninety. Then I pulled the stick back quickly. The nose swung up, the earth slipped away below the tail, for an instant I lost it, and then it re-appeared somewhere above my head. I switched off the engine and came swooping down out of my first loop. Nothing before or since has ever produced in me such a thrill as that first loop. This dreaded stunt had proved astonishingly easy and I did it again, and once again. I found myself singing and shouting in the air with the sheer joy of this unlimited, bird-like freedom.

Then I tried some Immelmann turns and found that they, too, were quite simple. To do this stunt, one foot on the rudder-bar is suddenly pushed forward and the stick pulled back. The machine rears up and rolls over sideways on to its back. Then the engine is switched off and the bus swoops back along its path.

Next, I attempted some vertical banks but did not succeed immediately with them. I found the nose dropping during the turns, so straightened out to think it over. We had never been given stunting instruction, so difficulties had to be solved as they cropped up. By a vertical bank is meant a very sharp turn in which the machine is banked over till the wings are practically vertical. In this position, of course, the elevator planes at the tail become the rudder, and it suddenly occurred to me that the rudder would naturally become the elevator. In making a left-hand turn, for instance, if the left foot were pushed forward on the rudder-bar (as would be done in a less steep turn) this would inevitably force the nose down as soon as the rudder took the place of the elevator planes. I now tried this turn again and succeeded at once, by putting the rudder-bar central. (Vertical banks were usually known, in R.F.C slang, as

WE ARRIVE IN ENGLAND

split-ass turns, and stunting, generally, was known as split-assing.)

Thinking that I might as well go through the whole gamut of stunts while I was about it, I now attempted a spinning nose-dive. I had frequently, from the aerodrome, seen Avros spinning, but had never been in a spin myself. I switched off the engine, pushed the nose down and tried various positions of rudder-bar and joystick. But the machine only began to vibrate horribly and would not spin. The vibration seemed likely to become dangerous, so I gave it up.

On landing I told Capt. Musgrave of my difficulty with the spin, and he cleared it up immediately. He told me to shut off the engine, to pull the stick right back and hold it there all the time, and to give the bus full left rudder, or right. The machine would then stall, flop over, and spin either to the left or to the right. So up I went again, and, after climbing to the safe height of about 3,000 feet, tried it again, this time successfully.

Stunting gives one extraordinary confidence in the air, and without perfect confidence one cannot fully appreciate the joys of flying.

One morning, after looping an Avro, I found that the pressure in the tank had fallen to zero. I pumped hard to get it up, but nothing happened. With my engine phut, I had to come down and managed to land safely in a large field. My prop. was still ticking over and I pumped hard to get up the pressure, but with no success. When I looked up several people were running towards the machine so I opened out the engine, but immediately I did so she failed again. The aerodrome was only about two miles off, and I was loth to go back without the machine, so I pumped hard once more, waved a farmer out of the way, and opened out again. This time she got off and reached the aerodrome. Captain Musgrave showed me how to adjust the release valve, which was all that was at fault.

One day, we had been posted for flying at two p.m. In the morning there was a fine drizzle falling from a uniformly grey sky. As there seemed no prospect of flying that day, Gibbon, Scott and I went in by the laundry tender to Market Drayton. Gibbon wanted to buy a new pipe, and I wanted to be measured for a new uniform. It was still raining when the tender went back so we stayed behind. While we were at lunch the sun peeped through a rift in the clouds. This was awkward. We did not know whether to get a taxi back, or chance the weather remaining dud.

" Let's get tight," I suggested, " then we won't give a damn."

The other two being agreeable, we proceeded to do this. We had not made much progress when Gibbon spotted an R.F.C. tender pulling up across the road. He went out to investigate and found that the driver had come in for some supplies and was returning immediately. The clouds were definitely breaking up now, so we went back with him. When we got to the aerodrome, a few minutes after two, all the machines were out on the tarmac and flying had just commenced. As soon as Captain Musgrave saw us he called out:

" Vee, will you leap into the atmosphere ? "

This was just what I felt like doing. The whisky I had consumed was enough to make me throw all caution to the winds and I took the Avro off the ground in a great climbing turn. The rest of the flight was on a par with the take-off, and every minute was glorious. But it was fortunate that the tender which had brought us back had not arrived any later in Market Drayton.

A number of cadets were having their first flying instruction at Shawbury on " Rumpeties " (Maurice Farman Shorthorns) and there were a good many crashes on these, but none of them fatal, at least while we were there.

Early one morning a few of us were watching a cadet doing his first solo on a Rumpety. When he came down

WE ARRIVE IN ENGLAND

to land, as one man described it afterwards at breakfast, he " made a perfect landing about a hundred feet up," that is, he flattened her out of the glide there, and pancaked the rest of the way. The Rumpety spread itself out on the grass as flat as a sheet of paper, leaving the cadet sitting unhurt in the middle of it.

On another occasion, some of us who were watching, caught our breaths when two Rumpeties flying side by side, came together in the air. They waggled a bit, and then, by a lucky chance, broke loose undamaged.

A Frenchman, Dulong, who was instructing on Rumpeties at Shawbury, was usually worth watching. He would throw them about most recklessly near the ground and would put them through unheard of stunts. One day several of us were lolling about watching the flying, when someone exclaimed, " Good God ! there's a man out on that wing." Looking up, we saw a Rumpety tearing about near the ground with two mechanics lying face downwards, one at each end of the lower wing. Dulong, of course, was the pilot.

After a while I was given some dual on Sopwith two-seaters, or 1½-Strutters as they were usually called, because there are one and a half struts between the upper and lower planes on either side of the fuselage. They were easy machines to fly. Once up in the air one could turn a wheel, on the right-hand side, which adjusted the inclination of the tailplane so that she would fly horizontally. After that the pilot could put his hands in his pockets, merely keeping his feet on the rudder-bar. To turn to the right, for instance, he would stretch out his right leg a bit and the machine would turn, putting on its own bank. The 1½-Strutters carried 110-h.p. Clerget engines. To come down, the wheel would be turned all the way back, and the engine shut off. The bus would then pick up its own gliding angle. Some of the days at Shawbury were very cold and it was rather jolly to be able to fly round with hands in pockets.

A story was told of a remarkable occurrence in France, while the 1½-Strutters were still in use there. One day a machine was seen to glide down into a field some seventy miles behind the lines. An officer in charge of a lorry-load of men, seeing the forced landing, walked across to see if the airmen needed any assistance. It was indeed a forced landing, as the petrol tank was empty, but the airmen needed no help. Both the pilot and the observer were dead.

Directly I had gone solo on Sopwith two-seaters I automatically graduated as a Flying Officer, for they were still considered " service machines," but I was still not entitled to wear wings. This was on the 26th November, but my graduation was antedated to the 16th October. The same thing was done with all the Canadian-trained pilots on account, it was said, of the sea voyage which had prevented them from graduating sooner. After graduation, flying-pay increased from four shillings to eight shillings a day. I was also given four days' graduation leave.

A few days before I went on leave, Gibbon, Scott and Leisk, who had already graduated, were transferred to a Camel Squadron on a neighbouring aerodrome, Tern Hill. Camels were fighting scout-machines used in France, right up to the end of the war. I flew over two or three times to visit them and had every hope of joining them on my return from leave.

I spent my leave with some Irish cousins in Belfast. They gave me a very jolly time and the leave slipped away only too quickly.

(iii)

When I returned to Shawbury, I discovered to my disgust that I had been posted to Netheravon, on Salisbury Plain. I had no idea what service machines

WE ARRIVE IN ENGLAND

they had at Netheravon, but someone told me there were R.E.8's there, and I feared that this meant that I should have to go out to France on artillery observation work. I badly wanted to go out to a fighting squadron. In case anybody should think this brave of me, let me explain that the fellows in fighting squadrons were far safer than the poor devils in artillery observation or in bombing squadrons. These were always exposed to much more intense anti-aircraft fire, because they had to fly low, and furthermore, if they were attacked by enemy aircraft they had little chance of defending themselves. The artillery observation people, especially, were in a bad way, for they flew slow, antiquated machines such as R.E.8's or Ack W's (Armstrong Whitworths, also known as Big Acks).

Well, in the Army one could not argue, so I left the same day for Netheravon. When I arrived at Bulford that evening a pretty girl came up to me, and asked if I were Mr. Vee. When I said I was, she told me that she had come to fetch me and that her tender was waiting outside the station. This was a pleasant surprise. She was the first W.A.A.C. I had met. On the way back, she told me, in answer to my very first question, that there were Bristol Fighters at Netheravon. I had not heard of these before and thought she meant Bristol Scouts, such as I had seen at Shawbury.

When I reported the next morning I was posted to No. 8 Squadron. As soon as possible I walked down to the hangars to see these Bristol Fighters. They were truly magnificent machines, and I was admiring their beautiful lines when someone clapped me on the shoulder, with a :

"Well, well! What are you doing here?" and there was Lynn Cameron, and beside him Lydell, the Philadelphian. They told me that there were some other Canadians at Netheravon, too. We were soon exchanging news about old acquaintances.

When Cameron and Lydell both assured me that Bristol Fighters were considered to be the finest fighting machines ever built, things once more took on a rosier hue. I should have been quite contented if only Gibbon and Scott could have been at Netheravon, too.

That first morning the Flight-Commander, Captain Tyrell, told me to take up a B.E.2.E. As I had already done some sixty hours' solo flying, I did not receive any instruction on it.

" Don't spin or loop it," he said, "as it won't stand it."

I found it an easy machine to fly and did several half-rolls (Immelmann turns) and vertical banks with it. It was very light and felt like a toy after the heavier $1\frac{1}{2}$-Strutters which I had been flying.

I put in several hours on these 2.E's, doing pin-point photography. I would be given the pin-points of about eight places, and a map, and would have to go up and photograph them. Once when I landed after two and a half hours of this, the photographic mechanic discovered when he removed the box of plates from the machine that he had forgotten to pull out the slide. He looked so crestfallen that I simply told him to fetch another box, and after having the tank filled, went up and took them all over again.

The aerodrome at Netheravon was large and there were several squadrons on it. One or two of these had Rumpeties and D.H.6's on which cadets were being taught to fly. The D.H.6 was a very slow machine. It was hideously ugly and there was no finish about it. It looked as though someone " had made it himself." It was commonly known as a " Clutching Hand," or a " Crab." I have seen Crabs flying against the wind with such low air-speeds that they were actually drifting backwards relatively to the ground.

Five days after I reached Netheravon I had a wire from Gibbon, at Tern Hill, saying that Scott had been killed, and asking me to go up for the funeral. The wire arrived

WE ARRIVE IN ENGLAND

too late for this but I wrote immediately to Gibbon. One grew very callous in the Flying Corps as so many good fellows were constantly being "written off," but Scott's death affected me deeply. I knew that Gibbon, in spite of his hard-bitten exterior, would be heart-broken.

Four weeks later Gibbon went out, too. Afterwards at Turnberry, McKinnan gave me the details. He had been at Tern Hill at the time. Scott went up one day, in a Camel, and after giving a wonderful display of stunting with the Camel, he spun into the ground and was killed instantly. Gibbon went on a blind drunk for about three weeks. His C.O., thinking that a change might do him good, sent him off to an aerodrome somewhere in the south of England. Here he was put back on D.H.6's, and one day, for no apparent reason, he dived straight into the ground from 2,000 feet.

After flying B.E.2.E's and B.E.2.C's I was put on to R.E.8's. An instructor, Lt. Kerman, flew me once round the aerodrome in one of these before sending me up alone. There was no instruction about this as the R.E.8's were not fitted with dual control. I took her up, flew round for about twenty minutes, and landed. It was the heaviest machine I had yet flown. Normally, I should have had to put in some time on R.E.8's, but fortunately, all the serviceable R.E.8's were crashed just about this time, and so I was put straight on to Bristol Fighters. Lt. Dobbie,* who was killed later in Egypt, flew me twice round the aerodrome in a Bristol. There was no dual control in this either. The pilot sat in the front cockpit and the observer in the rear one. He took off in a great climbing turn, with a split-ass turn at the top. When we landed, he said:

"All right, take her up, but don't do any climbing turns." So I climbed over into the pilot's seat, and opened the throttle. I felt at home at once in a Bristol even on this first solo. The engine, a 250-h.p. Rolls-

Royce, was infinitely more powerful than anything I had come across so far. It gave a full-throated roar and shot away across the aerodrome and then up, soaring into the air like a great eagle. She was a massive machine but so beautifully designed that she did not feel heavy on the controls. She responded superbly to the least touch of the stick or rudder-bar. After flying round for half an hour, I brought her down and landed quite smoothly. I felt that up to the present I had only been playing at flying.

Five of us, Cameron, Lydell, Bryan, Eldritch and I were in a wooden hut.

I got on very well with Cameron, Lydell and Eldritch: and Bryan, too, was quite an amusing fellow, but a hopeless lead-swinger. I could never understand why he had enlisted at all, as he dodged flying and all parades whenever he could lie himself out of them.

One morning, to give but one of many instances, Bryan sent word that he was sick, and stayed in bed. When the M.O. came round to see him, Bryan said to him, " Doc, my neck's stiff and if I try to move I get pains all down my back. It's hell, Doc! Can't you do something about it ? "

That good-natured fool, after an examination through which Bryan led him by the nose, pronounced it to be lumbago, and ordered Bryan to remain in bed till further orders. The M.O. was no sooner out of the room than Bryan was jumping up and down on his bed shouting,

" Hooray, fellers ! I've got lumbago ! "

No man could possibly have less sense of direction than had Bryan. He was quite useless at cross-country work and sometimes got lost within sight of the aerodrome. One afternoon we saw a machine about half a mile from the aerodrome go down into a field. Thinking that the engine had failed an instructor sent out a tender to investigate. When it reached the field the driver found Bryan standing next to the bus, the engine of which was in perfect order. Bryan had simply got lost.

WE ARRIVE IN ENGLAND

A funny thing happened at Netheravon one afternoon. The engine of one of the Bristol Fighters failed quite near the aerodrome, so the pilot brought her down safely in a field. Presently a beginner flying round in a Rumpety saw the Bristol in the field, and wishing to be helpful landed next to it, but wiped off his own undercarriage in doing so. The next victim was an R.E.8. The pilot, seeing the two machines side by side, shut off his engine and crashed beside them. A lady-driver, who was sent out in a tender from the aerodrome, no sooner reached the unlucky field than her engine caved in altogether. When two instructors eventually walked over, they found the three pilots tearing their hair and the lady-driver walking round her tender, with a spanner in each hand, weeping.

There were four South Africans at Netheravon. Two of them I hardly ever saw, as they were in a different squadron, just beginning their course. The third, Smiles, I got to know very well, as he and I went over to France together a few weeks later. The fourth, Andrews, met with a nasty accident. There was an aerobatics test at Netheravon, which all pilots had to pass before they could go up to Scotland for the final course. In this test the pilot had to loop, spin, side-slip and half-roll a Bristol Fighter. Andrews took off in a great climbing turn over the hangars without getting up sufficient speed. At the top of the turn his machine stalled and spun down, with the engine full on, into a macadam road which ran between the hangars and the stores huts. It was a ghastly crash, and the Bristol was completely smashed. Andrews somehow escaped with his life, but nearly every bone in his body was broken.

It was always rather nerve-wracking, watching beginners in the air. Several of us one afternoon were watching an instructor giving a pupil landings in a Rumpety. He came round again and again, and sometimes the pupil would make good landings and at other times bad ones.

At last the instructor got out and sent him up alone. After making a circuit the pupil tried to land but overshot the mark and put on his engine and went round again. This happened three or four times and the youngster then evidently lost his head for the machine began lurching about in an alarming way. Once, in making a turn, he stalled it, and it did an Immelmann turn. Goodness knows why the Rumpety did not spin! Some of the men watching this laughed and cursed in the same breath. In the end he crashed badly.

On another occasion I was watching a Crab coming in over the hangars, to land. The pilot evidently thought he was not going to clear the hangars, and, regardless of flying-speed, pulled back the stick. The nose lifted, the machine stalled, and then dived straight down into the hangar. The nose crashed through the roof, leaving the machine sticking tail-up into the air. Then the young pilot climbed out and ran along to the end of the roof, where he pulled out a pocket-kodak and snapped his own crash.

We spent a quiet Christmas at Netheravon. In the morning, Cameron and I went for a long walk. Lydell, who was a solitary fellow, went off by himself.

During our walk, Cameron told me that shortly before I arrived an S.E.5 (a scout machine) had landed one afternoon at Netheravon. Cameron saw it land but did not pay much attention to it as pilots from other aerodromes frequently visited us. On this occasion the S.E.5 taxied up to the hangars and the pilot beckoned to him. When Cameron walked over he noticed a line of ribbons on the man's tunic below his wings.

" Could you tell me if Captain Tyrell is here ? " he asked.

" Yes, he has just gone across to the mess for tea," said Cameron.

" I'd like to see him. We were in the same squadron in France. Would you mind giving me a hand in getting out of this bus ? "

"Sure," Cameron replied, rather surprised.

He helped him out and to his astonishment saw that the pilot had two artificial legs and one artificial arm!

(iv)

The Bristol Fighters in France normally did their patrols at 20,000 feet, so it was necessary for all Bristol pilots to pass a height test in England before going over. Some people could not stand the altitude. One man who went up on a height test from Netheravon fainted when he got above 15,000 feet. He came down out of control some thousands of feet, but came to in time to save himself.

On the morning of the 27th December, Cameron was sent up on his height test. He was told to reach 20,000 feet if possible. At Netheravon none of our Bristols carried 264-h.p. Rolls-Royce engines, they all had the earlier 250-h.p. type. These had a "ceiling" of barely 20,000 feet. Cameron reached 18,000 and as she was climbing very slowly when he reached that height, he came down.

After lunch Captain Tyrell said to me:

"You had better go up now, Vee. Take her up to 20,000 and see if you can do it in half an hour."

So I put on my sheepskin thigh boots, leather coat, helmet, goggles and fleece-lined gloves, and climbed in.

Just before I took off the mechanic said to me:

"There's only a quarter of an hour's petrol in the front tank, sir, so you had better fly on the rear tank."

The rear tank, I knew, would last for an hour and a quarter.

Cameron and I were great pals and there was always friendly rivalry between us, and so I was fully determined to beat his record. The visibility was good at three o'clock when I left the ground, and there was a slight

N.E. breeze blowing. I climbed in a wide spiral over the aerodrome, round and round and up and up, and the air gradually changed from frosty to intensely cold.

After half an hour I had only reached 15,000 feet so I went on, but noticed that a ground mist was beginning to cover the aerodrome. I merely noticed this and dismissed it from my mind, and continued to climb in the spiral. From now on I began to notice the altitude a bit, but it did not worry me unduly. I felt myself panting, but was not really uncomfortable. The higher the Bristol went the more slowly did she climb. At ten minutes to four I reached Cameron's limit, 18,000 feet. I was beginning to feel numbed with the intense cold. To climb faster I pulled back the stick as far as I dared and crawled up against the sky another 600 feet. Then she would not go any higher. Satisfied that she had reached her limit, and pleased that I had beaten Cameron's effort, I shut off and began to come down. I glanced at my watch and it was four o'clock. The mist, or clouds, had by this time covered everything down below. The afternoon was fading into twilight, and it was bitterly cold up there, so after closing the radiator I threw her over into a spin, to lose height as rapidly as possible. Down we spun giddily, head first, and the compass was spinning too and the altimeter oscillating.

After a while I pulled her out of the spin. We were still far above the clouds and the altimeter showed 12,000 feet. So back we went into the spin, and pulled out the next time at 8,000 feet. I could see that we were nearing the clouds now, so decided to glide down the rest of the way. It suddenly struck me, too, that I had better pump up the pressure in the tank as the gauge was registering nothing. To my dismay I could not move the pump handle as the oil had congealed round it. All this time the machine was losing height, and presently it entered the clouds. I thought that if she were still at a fair height after getting through the clouds I should be able

WE ARRIVE IN ENGLAND

to land her on the aerodrome without the help of the engine. Suddenly she emerged from the clouds and I put my head over the side immediately, to look for the hangars.

But below me lay the sea. Great waves were rolling along, for miles and miles, as far as I could see. I was still at 6,000 feet, but there was not a sign of land, or a single boat in sight.

I am no hero, and for about two seconds I panicked. Then suddenly the realisation that every second was precious poured over me. Undoubtedly the first thing to do was to get the engine going. The pressure pump was mounted on the left wall of the cockpit, and leaning backwards and to the left, and putting the joystick between my knees, I got both hands on to the pump. At first she would not budge, but after a great effort she moved very slightly. That was enough to start her, and I soon had her moving more easily. Then, with the stick still between my knees, I held down the release valve with my right hand, and with the left pumped literally for dear life.

The Bristol was dropping rapidly and, pump as I would, the gauge simply would not register.

Down we went, 5,000, 4,000, 3,000, 2,000, and I swore at the altimeter. There did not seem to be any possible chance of getting out of this, and I wondered how long the Bristol would float after she hit the water. Her heavy engine would probably pull her under immediately. I knew that a water surface was pretty solid if one hit it rapidly and I began to think of *crashing* the machine on to it in the hope of knocking off a wheel. The pneumatic tyre would save me from immediate drowning.

At 1,000 feet the engine sputtered into life.

It did not take long to get over the first feeling of relief. The rear tank would soon be empty and there was only petrol for another fifteen minutes in the front one. Furthermore, I had not the remotest idea where I was, there was no sign of life anywhere in sight, and it was beginning to get dark. It seemed to me that I was just as likely to be off the west coast as off the south, and I decided that the only safe course was to fly north-east.

I had paid no attention to direction while gliding down so now I turned slowly till the compass pointed north-east.

In an aeroplane, one is not conscious of wind, but there must have been a stiff breeze blowing, judging by the size of the waves. Also the air was frightfully bumpy. I have never experienced such bumps. Once the left wing and tail dropped so suddenly that the machine stalled and fell over into a spin. I pulled her out of it just over the waves. I dared not climb as I had to conserve my petrol. It was a nightmare ride over that grey, pitiless sea.

I wondered whether I could get further throttled down, thus using less petrol but flying more slowly, or with the engine full on. I decided to throttle down.

After flying north-east for fifteen minutes the rear tank gave out, and I switched over to the front. This would carry me on for another fifteen minutes.

For ten minutes the Bristol and I flew on through the gathering darkness, and she was pitching and rolling badly all the time. There was still no sign of land or boat and I felt sure now that I was " for it."

Mechanically I corrected her plunging. I wished impotently that I could let my people in South Africa know what was happening to me. They would simply be told that I had last been seen leaving the aerodrome at Netheravon, and then had vanished completely. Probably for weeks they would hope on for further news.

I kept glancing at my watch, and, after twelve minutes, spotted a boat ahead. Then I realised that there was still a chance. The Bristol was up to it almost immediately and I was doing some pretty rapid thinking, wondering how I could best make use of this last-minute opportunity.

WE ARRIVE IN ENGLAND

Twice I circled round the trawler waving to the men on board, and they waved back. It was tantalising to have them so near and yet so hopelessly far. The boat, now that I had found it, seemed so inaccessible that I did a foolish thing. I decided to make a last effort to reach land, and once more set off north-east. I had no sooner turned the machine than, luckily, the petrol gave out. The engine gave a coughing noise, and stopped completely. There was only one thing to do now, and that was to pancake the machine as slowly as possible on to the sea.

I slipped loose the belt that held me into the pilot's seat, glided down towards the trawler, flattened out about twenty feet up, and dropped the good old Bristol on to the water. She hit the water with a great smack and I was thrown against the cowling. The nose began to go down at once so I crawled out along the fuselage to the tail-plane and hung on to the rudder.

In the meantime, the trawler had turned and was coming towards the machine. I was very much relieved to see the name *Toronto* on her, as I had been dreading that she might be a German boat.

The men could see that the aeroplane was sinking rapidly, and they threw out a lifebelt. It must have fallen about fifty feet from me and I struck out at once for it. It was no easy matter swimming in a rough sea in full flying-kit, but I got there, and hung on while they hauled it in. When I was directly below them they let down a rope with a noose at the end and shouted directions to me to get it round my shoulders and then under the armpits. This relieved all strain from my arms, and soon the sailors were hauling me out of the water. It was good to look up into those honest faces peering down, and to feel that my responsibility for affairs was at an end now.

Two pairs of capable arms lifted me over the rail.

Someone was saying, insistently:

"Was there anyone else with you? Were you alone in the aeroplane?"

"I was alone," I answered.

"Lend a hand there, Jo."

"Never mind that, get him below."

"Oh, there she goes! See, my lad, there." A tall angular seaman, who had me by the arm, pointed to the aeroplane. I was just in time to see the tail disappearing. It was with a bit of a pang that I saw her go down, Bristol Fighter No. 4807. She and I had been through some tight places together that afternoon.

Soon I was down in a small cabin and they had stripped off my wet things. My teeth were chattering with the cold. Two of the men gave me a vigorous rub-down and a fat sailor came in with a pair of trousers and a vest in his hands. After getting into these and gulping down a hot, choking drink which was handed to me in a great mug, I began to feel more comfortable. My face had been knocked about a bit against the cowling when we hit the water. A cut in the lip was bleeding and I sat back on a box against the cabin wall while the angular man did first-aid to this.

A lantern was swinging backwards and forwards, and then violently sideways as the boat pitched and rolled. The cabin was small and rather close, but it was warm, and I was sorry when one of the sailors said:

"We'd better take him along now. The old man wants him in the saloon."

I got up, and the fat seaman said, gruffly:

"Here, I'll give you a hand."

"It's all right, thanks. I can manage now," and I followed the angular man down a narrow passage, along which the motion of the boat bumped us from side to side, to the saloon.

The skipper was there, and after asking how I felt, said:

"Well, if you feel up to it now, I should like to get down a few particulars as I shall be questioned about this."

So we sat down at the table and I gave him a short outline of what had happened, while he made a few notes.

WE ARRIVE IN ENGLAND

He told me that the Bristol had gone down about five miles off Portland Bill, and gave me the bearings of the spot, but he thought there was little chance of salvaging her as the water was very deep there.

It was fortunate that the light had been so bad before I found the trawler. Otherwise, I should have seen land, and tried to reach it, and the petrol would certainly have given out before I could do so.

Not long after this we all had supper together in the tiny saloon. They were a jolly crowd in the trawler, and after the hectic afternoon it was quite cheery to listen to the banter and rough thrust-and-parry that went on between them during the meal.

After we had finished, I was longing for a smoke, and when one of the sailors offered me some tobacco I gladly accepted and rolled a cigarette with it in some notepaper. But it was villainously strong stuff, and between this and the pitching of the boat I was very nearly sick.

One of the sailors told me they had thought I was a German, and when I flew round the boat they were waiting for the bomb.

"Well, for my part," I said, laughing, "I was relieved to see the name of your boat as I thought *you* fellows might be Boches."

"It's the name of my home-town," the skipper said. When he heard that I had recently been there, it established a new link between us, and we discussed Toronto for some time. He had not seen it for three years and it was clear that the names of the streets, theatres, parks and pubs were like music in his ears.

The trawler was on coastguard patrol and so could not put me ashore, but before long we came up with a large boat which had wireless on board. The trawler signalled to her, and she sent a message ashore. Shortly after, a launch came out from Weymouth to take me off.

My uniform and flying kit had been hung up to dry, and they put these, with the exception of one thigh-boot,

F

which had come off in the sea, into a sailor's kit-bag for me.

The skipper lent me a coat and cap, and then I said good-bye to these cheery fellows.

When we got to Weymouth I was told to report to the Garrison Adjutant, and a lad from the launch was sent with me to show me the house. It was only a short walk from the harbour and presently he stopped and said:

"This is where Captain Smythe lives, sir."

"Thank you," I said. "Good night."

"Good night, sir."

As he turned to go I rang the bell.

For quite two minutes I waited, and was just going to ring again when the door opened. An officer, smoking a pipe, and holding a newspaper in his hand, stared at me.

"Well," he said, curtly.

"I came down in the Channel in an aeroplane this afternoon, and have been told to report to you."

He looked me up and down slowly, and then said:

"Your name?"

"Second Lieutenant Vee, No. 8 Squadron, Netheravon."

"What the devil are you——" he began, then, "Come inside."

He led the way into a cosy-looking room. In the grate a cheerful fire was burning. Near the fire stood a tall lamp with a red shade over it, and this was the only light in the room. To my distress I noticed that, beyond the lamp, a woman was sitting in a low armless chair before the fire. She was knitting something with long white needles. She glanced up as we came in, and the light from the lamp fell on a friendly, attractive face. I was in no condition to meet any woman, pretty or otherwise. With my baggy clothes and battered face, I must have presented a sorry spectacle. She could not see us in the shadow beyond the lamp, until the Captain pressed a switch and flooded the room with light.

WE ARRIVE IN ENGLAND

"Lt. Vee," he said. "My wife."

"How do you do—Oh!" she exclaimed, jumping up and putting down her knitting. "You poor man! Whatever have you been doing?"

Before I could reply the Captain said:

"Pull up a chair and let's hear about it."

He was already back in his club easy, on the near side of the fireplace.

I pulled up a chair and sat down, and tried to hide my feet, with the fat sailor's enormous boots, under it.

"Have a drink?" Captain Smythe asked, without moving.

"No, thanks," I replied.

Then I gave them what was intended to be a very brief sketch of the mishap, but Mrs. Smythe kept interrupting with so many exclamations and questions that eventually they had the whole story. Mrs. Smythe was a most interested and sympathetic listener, but I do not think the Adjutant believed a quarter of what I said.

When I had finished I asked him what I had better do next. He said that in the morning I should have to report to the Major and in the meantime there was the Hotel X nearby, where I could spend the night. I had to tell him that I had no money with me, and to ask him if he would vouch for me at the hotel. I told him that I would return the money to him as soon as I got back to my squadron.

Thereupon he pulled out a notebook and wrote a chit to the hotel proprietor. This he handed to me and rose. I rose too, and saying good night to Mrs. Smythe, walked towards the door.

"But you can't go off like this," I heard her say, but the Adjutant was just behind me and accompanied me to the front door. Here he handed me five shillings.

"You'll want that for cigarettes," he said. "You can post it back if you want to."

He then explained to me how to find the hotel.

After adding, " Don't go having any champagne suppers there," he went in and shut the door.

I had not gone very far when I heard a shout behind me, and looking back, saw the Captain striding after me. I waited till he came up.

" Look here," he said, " my wife and I don't feel that we can let you go to the hotel. If you'll be content with a shake-down we can put you up for the night."

I suppose I should have told him to go to the devil, but guessing that his wife had sent him I could hardly do that, and, besides, I was far too weary for any arguments.

So I went back with him.

When we got to the house, Mrs. Smythe must have been busy preparing a room. She came in presently, and smiling brightly said :

" I'm so glad you've come back. Hotels are such cheerless places, aren't they ? Now you must first have a night-cap with us."

She poured out three glasses, and produced some cigarettes. We returned to the fire with these and she chatted on pleasantly for a few minutes. Then she said :

" I expect you're dead beat, and dying to go to your room. There's only a camp-stretcher there and I'm afraid you'll find everything rather rough and ready, but if there's anything you want you'll say so, won't you ?"

" I think bed is indicated, Mrs. Smythe," I replied. " I'm afraid I am being rather a nuisance, but I am jolly grateful, you know. Good night."

The Captain rose to show me to my room and as we left she called out :

" There's some ointment on the dressing-table. Put some of it on those bruises."

" All right. Thanks awfully. Good night."

He led the way upstairs, and opening a door, switched on the light.

" Here we are. Got everything ? Good night."

As the door closed behind him I noticed a pair of his

WE ARRIVE IN ENGLAND

pyjamas on the pillow, and I wondered how this extraordinary woman managed to think of everything.

Then I lost no time in tumbling into bed.

When I came down to breakfast the next morning, Captain Smythe was chipping an egg. After a curt "Morning," he returned to his newspaper, which was propped against the cruet. His wife, looking fresh and pretty, more than compensated, by her cheerful patter, for her husband's silence.

After breakfast, I said good-bye to my hostess, and, grasping the kit-bag, set off with the Adjutant for the Orderly Room. On the way he told me that he had sent off a wire to my C.O. at Netheravon, the previous night.

As we entered the Orderly Room, I grinned, wondering suddenly whether I should salute, in sailor's trousers and a skipper's cap.

The Major was a very kindly old chap, and during the narrative, which I condensed as much as possible, he kept exclaiming:

"What an adventure! What an experience!"

He questioned me a good deal about it and was far more sympathetic than his supercilious subordinate had been.

After giving me a railway-warrant back to Bulford, he shook me very warmly by the hand, and called a clerk to carry my kit-bag and to accompany me to the railway station. Outside the Orderly Room, this youth picked up the kit-bag and with a curt, "Come along," led the way.

He seemed put out about something and we walked along in silence. Suddenly he stopped and turning to me excitedly, said:

"I say, sir, are you the officer who came down in the Channel last night?"

When I nodded he became very apologetic.

"I'm awfully sorry, sir, I didn't know that you were an officer. Did you have a very bad time, sir? It must have been an awful experience, sir. I heard something about it from Corporal Lock who had to send off a wire for the Adjutant last night."

He chattered on till we got to the railway station. Here he put my bag into the train, and I shook hands with him and thanked him. And then I was awfully touched when, after stammering a bit, he suddenly blurted forth:

"I say, sir, if you wouldn't think it cheek of me, could I lend you some money till you get back?"

I thanked him very warmly but told him that the Adjutant had already lent me five bob.

The journey back was slow. I had to wait two hours for a connection at Salisbury, and it was late afternoon when I got to Bulford. I had been amused in the train by the looks of annoyance on the faces of the other officers in the compartment. No doubt they wondered how a seaman who had evidently been in some drunken brawl had found his way into a first-class carriage.

Outside Bulford Station a tender was waiting to take some officers, who had arrived back from leave, up to the mess. It was fairly dark by this time and nobody in the tender raised any objection or made any comment when I got in, too, with my kit-bag. The tender stopped at the mess, and I walked across to our hut. As I went in, Lydell, curious fellow, was walking up and down the bed in his socks. What on earth he was doing it for I do not know, but when he saw me he stopped in the middle of the bed and a look of blank amazement came over his face.

"What the hell—hi, Cameron!" he yelled.

When Cameron came in they wanted full details. When I had finished the tale, I added:

"Well, anyway, old man, I beat your record."

"You're welcome," said Cameron.

"It's almost time for dinner," said Lydell. "Come in those duds, Vee."

"Yes, be a sport!" urged Cameron, "and come on over like that."

WE ARRIVE IN ENGLAND

"No, you don't!" I said. "I'm longing to crawl back into my inconspicuous uniform once more, and you can both go hopping!"

In the morning, I walked down to the hangars and reported to the Flight-Commander. He and the other instructors took quite a cheery view of the incident, and Captain Tyrell then took me along to the Squadron Commander.

The Major "strafed" me good-humouredly, and told me that I should have to go before the Wing-Commander in the morning.

The next day I appeared before him. He was an old colonel who had been seconded from some Scotch regiment and had never done any flying himself. He was furious about the whole affair and accused me of rank carelessness in losing the Bristol. My Flight-Commander let me down rather badly here. When asked for his version of the affair up to the time I had left the aerodrome, he stated that he had told me to climb for half an hour and to see if I could reach 20,000 feet in that time. I protested against this and said that I had been told to climb to 20,000 feet, and to see if I could do it in half an hour. But the Colonel was far too angry to listen to anything I had to say, and, in any case would probably have accepted the word of my superior officer.

After a great deal of talk the Wing-Commander summed up the position:

(i) Directly it became cloudy I should have returned to the aerodrome.

(ii) It was extremely careless of me not to have allowed for the north-east wind which was blowing, and, by continuing to fly in spirals, to have allowed myself to be carried out to sea.[1]

---

[1] As I had been flying north-east for approximately half an hour on half-throttle before finding the trawler, the wind, which had risen considerably after I left the ground, must have carried me fully forty miles out to sea.

(iii) I had thus been guilty of gross carelessness, which had caused the loss of a valuable machine.

Finally:

(iv) In view of the severity of the experience I had already been through, he would not impose any further punishment.

A few days later I saw the finding of the Court of Enquiry which had sat on the loss of the camera-gun attached to the ill-fated Bristol.

The Court of Enquiry found that camera-gun No.—, of the value of £30, attached to Bristol Fighter No. 4807, had been sunk in — fathoms of water, at latitude —, longitude —, and the said camera-gun proving irrecoverable, was to be written off forthwith from the establishment of Squadron 8, Royal Flying Corps, Netheravon, Wilts, the loss of the said camera-gun to be borne, etc., etc.

I returned the seaman's kit-bag and his voluminous clothes, and also the skipper's coat and cap. I also had a large quantity of cigarettes sent down to those good fellows of the trawler.

A few days later I had a letter of acknowledgment from the skipper, and he wrote that one of his men had picked up a wheel that had been seen floating after the aeroplane hit the water. This he would return if it was required, but otherwise he would like to keep it as a memento.

I took it upon myself to write at once asking him to keep it.

And so the matter ended.

On the 31st December, I flew again for the first time after the mishap.

Now this being a veracious record, I feel compelled to admit, even at the risk of being charged with common or garden funk, that when I found myself sitting once

WE ARRIVE IN ENGLAND

more in the pilot's seat of a Bristol Fighter, my knees were knocking together and it was all I could do to wave the mechanics away and open the throttle. But from watching three or four similar cases of nerves during the previous six months, I knew that if I gave way now I should inevitably crock up altogether. So that afternoon I stayed up for an hour, and forced myself to put the Bristol through all her paces. I looped her, sideslipped her, half-rolled, stalled, and finally, towards the end of the hour, I spun her. Unfortunately she was loosely rigged and I had some difficulty in pulling her out of the spin, and this, to some extent, destroyed the confidence which had been coming back to me.

But after this I flew regularly and soon felt quite at home again in the air.

CHAPTER V

THE LAST LAP, IN SCOTLAND

EARLY in January, Smiles, the South African, and I were sent up to Turnberry, on the south-west coast of Scotland.

We travelled together from London and reached our destination on the evening of the 9th. At one of the stations in Scotland, on the way up, some women and girls gave us some piping hot tea and scones. We were very grateful for these as it was a bitterly cold day. We had never come across anything like this in England. Frequently at the stations there the men were given tea and sandwiches or cakes, but never the officers.

At Turnberry we were billeted in a very large, comfortable hotel, overlooking the sea.

Directly a pilot reached Turnberry he was entitled to put up " wings," and Smiles and I lost no time that evening in sewing ours on.

Turnberry was a great place for meeting old acquaintances. There was a large number there when we arrived, some of them fellows whom I had not seen since leaving Canada.

All fighting pilots had to pass through Turnberry before going to France and men were leaving every day and others arriving.

Our quarters left nothing to be desired, but for the rest our stay there was not a very pleasant one. For the first week we were out all day on the range, either firing, or in some little hut attending lectures on the Constantinesco gear or the Vickers gun. We had already had a considerable amount of instruction in these subjects

THE LAST LAP, IN SCOTLAND

in Canada and also in England, but we went through it all again in great detail. It was of importance for us to be thoroughly familiar with every detail of the mechanism of both gear and gun. We also had a lecture on the Aldis Ring Sight. In appearance it resembled a telescope, and carried two lenses and a glass screen on which the ring was drawn. The lenses neither diminished nor magnified the object looked at, and their arrangement was such as to avoid the necessity of aligning a bead with the centre of the ring, as in the earlier type. It was mounted directly above the Vickers gun in the Bristol Fighter.

The weather was bitterly cold. There was snow on the ground nearly all the time, and usually there was a howling wind. The huts on the range provided very little shelter against the weather and we were half-frozen all day. It was a great, blessed relief to get back to the warm hotel at night.

A couple of days after we reached Turnberry, Cameron arrived from Netheravon.

When Saturday came round we were washed out for the afternoon, so four of us walked to Girvan. It was a pretty walk of about five miles along the coast. Part of the time we were tramping through a snowstorm. After an enormous tea at Girvan we got a train back.

At the end of a week, we sat for a test on the work we had done and, on passing this, were sent to the aerodrome.

We spent another week here, never flying the machines ourselves, but being taken up by other pilots to fire at silhouettes, at tow-targets, and at rafts in the sea.

On the 23rd of January, Smiles and I were sent to the School of Aerial Fighting at Ayr. This was a very different story from Turnberry. Our quarters, at Westfield House, were not so palatial as those at Turnberry, but the course was intensely interesting. Also we had a very fine C.O. in Captain Birmingham, M.C., an Australian.

At Ayr I met a South African, Lt. Shirly Samson, whom I had known many years before as a small boy in Pretoria.

Captain Birmingham did not believe in any red-tape or other forms of "hot air." If, at breakfast-time, the weather looked threatening, he would say :

"It's dud this morning, boys. Wash out for the day."

But when we did work, we got down to it very thoroughly. The racecourse at Ayr was the aerodrome. Parts of it had been ploughed up and as there had been a good deal of rain the ground was horribly soft. We flew Bristols here and it would often happen that, after a good landing, a machine would turn up on its nose while taxi-ing in to the hangars. It was not unusual for four to turn up in one morning.

Captain Birmingham insisted on our stunting all the time that we were in the air. He would not allow any pilot to fly straight for more than a minute at a time. If he did he was cursed roundly when he came down.

One rainy morning, after breakfast, four of us were standing about in the ante-room, when our skipper walked in.

"Nothing doing to-day, boys," he said.

"Show us how to play poker, sir," said Samson.

With a smile Captain Birmingham walked across to a bookshelf and picked up a pack of cards lying on it.

Within a couple of minutes he had arranged the cards as he wanted them, and he asked someone to cut them. Then he dealt us each a hand. The first man held a straight, the second a full-house, the third four of a kind and the fourth a straight flush. He himself turned over a royal flush.

"Show us how you did it, sir," someone asked him.

But he grinned and walked off.

There were a few lectures on aerial tactics but most of the fighting instruction was given by actual demonstration in the air. Captain Birmingham, or one of the other instructors, would frequently take one of us as a passenger

THE LAST LAP, IN SCOTLAND

and attack some machine which had come up for the scrap.

Also, we were always challenging one another to air-fights. The man who first " got a bead " on the other was considered to have won the scrap. These practice fights were very exciting as they involved continuous stunting. Also the knowledge that we should soon be involved in actual scrapping, over the line, added a certain spice to them.

One machine, a white-nosed Bristol, was always giving trouble. Its engine would mysteriously fail about three times out of five, but it never let its pilot in for a bad crash. The mechanics never seemed able to solve its mystery.

It was on this machine that Captain Birmingham put up such a good exhibition of turning back into the aerodrome, with a dud engine, which I have described earlier in the book.

One day I was out on the aerodrome when he landed. He beckoned to me and showed me a fly sitting on the back of a strut in the inner bay. He told me he had noticed the fly there while he was running up his engine before taking off. The fly had been unable to get away, being sucked against the strut by the back-pressure of the air because the strut was not perfectly stream-lined.

One afternoon a good exhibition of upside-down flying was given by a Camel pilot. First of all some S.E.5's came streaking across the aerodrome, zoomed up three hundred feet and looped at the top. Then the Camel pilot came along. He began by putting his little machine through all the usual stunts and then through a good many more of his own devising. At last, after beginning a loop, he held his little bus at the top of it, upside down, and in that position began gliding down to earth. Lower he came and lower, till we caught our breaths, thinking that he must crash into the ground. At the last possible moment the nose swung down and round sharply and the machine, right way up, grazed the ground.

On dud days we often went for long walks into the country, or along the coast. And, of course, we visited Burns's cottage.

Our ten days of the final course were happy ones. There was a feeling of good-fellowship in the air, and I think Captain Birmingham, our genial little skipper, had a lot to do with this. I daresay the knowledge that within a few days we should be in France, gave an added zest to life.

Samson left us on the last day of January. We always gave the departing pilots a good send-off, and as Samson had been particularly popular the bar was kept busy from the moment it opened. There was a lamentable lack of whisky and brandy in the bar that night, but an abundance of port and various liqueurs, and so we did the best we could with them. It was a sickly-sweet binge that night, and for months afterwards my stomach turned at the thought of it. By the time the car came for Samson I do not think he knew, or cared, whether he was going to France or to the moon.

Three days later Smiles, Cameron and I left for London.

On reporting at Bolo House, in the Strand, we were told that we were leaving for France on the 6th February and were given leave till then.

Cameron and I went back to Netheravon to collect some kit which we had left behind when we went up to Scotland. When we got to Netheravon we heard that Lydell, whose nerves had been playing tricks with him for some time, had crashed badly and broken his leg. He was in hospital at the time but we were not allowed to see him.

We travelled up to London again the next morning. Cameron wanted to get a folding-bed and a flea-bag, and I had one or two small purchases to make.

When we had finished our shopping we were walking along the Strand towards Trafalgar Square when I spotted a fat youth in Flying Corps uniform coming towards us.

THE LAST LAP, IN SCOTLAND   95

"I say, Cameron, don't we know this little bird? He seems vaguely familiar."

"Well, well!" said Cameron, "if it isn't our young lead-swinger from Toronto." This youngster had wangled a drill-instructorship in Toronto when the rest of us were posted off to our first flying-camps. "I say, young feller," he remarked as we came up to the youth, "what are you doing so far from home?"

The fat boy stared at us for a couple of seconds, and then, "Ah, yes," he said, "I met you fellows at Burwash Hall. And what are you doing, slacking in England? Don't you know there's a war on?"

"Waiting to be asked to have a drink, and then going to Cox's."

"Well, if you'll come with me while I have a hair-cut I'll stand the drinks and then go to Cox's with you."

"You have got a nerve," said Cameron. "Anyway, we're killing time ourselves, so we'll hold you to it. Let's go with him, Vee."

So we followed him into a barber's. Cameron looked at a *Tatler* and I at a copy of *Punch* while the youngster had his hair cut. Then we swopped papers while he had a shave. When I looked up ten minutes later he was having a face-massage.

"The young sweep," I said. "Look at that, Cameron."

"This is too much," he remarked. "It's not worth a drink, Vee. When you've finished that," he said to the barber, "get a big kettle and boil his head," and we left.

After lunching at a comfortable little place in Regent Street, we took a bus out to Hendon and watched the flying for a while. We got back in time for cocktails before dinner, and that night we saw a charming play by Barrie in a tiny theatre.

And then to bed.

The next morning we joined Smiles at Victoria Station.

PART II

CHAPTER VI

FRANCE AT LAST

(i)

It was a quarter past seven when we got to Victoria Station. A woman porter took our valises in a hand-truck to the Folkestone train, which was already fairly crowded. None of us had anyone at the station to see him off and we were glad of this. It was pathetic to see the farewells that took place just before the train left. A pretty girl had been standing next to our compartment, talking through the window to a young subaltern, and as the train moved off, she cried out, " Cheerio, Jack, oh, cheeri-awfully, oh ! " and she ran a few steps after him, dabbing her wet eyes with a little handkerchief.

It was a grey morning and there was a depressing drizzle falling. After the train had started we went along to the saloon and had breakfast. Afterwards we sat on for a while in the saloon, over cigarettes, watching the fields flashing past.

" That," said Smiles, pointing " wouldn't be a bad field for a forced-landing."

" Provided the wind was right," amended Cameron. " Otherwise you would have to side-slip down pretty sharply over those trees."

For some time we commented on the merits and demerits of various fields as landing-grounds.

We wondered whether we should all be sent to the same squadron in France. It seemed quite likely, as we were going over together.

" You never can tell," said Cameron. " There's only

one thing, you know, that the army can't do to us. Anyway, I hope we all get to fighting squadrons. I should hate to have to do contact patrols or art. obs. after once having felt a Bristol between my knees."

It was still raining when we got to Folkestone, so we walked along to the Queen's Hotel where we waited in the lounge, looking at papers and scribbling off one or two letters. We had been told to report at a quarter past one, so after an early lunch we went down to the boat. It was about two o'clock before we sailed. It was with a sinking feeling that I saw the shores of England fading into the mist behind us. Then I began looking round at our fellow-passengers. When I saw the hardened veterans among them, some with wound stripes on their sleeves and others with ribbons on their chests, I felt rather a thrill at the thought that at last we were to have a whack ourselves in the great game. The passage across the Channel was calm, and we had a destroyer on each side of us.

It was some time before we could make out the coastline of France through the haze that still hung about although the rain had stopped. For some reason we did not go in at once to Boulogne harbour, but hung about till it was nearly dark. It was fairly cold on deck and I went below.

When at last we landed the A.M.L.O. told Smiles and me that we had to leave that night for the Pilot's Pool at Candas. Cameron was told to report again the following day. We enquired the way to the Officers' Club and the three of us had dinner there. Our train was due to leave at eight o'clock, and we went down early to secure seats. We found seats in a carriage of which the windows were broken and the doors wrenched off. Remembering a hint given to us by an officer on the boat we took our valises into the compartment with us. There was no knowing when the train would start, and after waiting till half-past eight, Cameron said good-bye to us and

FRANCE AT LAST

returned to the Officers' Club. The carriage was in total darkness, but after we started, a French officer produced a short piece of candle and lit it. There were three French officers in the carriage, and as they could not speak English and we could not speak French, the two of us soon relapsed into silence and watched them talking animatedly and gesticulating. It was a miserable journey. The wind was very cold and the rain beat in freely. Before long the candle which the Frenchman had kept sheltered in a corner, burnt out. The train stopped frequently at small stations and sometimes in between stations. We dozed, woke up shivering, and dozed again. After what seemed hours and hours we came to a big station and once more the train stopped.

We got out to restore some circulation in our legs, and an English officer told us the train would remain here for at least an hour. He suggested our going along with him to the officers' resthouse, a short distance along the platform. It was a godsend to be able to get hot coffee, boiled eggs and bread-and-butter here. We were much warmer and more comfortable when the train started again.

In the morning when we awoke, the train was standing in a small station. Several officers from the train were strolling about. One of them told us that the engine driver had said that the train would remain here for two hours, so Smiles and I, after a cup of black coffee at a small *estaminet*, set off on a brisk walk. As we came to a crossroads, we saw a column of Indian troops approaching on horseback. They were fine-looking men. As they passed us we noticed with surprise that the great majority of them were sergeants! When we returned to the train it was with a comfortable glow throughout our bodies.

We reached Candas late that afternoon, rather weary and very hungry. After dinner, Smiles got into a bridge four, and I sat with some other flying officers in front of a fire. A few of them were out for the first time, like myself, but a number of them had been out before. Some of these had been in hospital, others had been to England on H.E.[1] duty for some months and all of them were now waiting to be posted off to some squadron.

I listened to the talk round the fire for a while and then turned in. It was a quiet night and the distant rumble of the guns could be heard distinctly. Well, this was what all our training had led up to and it was exciting to be so near the scene of action at last. Occasionally, a louder report than usual could be heard, and I lay wondering how the P.B.I.[2] were faring. The plight of those poor devils was indeed much worse than ours. Before long I fell asleep.

In the morning, after breakfast, about a dozen of us were sent off to censor the men's letters in a room next to the orderly room.

After an hour and a half of this we were free for the day. I returned to the mess and was delighted to find Westlake there. He told me he had left Canada shortly after we had, with the next draft, in fact. He had come out to France as a Camel pilot. We sat together for a long time talking about mutual friends. After lunch we went for a long tramp together.

The next day Westlake was posted off to a Camel squadron.

"You're a lucky dog," I said laughing, "getting here after us and leaving before."

"I guess it means," he replied, "that the Camel merchants are being killed off faster than the Bristols."

On the third day, Smiles and I were posted off to A Squadron and were given railway warrants to Peronne.

When we reached Peronne, after another very tedious journey, the R.T.O. there told us that our squadron was at Guizancourt, and he 'phoned them and asked for transport for us.

[1] Home Establishment.   [2] Poor Bloody Infantry.

FRANCE AT LAST

While we were waiting we went to the Officers' Club in Peronne for dinner. The club was in a building which was about the only one in Peronne that was not completely wrecked. There were a great many officers in the club for dinner that night and a talkative waiter pointed out a large number of important people to us.

"That officer just sitting down at that small table is an Italian general. Potatoes, sir? That's a Field-Marshal talking to those two French officers over there. Yes, sir, there's always plenty of brass hats passing through Peronne."

(ii)

Shortly after dinner our tender arrived and took us to Guizancourt. Smiles and I were put in different huts. The Orderly Officer took me along to a very large Nissen hut. Five officers were playing poker at a table on the far side of the hut.

"Lieut. Vee," said the Orderly Officer, "a new pilot."

They looked up as we entered but immediately returned to their game. Two more fellows were in bed, reading.

"You can put up your bed here," said the O.O., indicating a space near the door. "Good night," and he went out. Nobody took the slightest notice of me. I pulled out a cigarette and sat down on one of the beds, smoking it. Presently an Ack Emma[1] came in and dumped my valise on the floor. He unrolled it, put up my bed and made it, and then he too went out.

The light in my corner of the hut was too poor to read by and I did not feel like asking my future comrades-in-arms for a candle, so I went to bed. I was tired after the day's travelling and soon dropped off.

In the early hours of the morning I was awakened and, for a moment, thought I was back at Mohawk when I saw a mechanic with a lantern, shaking men by their arms. Suddenly I remembered where I was and I

[1] A.M., Air Mechanic.

guessed that these men were being called for the dawn patrol.

There was a scuffling noise for a few minutes as they dressed and then one by one they passed my bed on their way out. The last man was late and ran out after the others. It was quite dark in the hut. Outside I could hear engines sputtering into life and then clip-clopping as they ticked over. Then one after the other they roared as they were run up. After two or three minutes they were all clip-clopping again. I lay listening for them to take off. Presently one machine gave a great roar, which diminished rapidly in volume as the machine sped away. Then I counted five more taking off, and after that everything was quiet once more in the hut.

It was broad daylight when I woke again. Two or three fellows were stirring and one of them asked another for a gasper. A man near me was dressing. He looked across and seeing me awake said :

" Morning ! "

" Morning ! " I answered.

" How long does the early patrol stay up ? " I asked.

" Oh, a couple of hours."

Presently they came in, walking clumsily in their Sidcot suits and thigh boots.

" See any E.A. this morning, Mac ? " asked the man who was dressing.

" Ran into eight of 'em over Guise. Brookes got one and the rest cleared off."

" Good egg ! "

Our aerodrome, Guizancourt, was only about eight miles west of St. Quentin and the intermittent gun-fire could be heard very clearly. I was conscious of it all the time but no one else seemed to pay the least attention to it.

When I had dressed and shaved I went out and found Smiles smoking an early pipe.

" The O.O. told me last night," he said, " that we

FRANCE AT LAST

had to report to the C.O. immediately after breakfast."

And so after breakfast, Smiles and I went along to the orderly room to report to Major Field.

Smiles was called in first. He was in the orderly room for about ten minutes. Directly he came out I was sent in.

The C.O. told me that for three weeks I should not be allowed to cross the lines, but could do a good bit of flying (with sandbags) so as to become thoroughly familiar with " the lie of the land " and should also have to do some aerial photography and some line-patrols. Then he asked me whether I wanted to do O. Pips[1] or to join the Photographic-and-Reconnaissance Flight. Having succeeded in getting to a fighting-squadron I thought I might as well go the whole hog, and answered that I should like to do O. Pips.

" Think you'll be any good at knocking Huns out of the sky ? " asked the C.O.

" I don't know, sir, but I should like to have a go at it," I answered.

" All right," he said. " Report to Captain Sotheran, C Flight."

Outside, Smiles was waiting and he told me that he, too, had been put into C Flight.

We reported to Capt. Sotheran and he told us each to take up a machine, with sandbags as ballast.

A number of observers watched us take off. The observers always watched the first performance of each new pilot with anxious interest.

We kept in sight of each other and flew round for about an hour taking note of all the principal landmarks in the neighbourhood.

The aerodrome at Guizancourt was a large one. There was a Camel squadron and also an S.E.5 squadron on it,

---

[1] O.P.s, Offensive Patrols.

and that evening, Smiles told me that he had seen Westlake at the Camel squadron. As soon as I could I went across to visit him. Their huts were only a couple of hundred yards from ours, so we were able to see a good deal of one another.

Every day, weather permitting, we did some flying and soon got to know the look of the country around Guizancourt. The roads stood out most clearly and could be seen far more easily than railway lines.

All the country in the neighbourhood, and along the Somme particularly, was pitted with shell-holes. It all looked very desolate.

At last, one day I was sent up with an observer, Sergeant Heather, in the back seat, and was told to take an overlap of a certain region in the neighbourhood of Ham. This was the first time I had ever flown with a passenger, and I felt a bit nervous with the responsibility of it! The sergeant looked very warlike as he came waddling along in his Sidcot-suit, carrying two drums of ammunition for the Lewis gun.

I secretly hoped that we might come across a stray Boche during our flight. But nothing of the sort happened. We got the overlap (the observer took the photographs) and then returned tamely to the aerodrome.

After this I always flew with an observer. Sometimes we would fly down to the silhouettes floating in the marshes at St. Simon, near Ham. I would dive steeply on them, firing with the Vickers gun as we went down, and on pulling out in a climbing turn the observer would fire with the Lewis gun.

New pilots were also sent on line patrols. Two machines would fly towards the line and meet two Camels at a pre-arranged spot. One Bristol, accompanied by a Camel, would fly down the line from Gouzeaucourt to La Fere, at 5,000 feet. The other Bristol would fly at 2,000 feet, accompanied by the other Camel. The upper Bristol would fire red Very lights and the lower one green lights.

"... IT ALL LOOKED VERY DESOLATE. ..."

[*Royal Air Force Official—Crown Copyright Reserved*

FRANCE AT LAST

This was to give our infantry an idea of what the machines looked like at these heights.

Smiles was unlucky from the start. While he was doing one of these line patrols two Boches dived on him, shot through his petrol tank, and wounded his observer, Sergeant Heather, in the leg. He glided back and picked out the smoothest-looking field he could find, but it had a good many shell-holes in it, and on landing his left wheel dropped into one of these and pitched the machine over on to its back. He and his observer arrived back in an ambulance while we were at lunch. Sergeant Heather was attended to by our M.O. and then sent off to the nearest C.C.S.[1] Smiles was unhurt and came in to lunch.

About a week after this Smiles flew down on a very dud day to St. Simon to fire at the silhouettes. While he was out a heavy snowstorm came on. He was caught in this, and being unable to see, flew into the side of a hill. The machine struck with great violence and he and his observer were thrown out. This was fortunate, for the machine immediately burst into flames.

After the first couple of days at Guizancourt I felt quite at home in my new surroundings. The officers in the squadron were a good crowd, and when the first reserve had worn off I found them very friendly. Two of them in particular I took to from the start. One was Lt. Alec Scott, a tall Scotch observer, and the other was Lt. Tomkins, a pilot, known as Tommy by everyone in the Squadron. Tommy had large brown eyes and a shy manner. He was a comical fellow. The immaculate Burrowes, observer to Tomkins, was a man who improved on acquaintance. His supercilious manner was rather inclined to repel strangers. I soon discovered that this was purely superficial, and found him to be a most likeable fellow.

McDougall, about a week before, had been made observer to Captain Sotheran, our Flight-Commander.

[1] Casualty Clearing Station.

Offensive patrols usually went over three times a day. Frequently the patrol came back with a Boche or two to its credit.

On dud days we did no flying and occasionally some of us went out in a lorry to collect firewood. At other times we would take revolvers and go off rat-hunting in some of the shattered houses in the neighbourhood.

There had been a few casualties shortly before Smiles and I arrived, and before long some new pilots and observers were posted to the Squadron to replace these. So we were no longer the juniors in the Squadron.

A little Canadian, called Parrish, who had arrived some three or four days before Smiles and me, went farther afield than usual one day, and got lost. He landed in a field near a village to find out his whereabouts. He had no sooner got down than a Frenchman, flying a Spad, attempted to land in the same field but struck a hedge and turned a complete somersault, wrecking his machine. Parrish told us that the Frenchman crawled out from underneath his machine quite unconcernedly and, walking up to him, shook hands. He began talking very rapidly but Parrish could not understand a word he said. Soon a crowd of villagers collected and the Frenchman turned to them, gesticulating and shouting, and pointing to his machine. About twenty of them walked over to the Spad, picked it up and marched off with it on their shoulders as though it were a perfectly natural proceeding. Parrish had very little petrol left and by pointing to his tanks made the villagers understand that he wanted more. A French officer who had arrived among them sent off to the village for some petrol and Parrish strained this through a silk handkerchief into the tanks. They gave him the direction of Peronne and he took off and soon found his way back to the aerodrome. Major Field was so pleased with the way he had conducted this forced-landing, and particularly with the fact that he had strained the petrol, that he

FRANCE AT LAST

allowed him to commence war-flying a week before his probationary period of three weeks was up.

There were five South Africans in A Squadron. Another, Second Lieut. A. W. Beauchamp-Proctor*, was in an S.E.5 squadron not far from us, and was already distinguishing himself. His toll of enemy aircraft and balloons was mounting steadily. It was not long before he was awarded the Military Cross, the first of his many decorations.

About this time a certain Major Wood arrived at the Squadron. The adjutant told one of the pilots that Major Wood was going to bring over a new Bristol Fighter squadron from England before long and he had come to us to learn how to run it. We did not think he would make a very inspiring C.O. He used to moon about the place with his hands in his pockets most of the day. After about a fortnight he disappeared, but I was to meet him again later.

Occasionally, French airmen visited the aerodrome. Most of them were very good pilots, but they were unconventional and usually amusing. One afternoon, five of them landed in Spads. We took them into the mess for tea and shortly afterwards they returned to their machines. Our mechanics swung their props, and then instead of first running up their engines and taxi-ing out so as to take off into the wind, as soon as their engines started they waved the chocks away and immediately took off in whichever direction they happened to be pointing. One of them choked his engine, pulled back the throttle, opened her up again and after bumping pretty badly, got off.

One morning just after breakfast the C.O. sent for me.

"Morning, Vee. Twelve E.A. have just crossed over, going towards Amiens. They will probably be back within the hour. I want you to go up and intercept them. Take Corporal Fulton with you. Go up in Number 18."

The C.O. said this all very crisply and without a smile on his face.

"Thank you, sir," I said and saluted and went off to find Corporal Fulton. Fulton was an observer who had done a good deal of war-flying and when I had found him he listened to the message without twitching a muscle. I watched his face, for at the back of my mind had been a feeling that the C.O. might be pulling my leg.

Number 18 was one of the older machines with a 250-h.p. engine. We climbed as fast as possible, but the old bus had a ceiling of 16,000 feet. All the time I was scanning the skies for a sign of the returning Boches, but not a machine could I see. At last I caught sight of nine little specks coming eastwards, some distance above us. I flew towards them, thinking I might zoom up and fire at them as they passed, but Corporal Fulton must have guessed my purpose for he touched me on the shoulder and shook his head. After we had been up about an hour he pointed towards the aerodrome and so, half-disappointed and half-relieved, I shut off and glided down. When we landed he told me the nine machines were S.E.5's which had been gaining height and were crossing over on an O. Pip! I told one of the older pilots about this episode, and by the way he grinned I guessed that I had been "had."

One morning, about eleven o'clock, a dreadful thing happened. Half a dozen of us were in the hut when a terrific "crump" was heard outside.

"My God!" said one of the men, "somebody's gone west for certain!"

I have never had any psychic experiences at any time, but I felt perfectly certain at that moment that Westlake had been killed. We ran out of the hut and round the mess to the aerodrome.

"A Camel merchant has written himself off," said an officer as we came on to the aerodrome.

"Do you know who it is?" I asked.

"Westfield or Westlake, I heard someone say," he answered.

Westlake had been flying round and doing some steep diving. After one of these dives he had pulled his machine out far too quickly and the wings had simply folded up. Then the fuselage had dropped like a stone. He had fallen out before reaching the ground.

After all his training to go out like this before he had even crossed the lines!

That evening I wrote to his mother. Long afterwards I heard from her and also from two of his brothers. Owing to some unaccountable delay, the cable which had been sent to them by his C.O. had only arrived at the same time as my letter. His mother particularly wanted to know if he had done any war flying before being killed.

I do not think I am more partial to falsehood than most men, but when I answered her letter I lied to her for the second time. I told her he had crossed the lines on two or three war-shows before his death. There are degrees in lying, and I could not quite bring myself to tell her that he had brought down any Boches, though I was tempted to do so. I know from what she wrote later, that my letter had comforted her.

It was about this time that a new pilot, Lt. Powell, an American, joined the Squadron. He was an exceptionally tall fellow and he had much vigour and a spice of originality in his make-up. It was from him, I think, that we first heard the story, which went the rounds of all the aerodromes in France, of the American pilot who, after crashing on a strange aerodrome, walked into the C.O.'s office with:

"Say, Bo! Are you the big noise round heeah? Wal, I dropped my gasoline kite on your lawn and I've come to say I'm sorry!"

(iii)

When Smiles and I were almost due to begin our war-flying, the Adjutant told me one morning that I had been chosen to go to Bromley, Kent, for a week's course in wireless telephony. Occasionally one of the newer pilots would be sent off for this course, but I was bitterly disappointed that it should have been my lot. I was very near the goal to which all my training had been leading, and being young, and new to the game, I regarded this as a nasty back-hander which Fate had dealt me.

And so one morning I received my railway warrant and set off by tender for Peronne. At Peronne Station I forgot to exchange my warrant for a railway ticket, and after finding an empty compartment in a remarkably good state of preservation, I settled down for the weary journey.

Presently the conductor came round for my ticket. I produced the warrant. He said a long sentence very rapidly in French.

"Nong comprong," I said, when he had finished.

Thereupon he took a deep breath and started off again faster than ever, waving his hands to heaven and then towards my warrant, and talking continuously for about three minutes. This gave me time to think what line I should take with him. I was not defrauding his railway in any way and so when he stopped for breath I said:

"Nong comprong," once more. And so it went on. Every time I repeated my formula it acted as a spur to a tired horse. But even a spur will lose its power in the end, and at last, flinging up his arms dramatically he went out and slammed the door.

After a while two Frenchmen entered the compartment, and still farther on a young Flying Corps officer got in. He was a cheery young fellow and was going back to England on leave.

We got into conversation and I found out that his bag

FRANCE AT LAST

up to date was ten E.A. For this he had just been awarded the M.C. He was very proud indeed of his brother, one of our greatest airmen, the famous Major McCudden, who was shortly after awarded the V.C.

I persuaded him to talk about some of his fights and he was most interesting about them. The Fokker triplane was being used extensively on the Front at this time. A few days before, he had seen and given chase to two of these " tripes." When he fired at the first it did a half-roll, and spun down. Then he tackled the second. This also spun, but he followed it down. Presently he saw the first one pull out of the spin and fly off, but when the second pulled out he tackled it again and fired till he saw it crash into the ground.

Now and then the Frenchmen and we made a polite exchange of amicable sounds.

The train made frequent stops, and once or twice we got out and stretched our legs. When it got dark, the Frenchmen dropped off to sleep.

McCudden had removed his collar and was bending down taking off his boots, to make himself as comfortable as possible for the night, when one of the Frenchmen began to snore. Every time he snored, McCudden imitated him, with a funny little whistle at the end. There was little temptation to try to sleep in our uncomfortable positions so we chatted on till late into the night. Then at one of the stations we found an officers' resthouse and were able to get coffee and something to eat. After that we dozed intermittently till morning. McCudden was a good travelling companion and I was sorry to say good-bye to him the next day at Boulogne. As he was going on leave and I on " duty," we had to travel over on different boats.

Shortly after he got back from leave he was reported missing, and I heard that on the day Major McCudden got the V.C. news came through that his brother had been killed.

H

The course at Bromley only lasted a week and we had an easy time of it, but I was glad when it was time to leave.

On the last day, I went up to Town. Here I ran across a fellow, called Crossley, whom I had known at one of the training camps in Canada. I noticed that he was walking very awkwardly and when I questioned him about it he told me that he was braced up in a sort of metal corset. He had taken up a mechanic one day in an Avro, fitted with dual control, and after doing some stunting he had spun the machine down. The Ack Emma had got "wind-up" during the spin and had grabbed the dual joystick and pulled it in tightly to his stomach. It was coupled, of course, to Crossley's joystick and when Crossley had tried to push this forward to come out of the spin he could not move it, and they had spun straight into the ground. The Ack Emma had been killed, and Crossley had spent three months in hospital.

The day after I got back to Guizancourt, B and C Flights, each flying six machines, raided a German aerodrome at Busigny.

Captain Mills in command of B Flight was detailed to attack the western portion of the aerodrome, and Captain Sotheran, of C Flight, the eastern portion. Three machines, led by Major Field, flew above the twelve raiders as a guard against E.A. These three machines carried cameras, and each of the fifteen machines carried four 25-lb. bombs.

Busigny aerodrome was about seven miles behind the lines. The machines, flying at 8,000 feet, crossed the lines near Bellicourt at two o'clock in the afternoon and began gliding down towards Bohain. Then they turned towards Busigny and with their noses down and their engines full on, roared towards the aerodrome. B Flight, led by Captain Mills, dived from 3,000 feet on the western hangars. Five Rumplers were seen on the aerodrome outside the hangars, and also a number of men.

FRANCE AT LAST

The six machines poured streams of bullets from their Vickers guns into the hangars, the Rumplers and the men of the German squadron. They also released some of their bombs. The men on the aerodrome were taken completely by surprise. When they realised that these were English aeroplanes diving on them they scattered in all directions, but it was too late, and many of them were seen to fall. Direct hits with the bombs were observed on some of the machines and hangars. The machines continued diving to within 100 feet of the ground and then zoomed up in a great left-hand turn. This gave the observers the chance to bring their Lewis guns into action and they sent more streams of bullets into the aerodrome.

In the meantime, C Flight, led by Captain Sotheran, had attacked the eastern hangars. Lined up in front of these were nine machines, some of them two-seaters and some of them scouts. Many direct hits were again observed with the bombs, and the nine E.A. on the ground were riddled by the streams of machine-gun bullets. Each Bristol dived twice on the aerodrome, and in the " report from Major Field, the officer commanding the Ath Squadron, R.F.C., in the Field, to Colonel Wiggett, the officer commanding the Dth Wing, R.F.C.," Major Field stated that 4,000 rounds had been fired into the aerodrome, fifty-two bombs dropped and twenty-seven exposures made over the area.

This concise statement was the summary of the report, which consisted of the individual reports of eleven of the pilots who had taken part in the raid.

The Bristols next turned their attention to the roads in the neighbourhood of Busigny. On the main road leading north from Busigny were large quantities of motor transport and horse transport, and some of the machines dived on these, causing utter confusion. Many of the motor-vehicles overturned, and all the wagons were observed to fall into a ditch running along the side of the road. Men scattered in all directions and many were seen to fall. An officer on horseback was shot from his horse. One pilot dived on a motor-cyclist tearing along the road, and the cyclist either through fear of death, or death itself, crashed into the ditch.

Then Captain Mills and Sotheran gathered formation and returned to the lines, climbing as they went.

B Flight crossed the lines near Le Catelet, at 6,000 feet, and were heavily archied. C Flight, with only five machines, crossed slightly north of Le Catelet and flew over a flaming-onion battery. This sent up its green cones of flaming onions at them but obtained no direct hits on them. Eight of the eleven machines had holes in them, caused by anti-aircraft fire, when they reached the aerodrome. The sixth machine of C Flight had been observed by the other members of the Flight flying back towards the lines at less than 1,000 feet, diving on troops and transport all the way back. The pilot of this machine was Lt. Staines and the observer Lt. Dickson. As it crossed the lines a bullet from the trenches passed through the pilot's heart. The machine reared, and plunged into the ground, just behind our lines, with the engine full on. Lt. Dickson miraculously escaped death. A field-battery sent him back in a car to the aerodrome. He got out of the car himself, but seemed half-dazed.

"Give me some whisky," he said, but before his wish could be granted our M.O. got hold of him and led him away. That same day he was sent off to hospital.

Dickson could carry an extraordinary quantity of whisky. He was a fat chap and his eyes were usually half-closed, giving him a "muzzy" look, but he was very much awake for all that. He spoke almost in a whisper, but rapidly and clearly, and his tongue was like a two-edged sword.

Nine days later Dickson walked into the ante-room of the mess one evening just before we went in to dinner. He looked weary and dusty. Shouts greeted him from all over the room. He grinned here and there, and, walking across to the C.O. said in his rapid whisper :

" I'm reporting back for duty, sir."

" Glad to see you back, Dickson. All right, again ? I was not notified that you were posted back to us."

" I wasn't, sir. I lorry-hopped back from the —st C.C.S."

" Oh, good man," said the C.O.

Dickson, of course, should have gone to the Pool on being discharged from the Casualty Clearing Station, there to be posted to some squadron to which the Powers-that-be might have thought fit to send him. But Dicky was taking no chances on getting sent to the wrong squadron, and Major Field was so pleased at getting him back, that he squared matters with the authorities, and Dickson was allowed to remain.

CHAPTER VII

OVER THE LINES

(i)

Two days after I rejoined the Squadron, Captain Sotheran told me that I could go up with the afternoon patrol. Scott, who had already done a good many war-shows, and whose regular pilot had been wounded a few days before, came with me as an observer.

Experienced observers were always sent up with new pilots, and new observers with old pilots.

There were five machines on this O. Pip, and we flew in a V-formation. Scott and I were on the outside right. Before leaving the ground, each pilot was given his position in the formation. We took off singly and linked up in the air.

We flew west along the Somme for about twenty miles, gaining height, then we turned east, still climbing steadily. We crossed the lines at 18,000 feet, a short distance south of St. Quentin. It was a beautifully clear day and the visibility was good. But it was bitterly cold at that altitude and particularly at that time of year, the beginning of March. My hands were rapidly becoming numbed with the intense cold. It was the first time I had crossed the lines, and I was keyed up to concert pitch. I kept glancing at the other machines to see that I maintained my correct place in the formation, and the rest of the time I was looking eagerly ahead for signs of any enemy aircraft. Occasionally I fired short bursts from my Vickers gun by pressing the Bowden lever on the joystick. This had to be done to keep the oil from congealing. From time to time, too, I heard Scott's gun in the back cockpit.

OVER THE LINES

While doing line shows I had occasionally received spasmodic attentions from anti-aircraft batteries, but had never realised what they could do when roused. Suddenly as we crossed St. Quentin, there was a terrific " wonk " just under us. The bus rocked about violently. Then " Archie " really woke up and got busy. Crump—wonk —bang—click. It must be remembered that each Bristol used for war-shows carried a 264-h.p. engine. The short exhaust pipes from this, one on either side, ended just next to the pilot's cockpit. The noise from the engine was thus deafening. Only those anti-aircraft shells which exploded near the machine could be heard at all. Even a click indicated an unpleasantly close burst.

Some brave fellows one reads about do not seem to mind being under heavy fire. But I did. I minded very much. For two pins I would have cut and run. However, the other four Bristols kept steadily on, so for very shame, I did too. The sight of them restored some of my confidence. A Bristol Fighter in the air is a glorious sight. It is like a flying tiger and it is an inspiring thing to look upon.

Archie was in a bad temper. Every time I heard a bang I looked over to see if the wings were still on. Frequently we were flying through the black, acrid smoke of the bursts. Then as we drew away eastwards, Archie reluctantly gave us up. We flew about twenty miles east of St. Quentin, looking for enemy aircraft, but never a Boche did we see. For three-quarters of an hour we hunted backwards and forwards and then, before we got back to St. Quentin, we turned south. Just after we turned I was lagging behind a bit. Suddenly I heard Scott's gun firing a longer burst than usual. Just for an instant I paid no attention, thinking that he was merely warming it. Then I felt the bus quiver and at almost the same moment the machine in front of us, flown by MacLaren, did a half-roll and dived back under us.

Then it dawned upon me that we had been attacked

and I, too, turned back. But by this time the two Albatros scouts who had dived on us out of the sun had got away. I looked round now for the rest of the formation, but could see no sign of them. MacLaren, too, seemed to have disappeared. It is extraordinarily difficult to see distant machines in the unlimited sky, and the knack of spotting them only comes after long experience. Each of us carried a map of the neighbourhood pasted on to a sheet of three-ply so, as I knew where I was, I decided to return to the aerodrome.

As we began gliding down Scott hit me on the shoulder and pointed to the right wing. Both struts in the inner bay had been splintered by the Boche's bullets and the drift wires had been cut at the point where they crossed. The four ends were flapping in the wind. When I saw this I glided very slowly so as to put no unnecessary strain on the wing, and we got down safely a few minutes before the rest of the patrol.

"Scotty," I said, as soon as we landed, "why the devil didn't you tell me those Boches were on our tail?"

"Vee, old sport," he answered, "I thought that if I told you, you might start split-assing the bus, and I shouldn't have been able to get such a good bead on them." MacLaren had had no luck either when he turned back, and both the Albatri had got away.

And so my first encounter with the enemy was over before I knew that it had taken place. I came in for a good deal of chaff about this and Captain Sotheran said good-humouredly that it would teach me in future to keep a look-out behind as well as in front, and not to leave the whole back view to the observer only. Scott was rapped over the knuckles too, for not telling me of the approach of the Albatros scouts.

Most of us were in the same hut, and as we walked across to change nobody even referred to the attentions we had received from Archie at the beginning of the patrol.

"Mac," I said as we were getting out of our flying-kit, "wasn't Archie pretty bad over St. Quentin this afternoon?"

"Oh, nothing much," MacLaren replied indifferently, "we strike much worse patches than that, sometimes."

The following evening, as we were sitting round the fire in the mess, Captain Sotheran told us of a rather sporting fellow whom he had encountered over Peronne that morning. He had gone up with an observer, intending to nose round for stray E.A. near the lines, and was flying east over Peronne after gaining his height, when he met the black-crossed machine. He had immediately attacked and the Boche had responded gamely. They split-assed round one another, banking and half-rolling, each doing his best to get a bead on the other. Sometimes their machines almost collided, and occasionally they fired short bursts at one another, but with no decisive results. After half an hour of this, Captain Sotheran ran out of ammunition. Probably the Boche had exhausted his supply too, for presently he waved his hand to our Flight-Commander, who waved back to him, and then they parted, the Boche flying off eastwards.

When Captain Sotheran landed he saw two little streaks of fresh blood on one of his wings. Neither he nor his observer had been hit, so the blood must have come from the Boche!

Two days later, Brigade wanted some information about gun transport on two main roads several miles behind the lines. Captain Sotheran went off on a lone reconnaissance to get this information, but he never came back. Often when we lost machines the Germans would drop messages on our side of the lines, saying what had happened to the occupants, and we always did the same for them, but we never heard what had happened to Captain Sotheran and his observer, Lieut. McDougall. A few days later Captain Pitts, a pilot from E Squadron, arrived to take over the command of C Flight.

(ii)

For some days the weather was very bad and no patrols were carried out. There was a good deal of snow and rain and the surface of the aerodrome became spongy and slushy. Most of the time the clouds were within a hundred feet of the ground, but when they lifted a bit we got in some flying.

On several occasions Scott and I went up purposely so that he might get some practice in handling the bus in the air. In his cockpit there was a spare joystick which could be slipped into a socket at his feet. There was no dual rudder-bar for him, but the two control wires from my rudder-bar passed through his cockpit on their way to the tail of the machine. He could move these wires by hand, and so to control the bus he would have one hand on the joystick and the other on one of the rudder wires.

Observers were not taught to fly an aeroplane during their training, and this meant that if the pilot were hit the observer was doomed unless he could control the descent. We arranged that if ever I were hit, Scott was to lean over and shut off the engine, then slip in his joystick and try to glide back to our lines. He would probably crash when he got down as he had never had any practice in landing, but that we agreed to leave in the lap of the gods. It was too risky to practise landings with the insufficient controls in the back cockpit.

During the bad weather a few propellers were damaged as the machines turned up readily on their noses while they were taxi-ing out to take off, or taxi-ing back to the hangars.

One of the new pilots, Stockdale, tried to get up one afternoon and just after he opened his engine the wheels sank deeply in a soft patch and the machine whipped right over on to its back. The propeller, the top plane and the rudder were smashed, but the pilot's belt held, and Stockdale was not hurt.

Once or twice the weather showed signs of breaking, and one day we managed to send over two patrols, in between showers, but there was little activity in the air, beyond the lines, that day. Then on the following morning, when I woke, I heard rain pattering once more steadily on the roof.

I wondered lazily what the time was, and tried, without getting out of bed, to reach the chair on which my watch was lying, but could not manage it. MacLaren was snoring spasmodically in the adjoining bed. Otherwise the silence was unbroken. Presently a silk pyjama'd figure emerged from its blankets and I called out :

"What's the time, Burrowes ? "

He groped under his pillow, pulled out his watch and exclaimed :

"Gad's teeth ! It's 9.20. Up, you lazy lubbers," he shouted, " and after the victuals ! Ten minutes to go."

"Eh ? What's that ? Ten minutes ? " asked MacLaren, sitting up dazedly in bed and rubbing his eyes.

"The C.O. has sent for you to do a lone reconn.," said Burrowes briskly.

"You have to leave in ten minutes," added Tomkins.

"Oh, Cripes ! " said MacLaren. "Good Lord ! it's raining. Go to hell, Tommy ! "

For the next six minutes there was a hasty stropping of razors and lathering of faces. Then Sidcot suits were hastily drawn on over pyjamas and at 9.29 there was a stampede for the mess. It was a rule in the Squadron that no officer, unless detained on duty, could enter the mess for breakfast after 9.30.

Forty minutes later we straggled back to the hut.

"Who's for a game of poker ? " asked Parrish.

"My soul revolts at the thought of it," remarked Scott.

"It would take more than that to tarnish your lily-white soul. What about bridge, then?" said the amiable Parrish.

"Now you're talking. But the first thing is to get the fire going."

The junior members were sent off to fetch wood for the little stove in the hut. When they returned the stove was packed and some petrol thrown down it. Then everyone retired to the doorway and threw lighted matches at it. Presently a direct hit was obtained and the stove went off with a bang, blowing out the chimney which led from the side. This was pushed back into place and soon the wood was blazing merrily. Scott, Burrowes, Tomkins and MacLaren settled down to a rubber of bridge on one side of the stove, while five others started a poker school on the other side. I sat in my Sidcot at a box, trying to write letters. But the bridge was chatty and the poker noisy.

After a while Murdock, from the poker school, was sent out to report upon the weather.

Everybody looked up as he came in, beaming.

"Dud as hell, boys. Carry on."

"Send it down, John," added Scott, piously.

I made one more attempt to get on with my letter, then, putting away the pad in despair, I watched the card-players for a while. Half an hour later, Captain Pitts came in.

"Sorry to interrupt you chaps, but will you, Tommy, and you, Vee, go off to fetch the new machine? The rain has eased off and I think you can manage it if you hedge-hop," and he went out.

"And I sitting here with a cast-iron hand," said Scott, as we got up. "Everything that opens and shuts!"

Tomkins and I got our goggles and gloves and went off. The distributing depot was about sixty miles off.

Tomkins flew the machine. He hedge-hopped the first part of the way, but when we got nearer the depot the clouds lifted and we rose a bit. The new machine was ready for us when we got to the depot and we found Browne there too, one of the A Flight pilots who had just returned from leave.

They gave us some tea at the depot and then we started back. Browne got into the back seat in Tomkins' bus, and the Ack Emmas put sand-bags into the new one for me. Tomkins, who knew the country well, was to lead the way home, but just after we left the ground I saw him turn back. I guessed that he had engine trouble, and after watching him get back to the aerodrome safely, I decided to go on alone.

The clouds were breaking now and the visibility was improving. I knew the general direction of our own aerodrome and I knew, too, that I should be able to pick up landmarks when I got nearer to it. There were still some heavy, isolated showers over various patches of the country, but I was high enough to be able to see them, and fly round instead of through them. I flew south-east till I picked up the Somme. After that it was plain sailing. I followed the Somme to Peronne and as I was familiar with that part of the country I had no difficulty in finding the aerodrome.

When I got back, Captain Pitts told me that I could keep the new bus as my own. I was very pleased at this, as up to that time I had been flying various odd machines. Now Bristol Fighter No. 22 belonged to me. Scott and I were to fly together regularly now, and of course we had our own rigger and fitter, whose business it was to see that our bus was always in tip-top condition.

One evening, Major Field had a visitor at dinner. When cigarettes had been lit the C.O. got up and announced that he wanted us all to collect in the ante-room after dinner, when Captain Mellish would address us.

Captain Mellish spoke on methods of escaping from Germany. He spoke with quiet confidence, and his account of how various prisoners had escaped was most interesting. He himself had spent many months in a prison camp. So much of our work was done many miles behind the Boche lines that we all ran some risk of going down, some time or other, in enemy territory. Captain Mellish advised each of us to arrange a code with some non-combatant relative or friend, before that happened.

"You might, for instance," he said, " arrange with an uncle that if you begin a letter to him ' My dear Uncle Harry ' he is to accept the letter at its face value. If you leave out the ' My ' and begin ' Dear Uncle Harry ' he is to know that it contains some hidden message. With regard to the code, don't make it too simple. The Boches are rather good at spotting these things. They have a special staff of censors who do nothing else. If your letter looks at all suspicious it will never be allowed to go through.

"You might, for instance, arrange that the second, sixth, fifth, ninth, eighth, twelfth, eleventh, fifteenth, etc., words are to be regarded as significant. You will have plenty of time—months if you like—to write your letter and fill in the other words so that, as a whole, the letter appears to read smoothly—the sort of letter that any prisoner might write to his people."

When new prisoners first arrived at a camp, he went on, they were often put together, with a spy disguised as a prisoner among them. Captain Mellish warned us to be exceedingly careful of what we said in front of strangers. For that matter we had to be careful about talking even among fellows whom we felt sure we could trust for the walls often had microphones concealed in them.

Sometimes, he went on, a simple bluff would be successful where a more subtle effort might only excite suspicion. One of his fellow-prisoners wrote in code to his people in England for a black coat. To attempt to escape in uniform would be to make his chance of getting through infinitesimal. In due course the coat arrived, but was eyed with suspicion by the prison authorities. Captain Mellish's friend told them with a straight face that a plain black coat was regulation mess-kit in his regiment. This story was actually believed and the coat handed over to him. This officer had previously, with the help of a bribe, obtained a pair of civilian trousers and, patiently biding his time, he eventually slipped out of camp. He possessed a little money and a smattering of German, and with the help of these he travelled quite a long way towards the Dutch frontier. But the Fates were against him. In a crowded train he offered his seat to a German woman. This little act of courtesy was apparently so unusual that it attracted attention to him and led to the disclosure of his identity.

Two more of Captain Mellish's fellow-prisoners had been preparing for some months for their escape. Each of them had collected some very shabby civilian clothes, and they were now awaiting a chance to slip out from the prison. Prisoners who attempted to escape knew that they rendered themselves liable to be shot in the event of their recapture, so they could not afford to bungle the first step. At last one day a heaven-sent opportunity presented itself. Some outside workmen were busy in the camp, whitewashing buildings. At midday they left their ladder against a wall and went off to eat their lunch. The two officers hastily slipped into their shabby civilian clothes, and carrying the ladder between them, boldly marched straight past the guards and out of the camp. Such a bold bid for freedom deserved a better fate. They had barely got a hundred yards from the gates when the alarm was given and they were hauled back.

An attempt by another officer began grotesquely, but had a successful ending. The fence round the camp was not unscalable, but sentries were on duty continuously, day and night. One day, this particular officer strolled over towards the boundary beyond which a river flowed past the camp. He knew a little German and exchanged a few remarks with the sentry. Suddenly he pointed excitedly, and exclaimed in German :

" Look at that rabbit swimming down the river ! "

The sentry swung round to see this extraordinary sight and the officer promptly hopped over the fence and into the river. He alternately swam under water and hid under the bank of the river till he had made good his escape from the camp. Then he gradually worked his way, at night, towards the frontier, remaining hidden during the day because he was in uniform. Eventually he got through.

CHAPTER VIII

MARCH 21ST, 1918

(i)

For some time there had been vague rumours about a coming attack. Gradually these rumours crystallised into more definite form, and it became known that before long the Germans were to launch their Great Offensive along a wide front.

The knowledge did not make much difference to the mode of life in the squadron. Offensive patrols still went up daily, and exacted their toll of machines from the German Air Force. When tenders were available, we still went in to Peronne for jolly dinners at the Officers' Club there. Fellows still rushed in to breakfast at the last minute in their Sidcot suits.

It often happened that men would go up on the dawn patrol with only pyjamas under their Sidcots. Occasionally a machine would fail to come back. It must have been awkward for the occupants when they found themselves in enemy country without their clothes.

One afternoon Parrish, the Canadian, asked me to walk over with him to the Artillery Observation Squadron at Monchy le Gache, as he knew one of the pilots there. While we were chatting to his friend on the aerodrome, a " Big Ack " landed and to my joy I saw Cameron climb out. We had not seen one another since we had parted at Boulogne and I had often wondered to which squadron he had been posted. There had been some casualties in this Big Ack squadron just before we got to France, and although Cameron was a fully-trained Bristol pilot, it had been his misfortune to fill one of the gaps. He told me that a few days before, he had been shot down while doing a shoot. Neither he nor his observer had been hit, but the bus had crashed in a shell-hole when they landed.

We promised to visit one another frequently, but just after this the Offensive began and I did not see Cameron again. Once, long after this, I had a postcard from him while he was on leave in England.

A few days before the Armistice was signed, Cameron, who had got his captaincy by that time, was shot down in flames.

One of the patrols witnessed a very fine deed one afternoon. They saw a dog-fight going on between half a dozen of our scout machines and about ten enemy scouts, five miles behind the lines. The patrol immediately shot off to the assistance of the British machines. As they got near they saw one of our scouts suddenly burst into flames. Now it might have been just possible for the pilot of that machine to save himself by side-slipping very steeply. The flames would then have shot out between the fuselage and the wing. But not he. He turned round, blazing from prop to rudder, and scrapped the E.A. till he fell to bits. I do not think it would be an exaggeration to say that that was one of the bravest deeds of the war.

Near us was an Australian "Art. Obs." squadron. The "Aussies" flew R.E.8's which, at that stage of the war, were much too slow and out-of-date for fighting purposes. The pilots had strict orders to avoid scraps while doing shoots, and to confine themselves rigidly to the business in hand. But sometimes a Boche would come along and tickle an R.E.8's ribs. This was too much for the pilot. Shoot forgotten, off he would go like a lame terrier after a greyhound, till he had chased him into his own backyard. Then he would bethink himself of the fuming battery commander below, and return to his job.

MARCH 21ST, 1918

Our new Flight-Commander, Captain Pitts, shared our big hut with us, and we went to some trouble to improve its appearance.

On the 20th March, we heard that the Great German Offensive was about to start. It was generally suspected that the line could not be held at this point and that the Boches would most probably break through.

Towards evening, several of our pilots and observers drove off to the Officers' Club in Peronne for dinner. Shortly after they had left, a message came through from Brigade that the attack was expected at dawn the following morning. We were to hold ourselves in readiness to move to a new aerodrome at any time during the next day. Intelligence reported that the bombardment would start at 10 p.m. that night, the 20th March.

At dinner that evening, the C.O. addressed us.

"From now on," he said, "our job is to hamper the Boche advance. I need not tell you that this Squadron has as fine a reputation as any in France, and it is up to all of us now to maintain that reputation.

"The whole Squadron will go up at five ack emma to-morrow. Each machine will carry bombs. Wherever you see Boche troops or transport, dive on 'em, and give 'em hell! We can do an appalling amount of damage in this way. The Bristols will go over as low as possible and strafe debussing points, and all cavalry, infantry, an emma toc[1] on the roads. The Bristols will be the lowest machines as they can do most damage with their two guns and bombs. Camels and S.E.5's will sit above you to deal with E.A. Directly you have emptied your ammunition-belts come back, fill up and go over again.

"We shall move to Champien aerodrome some time to-morrow. From there we shall carry on the good work till we have to move again.

"I do not wish to be maudlin about it, but this is literally a time when England expects every man to do

[1] M.T., Mechanical Transport.

his duty. If the Boches get us on the run now, it will be the end of all things, and Germany will have won the war. We are not going to allow that!"

When the C.O. sat down the cheering nearly lifted the roof.

The mess was buzzing with excitement that night. Nobody felt inclined to play cards, and, instead, we stood about in groups, talking and speculating about the immediate future. Everyone was thoroughly optimistic about the final result.

After a while the groups began breaking up and we drifted off to our quarters to pack up our few belongings.

At ten pip emma, to the minute, the bombardment started. I had never conceived of such a racket. It was just one continuous deafening roar. No individual bursts from the greater guns could be distinguished, but this continuous roar waxed and waned, and kept on without a break. We wondered how the P.B.I. in the trenches were faring. It seemed impossible that a single man could escape with his life from that inferno.

All of us were wildly excited. It did not take us long to collect our few possessions and put them next to our stretchers, ready to be stuffed into our valises in the morning.

Captain Pitts was looking round the hut regretfully.

"Look here," he said, "do you think we should leave all this luxury for the Boches?"

We did not, and, in a few minutes, we had ripped off all our red decorations from the walls and ceiling and windows.

"I'm damned if they get my cupboard either," said Tomkins, and proceeded to kick it to bits.

At half-past ten the revellers returned from Peronne. We advised them to get to bed, as everyone had to leave the ground at five the next morning.

"Oh, I can't do that," protested Scott, with a comic gesture, "I don't get up till nine."

MARCH 21ST, 1918

We told the late-comers what the plans were for the morrow, and advised them to collect their kit as the squadron was moving to the aerodrome at Champien some time during the next day.

"I can't do that either," complained Scott. "My washing's down at Ham!"

Eventually we all got to bed, but there was not much sleep that night.

(ii)

At half-past four the next morning we were called, and hopped out of bed immediately.

It was pitch dark at first, but as it grew lighter we saw that there was an impenetrable fog over everything. Flying was quite impossible for the time being. It would have been out of the question to get a machine off the ground.

Shells were whining and exploding fairly near us, but none fell on the aerodrome. The ack emmas produced some breakfast and after that we rolled up our valises. Then there was nothing for us to do but to hang around waiting for the fog to lift.

At about eight o'clock we heard the throb of a German machine above the fog. He must have started from some very distant aerodrome, clear of the fog, but he was perfectly safe and also harmless up there.

Our ack emmas had been very busy, and everything on the aerodrome was packed up, ready for moving if the Germans got through.

It was a bit of a strain waiting for the fog to lift.

Shortly after breakfast a telephone message reached the Orderly Room that the Germans had broken through and were advancing rapidly. We also heard that shells were falling on No. 5 Naval aerodrome, and in Monchy le Gache.

We heard some fall in a wood near us.

Personally, at first I was in a blue funk. We all knew that we were in for a pretty rough time. Archie had been bad enough at 20,000 feet, and what he would be like at a few hundred was horrible to think of. Fortunately after a while this funk wore off.

At half-past twelve the fog began to break up.

All of us in C Flight were waiting about outside our hut. Presently Captain Pitts came along.

"Look here, you chaps," he said, "the original scheme of a squadron show has fallen through. The C.O. wants C Flight to go over first. We'd better get along to our buses. As soon as it lifts we'll go up."

Then he gave us our places in the formation. Scott and I as usual were outside right. This was because I was the newest pilot in the Flight, and new pilots were always put at the rear.

We did not put on Sidcot suits for this show, as we were to fly low. Scott and I slipped on our leather flying-coats, and walked over to the hangars, carrying our gloves and goggles. On the way we rehearsed the system of signals that we had agreed upon. For instance, if either of us saw E.A., or observation balloons, or troops, or transport, he was to point them out and shake his fist if he wanted to attack. Again, if I wanted Scott to fire a red light I was to hold up one finger, if a green light, two.

At five minutes past one the mechanics swung the props. and at 1.10 p.m. we left the ground.

We crossed the line near St. Quentin at about 2,000 feet.

Archie opened up as soon as we crossed over, but he was not nearly as bad as we had expected. Probably he was on the move himself and could not give us much attention. But though we had expected a hotter reception from him, the one we got was warm enough. Many "woofs" were unpleasantly close.

Just beyond St. Quentin our leader dived on an enemy scout but left him again after firing a short burst. The Boche put his nose down and went east as fast as he could. Then I dived on him and got in quite a long burst but with no effect, and as I did a climbing turn to rejoin the formation Scott fired at him, but we saw him streaking off hell-for-leather, apparently none the worse for our attempts. Just after this I noticed an observation balloon to our left. I was doubtful whether I ought to leave the formation to attack this, but at that moment Scott saw it and hit me on the shoulder, pointing to it and shaking his fist excitedly. This decided me, and I flew at it, getting in a long burst from my Vickers gun. The tracer bullets seemed to stream right into it. When we were fairly near it I did a climbing-turn over it and Scott fired at it. As we left it they pulled it down. It must have had a good many holes in it, but unfortunately it did not catch fire. Every fifth bullet in our machine-gun belts was a tracer, but tracers would not necessarily set a balloon ablaze.

I looked round for the rest of the formation but there was no sign of it now. Just north of us, and below us, I caught sight of an enemy two-seater of the L.V.G. type. I pointed him out to Scott and shook my fist and then, putting the nose down, I pressed the Bowden lever and poured a stream of bullets and tracer-bullets apparently right into him. I was too excited to remember to use the Aldis ring-sight and was guided simply by the tracers. It was always pretty useless to rely on these as a guide when firing at a moving object. The E.A.'s back gun was flashing at us continuously and the pilot was split-assing from side to side. I continued to dive and fire till my gun jammed. Then I turned off and Scott fired at him, but also with no effect. This was the first time that I had found and attacked a Boche by myself, and I was bitterly disappointed that he got away.

I cleared the stoppage and then we turned our attention to a large balloon on the ground. Little ant-like figures were swarming round it. I pushed the stick forward and swooped down on it with wires howling, firing as we went. I also released one bomb, but it fell short. As we passed over it I turned, climbing, and Scott got busy with the back gun. The little ant-like figures scattered in all directions.

When we left the balloon we began attacking troops and transport. All the roads were very busy and time and again we dived on motor-transport and on columns of men and saw them scatter wildly. We also dropped our remaining bombs. It was difficult to see what happened to these as we were so low. Unless we turned immediately after releasing a bomb our vision of the burst would be obstructed by our own machine. Each machine only carried four 25-lb. bombs on a rack mounted under the fuselage. Bristols were not designed for bombing purposes and carried no special sights for this work. The pilot simply sighted over the right wheel and when the objective was in line with the rim he pulled the release cable.

A Vickers gun normally fires about 600 rounds per minute but ours were fitted with special recoil springs which increased the rate to 1,000 per minute. When a road thickly covered with troops was sprayed with bullets at this rate the damage done must have been considerable. All this time we were being subjected to a good deal of rifle fire from below and were frequently shot at by Archie batteries. Then we got within range of a flaming-onion battery and this gave us a bad time. Great fans of the greenish flaming onions streamed up at us and at times they seemed to miss us only by inches. Actually they were travelling extremely fast but, as they were luminous, we could watch their approach from the moment they left the short-barrelled gun, and we would wait until they were nearly on us and then dive below, or zoom above them. It was exciting work dodging them. Archie had been unexpectedly quiet over St. Quentin but we struck some very fierce brothers of his near Fresnoy, just after we got out of range of the flaming onions. Black bursts surrounded us and each was accompanied by a terrific " woof " that made the Bristol shudder.

They became so bad that we had to fly west to escape them. Two small gashes were visible in our right wing, one near the tip and the other a few inches from the fuselage. Directly we had reached the line we turned north-east again and crossed the St. Quentin canal somewhere near Le Catelet. Then we proceeded to do some more ground-strafing till our ammunition gave out, and we returned to the aerodrome. We had only been up an hour on this show but it had seemed like three. The rest of the Flight had landed a few minutes before and I at once went up to Captain Pitts and apologised for having left the formation and explained the circumstances. He said immediately that he thought I had been justified in doing this and he thought, too, that we could do more damage on these low shows if we separated a bit than if we remained in close formation. I should explain that, whenever we went over on what was called a " peace-time war-show," that is, when we were not doing ground-strafing, it was unpardonable for any machine to leave the formation except with engine-trouble or with gun-jam. Every pilot had to follow the leader at all costs.

We learned now, on landing, that we were to spend another night at Guizancourt, and also that we were not due for another show till five o'clock. Glad of the breather, Scott and I adjourned to the mess for a small one.

" Happy days."

" Soft landings. Hullo, Mac," as MacLaren and his observer came in for a spot, " bag any Boches ? "

" Drew a blank. 'Dyou have any luck ? No ? The skipper got an L.V.G. over Bohain. As far's I know that's the only one brought down."

At five-fifteen the Flight took off again. My engine was running badly and I soon began to lag behind the formation. We crossed the line at 5,000 feet, some distance to the south of St. Quentin. Nine S.E.5's were sitting above us when we crossed. Very shortly after this they must have turned off. As it appeared later no one in the Flight noticed when they left us. Archie kept us pretty busy for a while. Suddenly Scott hit me violently on the shoulder. I looked round and there, up above us, were eight black triplanes. They were near enough for us to see the Maltese crosses on their wings distinctly. They were hideous little devils and looked like black crabs against the sky. This was the first time Scott and I had seen the famous Fokker triplanes. Almost as soon as we saw them they dived on us. Scott had no time to fire a red light to bring the other machines to our assistance. He began firing as hard as he could at the " tripes," while I pushed the nose down to 200 miles per hour, kicking on left and right rudder alternately.

All we could hope to do, with a badly running engine, was to get away from them by very steep diving. Scott's gun was firing in short bursts all the time. I kept glancing over my shoulder at them, and presently we both saw the foremost triplane go down in an almost vertical dive. At the same moment, to our unbounded joy, the rest of them turned back.

We were a long way below the rest of our formation by this time, and we could not get back to their level with our semi-dud engine. So we just kept below them, till they came down for ground-strafing.

We shot up troops and transport for almost an hour, and for most of the time were badly archied.

We got back to the aerodrome after being up an hour and a quarter.

When we were discussing the show, over sun-downers, we found that the other members of the formation had not see the triplanes at all. They had certainly seen the eight machines going down, but had paid no attention to them as they had thought they were the S.E.5's going down for ground-strafing !

In the evening a fog settled down again, but in spite of

this a Boche night-flier came over and dropped four bombs just off the edge of the aerodrome.

At dinner the Adjutant told us an extraordinary story. The C.O. had become very much annoyed with one of his clerks, who had become flurried in the bustle and excitement of the day. Towards evening the C.O. lost his temper completely.

" Clear out of the orderly room ! You're no damned good here ! " he yelled at him. " Take a rifle and go and shoot Boches ! "

The clerk took his words literally, got a rifle and walked off. Shortly afterwards a German formation passed overhead, flying low. The clerk put up his rifle and, by the grace of God, shot one of the pilots dead. The machine crashed three-quarters of a mile from the aerodrome.

(iii)

The next morning we were called very early. As it got lighter we saw that again a heavy fog lay over everything. One could barely see ten yards.

Our ack emmas managed to give us some breakfast. How they did it was a mystery, because practically everything was packed up.

After breakfast we sat about again waiting for the fog to lift. At about ten o'clock our heavy transport left for the huge aerodrome at Champien.

Shortly after midday the fog began to clear. The six pilots in C Flight were waiting on the aerodrome, Captain Pitts, Lts. Tomkins, MacLaren, Parrish, Smiles and myself, and our observers. At 1.15 the fog had broken up into patches and we took off. We could see below us, that the Boches had broken through on a wide front and were coming steadily westwards.

We climbed to about 5,000 feet before we crossed over. Near Cerisy we had a fairly lively five minutes with a flaming-onion battery. Just after we got clear of this, Scott hit me on the shoulder and pointed up. A huge formation of twenty triplanes was passing overhead, going north. The sight put me into a cold sweat!

Two of them turned aside at that moment and began diving on us. This time Scott had his Very pistol ready loaded with a red light, and he promptly fired this and then swung his Lewis gun round and opened fire on them. They immediately turned off and rejoined their formation. It was extraordinary that the whole formation did not come down on us. One can only think that the leader had not seen us.

Along most of the roads below us, troops and motorlorries and horse transport were advancing. Suddenly our leader put his nose down and I saw tracers streaming from his front gun. Then below him I saw an enemy two-seater with a pale-green body and yellow wings. In about two seconds it was all over. The Boche reared up and fell over into a spin. Some object, most probably the observer, left the machine and fell over and over through the air. The machine itself continued spinning till it crashed into the ground.

The rest of us had also dived in order to keep near our leader, but we had not fired as it was undoubtedly his pigeon.

Now we were fairly low, about 2,000 feet, but Captain Pitts continued to lose height, and gradually swung round to the west till we were flying above the road that runs westwards into St. Quentin. Some distance ahead, troops in grey were marching along the road. There must have been close on a battalion of them and ahead of these again was a considerable amount of motor-transport. We were watching Pitts' machine and directly he dived we followed suit. It must have been a bad moment for the troops when they looked round to see the six machines swooping down on them, each sending out a greenish spray of tracers, dealing sudden death along that road. When Bristol Fighters dived with their engines full on, the speed rapidly rose above 200 miles per hour and the howl from the wires rose in pitch to a piercing shriek.

Smiles and I were flying the two rear machines. As Scott and I dived, a machine in front of us obscured our view and we waited till it rose, and then opened fire. Below us lay many figures spread-eagled across the road. The remainder had scattered off the sides. The motor-lorries were pulling up but our guns were rat-tat-tatting and one of them rolled over into the ditch. The whole incident had only lasted a few seconds. After the dive we zoomed up again and rejoined the rest of our machines, but now we no longer flew in close formation. We kept within sight of each other and from time to time dived on columns of men who were marching steadily westwards.

Once two of us together attacked a troop of cavalry advancing along a minor road. The horses broke away in terror, rearing and stampeding, and soon there were only two left on the road, one lying still and the other on its back, kicking. It was a pitiful sight. No one ever respected the neutrality of the horses!

Practically throughout the show we were subjected to anti-aircraft fire, first from one battery and then from another. Frequently we dived to within a couple of hundred feet of the ground and then we heard the crack of the rifles as well.

At last Scott pointed out to me a white light, the washout signal, that had come from one of our machines. It was our leader's machine, as we could tell by the streamers from the outer struts. We turned west, but we were well separated now. Just after we had turned, I saw three E.A. coming east, about 3,000 feet above us. I pointed them out to Scott. He got his gun ready and we watched them. They had barely passed overhead when they half-rolled, and came at us. Scott immediately opened fire. But the Germans were not anxious for a scrap. Their dive was a half-hearted one, and as soon as they saw Scott's gun flashing they turned off again, and we watched them disappearing eastwards.

I looked round for our machines and could see the leader not far off, and three more in the distance. Pointing to our machines I held up four fingers. "Where's the other?" I yelled into Scott's ear. He looked round carefully, then shook his head.

When we got near the lines Archie became very bad. We crossed at about 4,000 feet, kicking on rudder continually, and the black bursts followed us round closely.

We got back to the aerodrome at a quarter to three. The first thing we heard on landing was that Tomkins had come back ten minutes before, with his observer dead. He was a fellow called Gould and had only been with us about a fortnight. Tomkins' regular observer, Burrowes, had been flying with Smiles on this show.

Captain Pitts walked straight over to the hut. Tomkins was there, looking pretty white about the gills.

"What happened, Tommy?"

"Archie got him," said Tomkins. "There was a deuce of a *wonk* and I felt the bus shiver. I looked round to see where we'd been hit and saw Gould lying in the cockpit with his head in a pulp. So I thought I'd better come back at once in case he was still alive."

"Yes," said the skipper. "Sorry, Tommy, old man. Well, I must go and report," and off he went to the orderly room.

As he left the hut we heard the B Flight machines taking off for a show.

I left the hut and walked back to the hangars. Some mechanics were filling the tanks of the C Flight buses and others were putting temporary patches over the small holes in the wings and bodies, caused by Archie and rifle-fire.

"Place is looking a bit bare, sir," said the Flight-

Sergeant to me. " Almost all our equipment has left already. There goes the last of B Flight now," he added, as a lorry passed, the men shouting humorous farewells to the C Flight mechanics.

" Aren't the B Flight machines landing here again ? "

" No, sir. Doing a show and landing at the new aerodrome at Champien. A Flight left here at two. Same programme."

" You've had a busy time packing," I said.

" Yes, sir. Nothing to do now but get these machines off and then we leave. When are you going up again, sir ? "

" I don't know," I replied. " Captain Pitts is in the orderly room now."

" Fine officer, that, sir. Knows his job too. He spent a couple of hours here himself last night. The men would do anything for him. Here, Corporal ! " he called out as a man from the orderly room appeared.

" C Flight machines to go up at four o'clock, Sergeant," said the Corporal. " Everybody to leave as soon as they're up."

It was half-past three, and I walked back to the hut. Some of the batmen were carrying off our valises. Scott had kept back my haversack with his own. We were to do a short show and land on the new aerodrome.

Our hut looked very bare and desolate. A few torn strips of our red decorations were hanging forlornly on the walls.

" What's to happen to the huts and hangars ? " I asked of Captain Pitts. " They'll be pretty useful to the Boches, won't they ? "

" They're not being left," he said. " The E.O. and six men are staying behind to fire them as soon as the last of the Squadron leaves. Tommy looks a bit more cheerful now, doesn't he ? Come along, you fellows ! " he called out to a group engaged in a noisy argument, " it's ten to four. We must keep in formation on this show," he said, as the Flight walked over to the hangars. "It's only to be a short one and we don't want anyone to get lost."

The Germans were getting very near now. As we were running up our engines a shell fell on the aerodrome. It sent up a great cloud of stones and dust, but it was too far out to do any damage.

Then we took off from Guizancourt aerodrome for the last time. I looked down and saw our last lorry standing in the road which ran past the hangars. Little figures were moving backwards and forwards near it. One solitary Bristol stood on the tarmac. The C.O. was going to fly this over to Champien when the lorry had left. A tender was standing near the orderly room. This was no doubt the tender which would take off the Equipment Officer and his six men, after they had done their job.

We joined formation and flew towards the lines, climbing as we went. We crossed at about 5,000 feet and shortly afterwards saw a great dog-fight going on below us, between triplanes and Bristols and S.E.5's. One triplane seemed to be going down like a falling leaf, but near the ground it righted itself and flew off east. Another triplane dived away from the fight, straight into the ground and a column of flame and black smoke rose from the spot.

I was wondering why our leader did not go down to the fight, when suddenly four Albatros scouts shot past in front of us, going down to the scrap. Captain Pitts had seen them coming but they had not spotted us as we were against the sun. At once he dived and we followed him. After a short burst, the skipper got one of them. It went down obviously out of control, but I lost sight of it, as I was watching Tomkins' machine in front of me. It was seen by other members of the Flight to crash. Tomkins was diving on a chequered scout in front of him and this suddenly broke up in the air. One wing folded back and the Boche plunged down like a stone. I never fired a shot as my field was obstructed by the two Bristols in front of me. The other two Albatri got away.

When we looked round for the dog-fight it had broken up. The remaining E.A. had scattered and we saw two of them streaking off east, pursued by S.E.5's, but we soon lost sight of them in the haze which was beginning to form. We saw no more enemy machines after this. Archie peppered us hotly for a while, and then we turned back and flew off to the new aerodrome at Champien.

(iv)

This aerodrome was enormous. After landing our skipper taxied up to where some other Bristols were standing, near the centre of the line of hangars.

Several squadrons had collected at Champien, and tenders and lorries were arriving all the time. There was a good deal of confusion everywhere, but after some enquiries a worried-looking adjutant pointed out two large huts to us.

" You'll find A Squadron over there," he said, and hurried on. As we got near them someone spotted Smiles and a batman carrying a valise between them over to one of the huts.

" Hi, Smiles! come and show us where we belong."

" Half a mo'," he replied, and pitched the valise through the doorway. " Look after it, Wake," he said, and came over to us. " God, it's a mix-up here. Where have you left your buses ? "

" Next to some Bristols belonging, I think, to Z Squadron. Are our hangars near ? "

" Just down here," said Smiles, and led the way.

After we had taxied our machines over we set off in pairs to look for our valises. But it was almost like looking for a few needles in a haystack. We tramped about from one lorry to another and at last Scott found his valise lying at the side of a road. Between us we began humping it back to the hut.

On the way back, a starved-looking dog sniffed at our heels and began following us rather doubtfully.

"Come on, Susie. Good dog, then, good dog," said Scott, and she needed no further encouragement. She followed us back to the hut, which we found again after some difficulty, and she entered close on Scott's heels. Then she got busy examining various cracks and holes in the floor, while we unrolled Scott's valise and put up his stretcher.

Just as we were finishing, a batman came in to tell us that dinner was ready. Susie came in with us and lay at our feet during the meal. The cook had managed to produce quite a jolly stew of bully-beef and potatoes. Dinner was not quite as cheerful a meal as usual that night, and the chatter at table was spasmodic. This was simply because we were all a bit tired and had not yet settled down to our new conditions of war flying. Ground-strafing was undoubtedly bad medicine for the Boches but it was a bit trying for us, too. From the moment we reached the advancing line of grey we were under continuous and sometimes heavy fire from Archie, machine-guns, rifles, and flaming-onion batteries. In the days to come we were often to think back regretfully on the peaceful high O. Pips that had formerly been the order of the day.

After dinner, we took Susie along to the kitchen for a feed. We saw her started on a basin of stew and went back to the hut. Presently she came waddling in, wagged her broken tail, belched loudly, and hopped on to Scott's stretcher.

Susie was an ugly brute. She was more like a bull-terrier bitch than anything else, but was too short in the leg. She had a very dirty white body, a heavy head, and a bent tail.

There were about thirty of us in the hut. Before

turning in we collected on three or four of the beds for a while, smoking and discussing the events of the day.

"I'm as tired," said Parrish, "as—as two dogs!"

We were all tired and before long we went to bed.

Several fellows had, like myself, been unable to find their valises, and were sleeping on the floor. Scott lent me his Sidcot suit and a blanket. I used my haversack as a pillow and so was quite comfortable.

The next morning we had to pack up again as we were to move to a new aerodrome later in the day. The Boches had already reached Guizancourt. We were helping one another in rolling up the valises when our skipper appeared in the doorway.

"C Flight, ahoy! We leave the ground in half an hour."

"Another low-show, Skipper?" someone asked.

"Of course," he replied, grinning. "We shall be doing low-shows now till we die of old age."

There was not much time for breakfast, and we hurried across, Susie following us.

"No time this morning, old lady," Scott said to her, "but we'll see what Merry can do for you."

After a hasty snack we hurried back to the hut for flying-coats and goggles.

"Merry," said Scott, "will you see to this lady's wants? And if her tummy isn't tight when we get back, God help you, my lad."

"Very good, sir."

"And Merry," I said, "find my valise and get out my Sidcot and blankets, will you?"

"Yes, sir," and off we went.

"Our job," said Captain Pitts, when we had assembled on the aerodrome, "is to shoot up the roads near the old aerodrome, Guizancourt. Take off as soon as you like. We won't fly in formation."

The machines took off singly, one after the other, and flew off to the north-east. I climbed to 3,000 feet and flew at that level for a while so that Scott and I could get a good view of all the roads below us. Archie was, if anything, worse than usual. We struck a particularly fierce patch about five minutes after starting. One burst succeeded another—*crump*—*wonk*—*woof!* We were tossed about violently. It seemed impossible that we could avoid being hit, and yet no holes were visible in the wings. And then, after half a dozen had crashed deafeningly close to us, there was a faint *click* from a far-off burst, and a gash, large enough to put one's hand through, appeared in the left wing. Gradually we drew away from this particular battery. Others took up the tale, but none of them was quite so bad as the first had been. Scattered groups of transport and troops were visible on the roads, and we dived a few times on these. Then we saw cavalry massed on a road leading from a wood near Guizancourt. We went down at them and the wires howled as we dived. They stood their ground gamely. When I pulled out of the dive Scott emptied half a drum into them. Then I dived again, and once more they stood firm, but one or two horses were down and the remainder were restive. How they controlled them I cannot imagine. We were very low and could see the cavalrymen distinctly with rifles to shoulders firing at us. When I had pulled her out of this second dive I looked over the side and they had all vanished, probably into the wood.

I happened to glance at the oil-gauge and noticed that the pressure was down to zero. I swung her round immediately and started back towards Champien. Luckily it was only about eight miles off, and I listened carefully to the engine all the way back, but she ran smoothly. As soon as we were within gliding distance I shut off the engine with a sigh of relief. The bus had shuddered rather severely once after a near Archie burst shortly after the gash had appeared in her wing, and it had felt as though some solid part had been hit.

On the way back Scott and I both scrutinised every bit of the machine that we could see from the cockpits but no serious damage was visible, so I feared that the undercarriage might have been hit and therefore landed her as slowly and smoothly as possible. It was just as well that I did so, for as soon as we touched ground the bus swung round to the right with a flat tyre. Scott got out and going to the wing-tip helped me to taxi her up to the hangars.

A chunk had been cut out of the right tyre. There was a bullet-hole through the oil tank and all the oil had run out. There was also the gash in the left wing, made by Archie, and in addition to this we counted six bullet-holes through various parts of the machine.

Our rigger and fitter got busy with repairs, and Scott and I walked off to the hut. Susie was sitting in the doorway and gave us, particularly Scott, a royal welcome. She had definitely adopted him as a master.

After getting rid of our flying kit we returned to the aerodrome to watch the repairs being made to our bus. As we reached the aerodrome we saw, to our amazement, a German two-seater calmly gliding down. Then we saw that it was being shepherded in by two of our scouts, one on either side of it. It landed in a field just beyond the aerodrome, and turned over on its back. The two scouts, having completed their work, flew off. Dozens of officers and men ran out to it and when Scott and I reached it the pilot and observer had just crawled out from underneath it. I was surprised to see that both of them were elderly men. The pilot was a bald-headed old N.C.O. and the observer an officer. Both of them looked rather bewildered. The officer explained in fairly good English that his brother had been missing since the previous day, and he had come over to drop a message of enquiry, when he was attacked, and his petrol tank shot through.

They were marched off under escort and I was glad to see that our people treated them very civilly.

Attached to the Squadron was an elderly mechanic who leapt, blushing, into fame on this day. Joe was a suspicious old man. He looked for, and found, in a latrine, torn bits of paper with German writing on them. These he collected and fitted together on a board. Then, having solved his jig-saw puzzle, old Joe marched off with it to the orderly room, with his head held high, though not entirely through pride.

The letter was translated and was found to contain useful information regarding the activities of two German squadrons.

The Wing-Commander visited Champien aerodrome during the day and laughingly shook hands with Joe and congratulated him on a useful piece of work.

Shortly after the L.V.G. had come down, Tomkins and MacLaren landed their buses.

" God ! " said Tomkins, pulling off his flying-cap, " if anyone tells me this is a strategic retreat, I shall call him a bloody liar."

Five minutes later the Flight-Commander got back. Captain Pitts had seen Smiles land in a field on our side of the line, and knowing that time was becoming precious had landed alongside him to find out the trouble. The timing of the Constantinesco gear in Smiles' machine had gone wrong, and during a long burst fired at troops on the ground Smiles shot away his own propeller. He was at 800 feet when this happened, but because of his diving speed, and a following wind, he was able to glide into our lines.

The skipper at once sent off a tender with a spare propeller and within an hour Smiles was back at the aerodrome. Tomkins and the skipper had each brought down a Boche during this show. Tomkins said that he had zoomed up to 1,500 feet after diving on some Emma Toc and was just preparing to dive again when he saw two black triplanes swoop down on the skipper's machine out of a low cloud-bank.

Said Tomkins, " They evidently hadn't seen me, for they paid no attention at all when I shot down after them. I couldn't help thinking of the old nursery-book picture of a dog chasing a cat and the cat chasing a rat."

" A rotten bad simile, Tommy."

" Oh, Lord ! yes, don't tell the skipper ! Well, by the sheerest fluke," went on the modest Tommy, " I managed to bag my feller. He must have fallen forward on his stick because he went straight down into some of his own Emma Toc on the road. As I zoomed up I saw the skipper having a hell of a scrap with the other chap. The tripe had green and yellow stripes along the fuselage and the pilot was evidently a bit of a crack judging by the way he handled his bus. They were half-rolling and split-assing round one another and all I could do was to hang round and watch. Once the tripe did an Immelmann and came down on the skipper's tail, and I thought it was all over bar the shouting. But, begad, the skipper wasn't having any. It was a pretty sight. He went clean round in a loop and came down on the tripe's tail. I saw tracer flickering from his nose and the next moment the Boche burst into flame."

(v)

It was three o'clock before the machines were ready for the air again. Each bus had several gashes in it and Captain Pitts' tailplane was riddled with bullet-holes.

At three we went up for some more ground-strafing near Ham. Archie was very bad from start to finish of that trip. The bursts succeeded one another rapidly and although we kept split-assing, and never flew straight for more than two seconds at a time, they followed us round closely.

It was always a marvel to me that Archie did not do more serious damage to our machines. But I was to see him get one of his few direct hits that afternoon. I had got separated from the rest of the Flight and was diving on troops on the road that runs westward into Ham, when I noticed an S.E.5 approaching. He passed close to me and waved cheerily. Then out of sheer high spirits the pilot looped his little bus before diving down on to the advancing hordes in grey below. Just at the top of his zoom Archie got him. A cloud of black smoke unrolled in the sky and the S.E.5 flew to pieces out of it, for all the world like a hit " clay-pigeon."

At four o'clock we all returned to the aerodrome. Captain Pitts had brought down another hostile machine during this show, bringing up his total to five since the Push started. Two of the squadrons at Champien had gone when we got back and the remainder were on the point of leaving. Our own Ack Emmas were busy loading up the last of our lorries. Merry, stout fellow, had saved some tea in a thermos flask for Scott and me.

" I found your valise, sir. I took out your Sidcot suit and blankets and put them in the hut, sir."

" Good man. You might take them and Mr. Scott's Sidcot and blankets, and our haversacks to my bus, No. 22. The valises can go in the lorry."

" Yes, sir."

" Where's Susie ? "

" Oh, the dog, sir ? She's in the hut, sir, very excited-like."

There we found Susie. She knew that something was on, but could not quite make out what it was, and in her doggy mind I suppose there was a large question mark as to whether or not she, too, was to take part in it. When Merry came in and carried off our kit Susie gave a howl. Scott petted her and fussed her a bit, but wherever he moved she followed him like a shadow, so closely indeed, that once she made him trip over his own feet.

At half-past five we walked down to the hangars and packed the kit in the bottom of the rear cockpit. Then we lifted Susie in and she sat proudly on the top blanket.

BRISTOL FIGHTER NO. 22 AT BERTANGLES.

Shortly after this the pilots ran up their engines, Scott climbed in next to Susie, and we took off for the new aerodrome at Bertangles, a couple of miles north of Amiens.

It had become very hazy, but we followed the straight road from Roye to Amiens and soon reached our new quarters. Susie was a model passenger and sat perfectly still during the trip. But this new experience had evidently excited her deeply. As soon as she was lifted out she jumped up against us, wildly delighted, and then, with her heavy head well down, tore off in a mad romp, doing marvellous split-ass figures of eight and circles over the aerodrome, finally returning panting to gaze up adoringly at Scott.

The aerodrome at Bertangles was large and the Nissen huts looked comfortable, but, of course, there was no dinner to be had that night as the lorries had not yet arrived. After leaving our kit in the huts, we walked down to the village to see what we could get there to allay the pangs. About thirty of us, nearly all the flying officers in the Squadron, set off to the village. The remaining four or five had had to wait for a tender as their machines had been badly shot about during the day and were not fit to fly.

The local *estaminet* had some bread but nothing else to eat, so we agreed to meet there again, and separated to buy up all the eggs we could get hold of. Within half an hour we reassembled with great quantities of them and Madame got very busy, turning out enormous and delicious omelettes for us.

After a royal feed we returned to our new quarters, spread our blankets on the floor and I, at any rate, was soon dreaming of triplanes, Archie-bursts and omelettes.

CHAPTER IX

MORE GROUND-STRAFING

(i)

During the next few days we continued to do low-shows, worrying the advancing troops as much as we could. On an average, each Flight did two shows a day and sometimes three. As soon as one Flight came in, the next went off, and we kept this up, in rotation, throughout each day.

A good many infantry officers passed through Bertangles every day, and we heard some very interesting accounts of the ground-fighting from them. The P.B.I. had been through hell since the offensive started.

One evening about a dozen very weary infantry officers reached Bertangles and we persuaded them to stay the night. They did not need much coaxing as they had nowhere to go to. They had got completely out of touch with their units, if indeed there was anything left of them.

Half an hour later an Ack W squadron, or the remnants of it, landed on the aerodrome and, of course, we offered them hospitality too. Our visitors we divided up among us. There were nineteen of us in one small Nissen hut that night.

" How have you chaps been faring since the show started ? " I asked one of the Big Ack pilots.

" Oh, nothing to complain of. We've moved three times so far—shelled out the second time. How have you been getting on ? Lost many buses ? "

We discussed our respective jobs for a while. He

told me that since the twenty-first they had lost nine machines on contact patrol work.

"That fellow, just beyond your Flight-Commander, was shot down to-day between the lines. He and his observer fired the bus and then ran like hell for our lines. The Boches fired everything at them they could put their hands on, but they got through."

"How did they fire the bus? They couldn't have had much time."

"Very pistol," he answered.

Five of us were sitting on my stretcher. Underneath it lay Susie, in a dreamland of her own. From time to time little grunts and whines escaped her. Presently a sixth man strolled across and joined us. This broke the stretcher's back and it collapsed with a crash. Susie below, in an ear-splitting howl, called upon high heaven to witness the calamity that had come upon her. Her frantic efforts to escape added to the general confusion. It was all very funny, except for Susie and a Big Ack pilot who got a nip in the calf of his leg just as Susie won through. When we had disentangled ourselves, I settled down near some of the infantry officers as I was anxious to hear their accounts of the "retreat." According to them we had been doomed from the start. Isolated machine-gun posts, with great gaps between them, were scattered along the line.

"The gunners were told to stick to their posts to the last," said one of the officers, "in order to cover the retreat. Of course, it was certain death for them."

"The South Africans," said another, "put up a good show at Gauche Wood. They were ordered to hold the wood at all costs, and, by God, they held it! They scrapped till they ran out of ammunition and then they fought with their bare fists."

We heard strange stories, too, from these officers, of men who suddenly appeared among them at the beginning of the offensive dressed in the uniform of British officers of high rank, who gave orders which caused grave confusion at this critical stage of the attack.

We turned in early as some of our guests were deadbeat. I noticed that the man I was looking after walked very stiffly and evidently with pain. When I questioned him about it, he said, rather apologetically, that it was only rheumatism.

"You see," he said, "I was standing knee-deep in water all last night."

My stretcher had "gone west" but I gave him the folding mattress and some blankets, as I had my Sidcot to sleep in. The poor chap was worn out. His head was hardly down before he was fast asleep.

In the morning the infantry officers went on their way, and the Big Ack Squadron flew off to a new aerodrome.

(ii)

The ground-strafing shows that we were doing every day were sometimes disappointing and unsatisfactory. With the line changing every day, it was often difficult to be sure which were our troops and which were Boches. When French troops were involved it became well-nigh impossible, as their blue uniforms could not be distinguished, at a height of a thousand feet, from those of the enemy. On one occasion, Smiles and I were sent over one forenoon to Nesle. We had to represent C Flight as the other machines of the Flight were temporarily out of action. The skipper's observer, Bannerman, went with Smiles, and Scott as usual with me.

While we were in the hut putting on our flying-kit, Tomkins, who was settling down to a poker game, asked us to guard jealously the reputation of C Flight.

"Yah!" said Smiles. "Flinking leadswingers."

"Which of you," asked MacLaren, "is going to be Acting-Flight-Commander during the show?"

MORE GROUND-STRAFING

" Go to blazes," said I.

The rest of the Flight agreed that it was essential for us to do the thing properly as it would help us to realise our responsibilities. And so Tommy gravely dealt us each a poker hand. Smiles picked up three sevens to my two pairs, and so word was sent to the Flight-Sergeant, to attach the streamers to Mr. Smiles' machine.

When we got near Nesle we saw troops in blue, or grey, marching westwards from the town. They looked very much like Boches and I was tempted to dive on them, but did not feel sure about it and held my fire. Over Nesle itself we got no Archie and presently we saw a fight in progress on a road running north-east from Nesle. The town was thus evidently not yet in German hands, so in this case our difficulty was solved for us. But on one or two other occasions it was not so easy. Once I returned from a late-afternoon show without having fired a single shot at ground troops.

Three or four of the infantry officers who passed through Bertangles told us how pleased the troops were to see our machines going over on low-shows. They said that it really had a cheering effect on the men. Just about this time, too, an order came out that when we were flying up to the lines on a show, or returning from one, we were to fly low and to wave to our troops. " Poor Bloody Infantry ! " They were brave fellows and they stood the whole brunt of the attack. They certainly deserved every encouragement, be it never so flimsy, that could be given them.

On the long straight road that runs west to Amiens, there was to be seen, at this time, a continuous stream of refugees, some walking next to a horse and cart loaded high with their belongings, others pushing handcarts, some carrying children, and practically all of them on foot.

It was a pathetic sight.

(iii)

"Do you remember Big Babe McLeod*?" Parrish asked me at lunch one day.

"Yes," I said, "I remember him at Borden. Why?"

"He put up a damned good show yesterday. One of the fellows from his squadron landed here this morning and told me about it."

McLeod was attacked while doing a patrol and his observer wounded. At the same time his machine caught fire. McLeod instantly pushed her over into a very steep side-slip, but the flames were scorching him, and so he jumped out of his cockpit on to the left wing and crouched low, with the joystick pulled hard over in his right hand. Then he smashed a hole through the fabric in the fuselage so that he could reach the rudder-wire with his left hand, and so he guided her towards the lines. The petrol was blazing fiercely but the steep side-slip sent the great flames clear of the fuselage and before long the machine crashed down in no man's land. McLeod was thrown clear, and ran to his observer, who was too badly hit to get out. Directly the machine crashed the Germans opened fire on it with machine-guns and rifles, but McLeod got his observer out and dragged him into a shell-hole. There they lay till it got dark. Then "Big Babe" carried his observer back to our lines.

Later, in the Royal Air Force Communiqués we saw that McLeod had been awarded the V.C.

One morning we saw a rather extraordinary thing happen on the aerodrome. A machine was taking off and the pilot, a new man, Griffin, was holding her down to get up speed for a climbing turn. He passed very low just beyond the last of the hangars, then, instead of zooming, he merely turned rather gradually, flew round the aerodrome, and landed. He said he had felt rather a jerk as the bus crossed the edge of the aerodrome and so came down to see what the matter was. We looked at

MORE GROUND-STRAFING

his machine and found a cut, about four inches wide, clean through his lower left plane, just next to the fuselage.

It had been made by a heavy iron standard at the edge of the field. During his subsequent flight round the aerodrome the whole strain on the left-hand planes was borne by the upper plane, without the help of any supporting wires !

Griffin did not get the usual three weeks' grace when he arrived at the Squadron. Every pilot was needed for ground-strafing, and after Griffin had been with us less than a week he was sent up with C Flight on a war-show. He did not really belong to our Flight, but was a spare A Flight pilot. The Flight-Commander asked Scott to fly with Griffin, and a new observer, Fitton, was sent with me.

The seven machines flew over in formation and, as arranged previously, we scattered on reaching our objective, Chipilly. It was a clear day, the visibility was good, and it was easy to distinguish our own troops from the Boches. We got fairly heavily Archied over Chipilly, and I spotted one of the Archie guns on the other side of a hollow just north of the village. It was on the edge of a large wood. This was the first time I had ever located an Archie-battery and it seemed high time to give him a dose of his own medicine. I pointed him out to Fitton, and then set the Bristol at him. Down she howled, with the front gun rat-tat-tatting. As we climbed again Fitton gave him a further burst with the back gun. At the top of our climb he was firing at us again, so we gave him a further dose. From a corner of the wood some machine-guns fired tracer at us, so we dived twice on them. We could not see them so had to fire into the wood in the direction from which the tracer came. This silenced them. Then we returned to the anti-aircraft gun, which was still firing, and dived again twice on it. The engine now began missing on the right-hand side, so I flew towards the lines. Before I reached them she picked up again and I turned back to Chipilly. The gun was still visible at the edge of the wood and I decided to loose my four bombs at it. I expected to get Archied as before, on this dive, but not a shot was fired, so we must either have driven off or killed the gunners. The bombs fell just short of the gun and made four big holes in the ground.

After this I dived twice on Boche infantry, and then my gun jammed. The engine began missing again rather badly, so I flew back to Bertangles. When we examined the machine after landing we found two holes in the left wing, just next to the fuselage, and another through the fuselage itself.

Captain Pitts landed a few minutes after we did. After seeing us all started at Chipilly he had gone farther afield and had come across an enemy two-seater. He dived on this, getting quite close to it, and putting in a long burst. The German observer had fired at him, but his gun had suddenly stopped—probably jammed—and Captain Pitts saw him hold up his hands. Our skipper, accepting this as a sign of surrender, at once stopped firing and flew round to head him off to our lines. The pilot, however, must have been hit, for immediately after this the two-seater fell over slowly into a spin, and spun down into the ground, where it burst into flames.

The next to return was Griffin, the new pilot. He was a good deal upset, and small wonder, for it was his first show, and he had seen MacLaren shot down in flames.

He had flown behind MacLaren in the formation, and Scott, who had been with him, told us that after the machines had scattered at Chipilly, Griffin had kept fairly near MacLaren's bus. They dived a few times, south of Chipilly, but rifle and machine-gun fire became so bad that they climbed to 4,000 feet. Suddenly Scott missed the other Bristol. He looked round and saw it a good way off diving south-east after an enemy two-seater. Scott instinctively looked up and, sure enough, four E.A.

MORE GROUND-STRAFING

scouts were streaking down out of the sun on MacLaren's bus.

Scott had a red light in his Very pistol and this he fired immediately, but if Anstey, MacLaren's observer, saw the warning, it was too late to save them. Scott grabbed Griffin by the arm and pointed to MacLaren's machine, but time is reckoned in seconds in the air, and by now the E.A. were on MacLaren's tail—the next instant the Bristol went down in flames. Griffin turned to give chase but the four scouts and the two-seater were too far off, going east.

It seemed curious that an experienced pilot like MacLaren should have been caught in the commonest of Boche traps.

A slow two-seater made a tempting bait for the trap. Its pilot and observer would need to be brave fellows, for they stood a remarkably good chance of becoming casualties before their comrades could wipe out the British machine attacking them. True they had the observer's gun with which to defend themselves but that was never so deadly as the pilot's gun. For the pilot had no allowance to make for his own speed when aiming, whereas the observer had to allow for his own speed as well as that of the machine he was firing at.

Parrish and Tomkins landed their machines shortly after Griffin, and a minute or two later we saw Smiles coming in. As soon as Smiles landed he stopped where he was instead of taxi-ing in, and beckoned to us, pointing to his observer's cockpit. We knew what that meant, and someone rushed for the M.O. while the rest of us ran out to the machine to help get the wounded man out. It was a ghastly sight. A chunk of Archie shell had smashed through the fuselage and had hit Corporal Fulton in the stomach. The M.O. came tearing out in " Hungry Liz " and was there almost as soon as we were. Corporal Fulton was still alive, but he died as we lifted him out.

L

Everyone, even the M.O., looked a bit pale as we put the stretcher into the ambulance.

As we walked back we had to make a detour to avoid the B Flight machines, which were taxi-ing out for a show.

Shortly after we landed an order came through that A Squadron was to move that afternoon to Yvremh, a landing-field a few miles west of Bertangles. The German advance had halted short of Villers Brettoneux and it was known that they intended launching another attack shortly. We were not unprepared for the move, and within two hours of receiving the order, some of our heavy transport was on its way.

Just before lunch the B Flight patrol returned, with one of their observers, Lt. Humphrey, killed by Archie. He had, strangely, also been hit in the stomach, but luckily death had been instantaneous.

We buried the two observers just beyond the village that afternoon. The day had started with a clear sky, but at midday, clouds had begun creeping up from the horizon, and after the Service, when the haunting notes of the Last Post were dying away, the rain came down.

C Flight had expected to do another show before leaving for Yvremh, but at four o'clock it was still drizzling steadily and the show was cancelled. A and B Flights, and most of our transport, had left for the new landing-field just after the burial service. At the hangars some of our mechanics were waiting to swing our props so we put on our Sidcots and carried our blankets and haversacks down to our machines. Scott carried Susie down, so that she would not ruin our blankets with muddy paws.

While the Ack Emmas were taking our five Bristols out of the hangars we noticed an S.E.5 gliding in, about 200 yards down the aerodrome. The pilot did not make a bad landing but bumped slightly as he touched ground, and then, by sheer bad luck turned up on his nose. Instantly, we saw flames leaping round the engine and in

MORE GROUND-STRAFING

a fraction of a second a great sheet of flame shot up and enveloped the machine.

The few people left on the aerodrome ran as hard as they could for the S.E.5, but were quite too late to be of any use. The petrol was blazing fiercely and the bullets in the machine-gun belt could be heard popping like a packet of crackers. The heat from the flames was terrific and it was quite impossible to get near the machine. Within a few minutes there were only some charred remains of the S.E.5 and its pilot.

The mechanics swung our props. and we took off. It was only a short distance to Yvremh but the trip was unpleasant because of the very bad visibility. We had to fly low to see the ground at all and our streaming goggles made this dangerous. Captain Pitts knew the route and we kept close to him, but on the way, first Smiles and then Parrish forced-landed with dud engines.

When we reached Yvremh, we flew low over the field to see what the surface was like before landing. The field was bad and there were several nasty holes in it. When we landed the skipper and I luckily escaped them but Tomkins struck one and went up on his nose. At the side of the " aerodrome " there was a cowshed, and two canvas hangars had been put up.

When we had taxied to the side of the field Scott took the blankets while I slung the haversacks round my neck and, with Susie in my arms, ran for the shelter of the cowshed. I had no sooner put Susie down than she tore off in a mad romp as she had done before at Bertangles, scattering mud and water as she went.

" The dirty little sweep ! " exclaimed Scott. " After all our trouble to keep her paws clean ! "

" Your bed will be in a hell of a mess to-night, Scotty," I laughed, as we watched her from the doorway.

" I'm damned if she comes on to my bed," said Scott, and we turned to the tea which the Ack Emmas, stout fellows, had prepared for us. There was plenty of hot tea, bread and butter, boiled eggs, and jam.

We were about half-way through this when Merry, our batman, appeared in the doorway, looking very agitated. He sent one of the mess-waiters to Scott, and I heard Scott exclaim, " What ? Susie ? " Then he ran out of the room, and I followed him.

Behind the cowshed, in the road along which the heavy lorries which had left Bertangles earlier in the afternoon, had just passed, we found Susie's ungainly body lying in a mud-puddle.

" Poor old lady," said Scott and he lifted her gently and carried her off the road.

(iv)

A repair-lorry had been sent off, directly we got down, to look for the two machines that had forced-landed. Both machines were found over on their backs, but the pilots and observers were unhurt. It was too late to do anything to the machines that night, so a guard was posted over each and the four officers brought on to Yvremh.

Two of our ground officers, Carruthers and Gould, had arranged for billets in the village, about a mile off, earlier in the day, and before it became quite dark, we set off in tenders from the aerodrome. The tenders stopped first at the village school, where C Flight was to be billeted. We got out with all our kit, and the tenders drove off with A and B Flights who were going on to the château of the Vicomte d'Omrigny.*

There was one large classroom in the school and into this we carried our kit. Those who had beds, put them up and the rest of us unrolled our valises on the floor and spread our blankets on them.

Then we set off for the *estaminet* in search of supper.

Madame soon put before us some tasty omelettes and bread and coffee.

" Très bon, Madame, oh ! very bon."

Madame withdrew, beaming maternally on us all, and we fell to with a will.

Once more the door opened, and Tomkins appeared.

Later, Madame brought us some bottles of a good white wine, and we dawdled over this for a long time, as the café was a cosier place than the bare schoolroom.

" Well," said Parrish, producing a tin of Gold Flake cigarettes, " this has been one hell of a day. Have one, Skipper ? Pass them round. First Mac and Anstey, then Corporal Fulton, then Humphrey. Then the S.E.5 pilot. I hear your pup got written off too, Scotty ? "

" C Flight's back to five machines again, if we can count the two that turned over to-night," said Captain Pitts. " It's a good thing we had a spare observer. Fitton, you'll fly with Smiles, please, in future. I'll ask A Flight to give us Griffin *avec* P.B.O. They're up to strength without him."

The room was heavy with smoke when, an hour later, the door opened and our C.O., Major Field, came in.

" No, don't get up," he said, motioning us down again. " I thought you'd like to see this list that came through to Bertangles just before I left this evening. No thanks, Pitts," he said, replying to an invitation from our Flight-Commander, " the drinks are on me this time. Madame ! "

When he had given the order, he read out the list.

" Military Cross : Captain Mills, Captain Pitts, 2nd Lts. Burden, Digby, Dickson, Anstey, Powell, and Sharman."

The reading of the list was interrupted at each name by rousing cheers from the nine of us in the café. Of the eight officers to receive the decoration, three were pilots and five were observers. This we considered was thoroughly sporting of our C.O., for the P.B.O's seldom got the recognition which they deserved. Of the eight decorations three came to C Flight, three went to B Flight, and two to A Flight. The three pilots were the Flight-Commanders of B and C Flights, and Powell the American in A Flight.

" I wish Anstey could have known about his M.C.," said Tomkins, as we walked back to our schoolroom that night.

A Flight did the dawn patrol the next morning. They reported rain and hail over the lines so C Flight, which was next for duty, sent up single machines. Our Flight Commander went first, and was away for an hour. When he got back Tomkins went up but returned almost at once with a dud engine, so Scott and I took off. We were Archied occasionally but apart from that there was little activity behind the lines.

In the afternoon the weather cleared and four of us from C Flight went up again. Griffin had been transferred to C Flight and made one of the four. Shortly after we crossed the lines first Tomkins and then Griffin had to turn back with dud engines. The skipper then dived down and I followed him. We raked all the roads on which there was any movement, and once we were dived on by three Pfalz scouts, but after firing short bursts at us they flew off east. My engine was not running well and as it became worse I decided to turn back. When I landed at Yvremh I ran into one of the holes and the bus went up on its nose. The propeller was chipped but no other damage was done. After a few minutes the skipper's bus came gliding in, and before it landed a red light was fired from it. Directly this was seen the M.O. was called and three or four of us who were on the aerodrome ran out to the machine.

Captain Pitts had turned and was taxi-ing back when we reached him. He was deathly white, and the first thing he said was, " Bannerman's been hit."

Bannerman was looking pretty wan and his right sleeve was soaked with blood. An explosive bullet had smashed the arm at the elbow. Captain Pitts looked

MORE GROUND-STRAFING

so ill that Scotty asked him sharply, " Have you been hit, Skipper ? "

" I've got it up the bottom," he said, and fainted.

The ambulance had arrived now and both the men were lifted out of the machine very gently. After some hasty first aid the M.O. decided to take them straight to the —th Casualty Clearing Station, which was only a mile and a half off, along a good road.

From the C.C.S. Captain Pitts was sent down to a base-hospital, where he lay in agony for two months, and then died.

Bannerman recovered eventually, but lost his right arm. He was a quiet, reserved fellow and none of us in the Squadron knew him at all intimately, but Captain Pitts had thought highly of him as an observer.

We felt keenly the loss of our skipper. He was an able Flight-Commander, and a thoroughly good chap.

Some months later I got an interesting side-light on his character, and it increased still more my admiration of him. Major Wells-Smythe, of M Squadron, a happy-go-lucky C.O., asked me if I had known Pitts in A Squadron.

" I knew him very well, sir," I replied, " he was my Flight-Commander."

" What sort of a chap was he, Vee ? Show any guts ? "

" He was one of the pluckiest fellows I have ever met, sir. During the 21st March show, he brought down nine E.A. within eight days, before he was hit. Also, he used to do the most amazing low-shows. He never talked much about these but we used to notice that his bus always had a good many bullet-holes in it, not Archie-holes, sir, but from rifle and machine-gun fire. It was rifle-fire that got him at last."

" It's extraordinary ! " said the C.O. " Pitts and I were pilots in the same Flight in E Squadron. He used to get a vertical breeze-up about crossing the lines at all. It was all he could do to go over with the rest of the Flight. On one occasion I know he turned back with a perfectly good engine. Well, they say you always get the best out of a chap by giving him responsibility. I was senior to him and got my Flight first, in another squadron, so I lost sight of him. But I heard that he had been given a Flight in A Squadron, and I was always curious to know how he had got on. Well, well! Have a drink?"

(v)

For the next few days we did low-shows regularly, in fine weather or foul. Tents were put up on the aerodrome and we left our billets in the village for these.

Scott and I shared a tent, and Merry produced a stretcher from somewhere for me.

" 'Ere y'are, sir," he said, proudly.

" Good work, Merry. Where did you get it?"

" Oh, I found it, sir," he answered vaguely, so I left it at that.

There was a moon at this time and on clear nights enemy bombers were always up. Twice they dropped bombs on the aerodrome but they did no damage beyond adding to the already numerous holes there.

It was always easy to tell them from our own night-fliers by the throbbing drone of their engines. Ours never made that throbbing sound.

One rainy evening sixteen of us went in to Abbeville, to have dinner at the Hôtel de France. It was nearly dark as we got into the tender and we saw two scouts come flying over our aerodrome. They flew round a couple of times like lost swallows and we could barely see them at a height of fifty feet through the mist and rain. Presently a huge fire broke out and flared up for a few minutes, and we knew that one of the scouts had flown into the ground. Men raced across the aerodrome in the hope that the pilot had been thrown clear, but his belt had held and he was burnt to death. The other machine had vanished.

MORE GROUND-STRAFING

One of the senior pilots from B Flight was posted as Flight-Commander to C Flight in Captain Pitts' place.

He had done well as a private in the infantry before joining the Flying Corps, and had received the D.C.M. and the Medal Militaire. I have never known a man so completely without fear as Captain Jackson. When he first came to us it was inevitable that we should compare him with his predecessor, Captain Pitts. Of the two I feel sure that Captain Pitts was the braver. He was more highly strung and sensitive than Captain Jackson, and realised danger in a job, but forced himself to see it through. Captain Jackson, on the other hand, would sail in gaily, with a complete absence of fear.

On the 2nd April, we heard that the Squadron was returning to Bertangles the following day.

" Thank God ! " said Tomkins devoutly. " Landing on this bally field is nearly as bad as doing a low-show. This evening there were two machines on their backs and three up on their noses—one of them mine."

" Fitton and I," said Smiles, " are sleeping in water every night. The only thing our tent does is to keep our blankets from drying during the day."

Our buses, standing out in the rain and sleet for several days, had been suffering badly. It frequently happened that three and even four machines had to turn back from a patrol with " dud " engines. Under ordinary war-flying conditions our Rolls-Royce engines behaved splendidly, but no man-made engine could stand up to the treatment ours received during this period.

When we awoke the following morning there was a steady drizzle falling. Merry came in for our boots and I asked him if A Flight had gone up.

" No, sir," he replied, " no machines has left the ground this morning."

At seven o'clock an orderly put his head through the opening. " Captain Jackson's compliments, sir, and the eight o'clock patrol is washed out."

"Good egg," I said, and rolled over for another forty winks.

Hours afterwards I woke up with a start as the faithful Merry appeared with two cups of tea.

"What's the time, Merry?"

"Eleven o'clock, sir. I thought as I'd better bring the tea, sir, as the mess lorry is the next to go."

"Scotty!" I called. No answer. "Scotty!" I shouted. Still no answer. "Give me that boot, Merry," and I lobbed it on to Scott's chest.

"Here—hi—what!" he exclaimed, sitting up suddenly and blinking. "Whazza time?"

"It's eleven o'clock," I said, "and the Squadron seems to be moving."

We drank the tea and Scott lay back, stretching and yawning. "Got any gaspers, Vee?"

"Not one. Merry, is it too late to get any from the mess?"

"I think I could manage it, sir. You see, sir, the mess Corporal's my uncle and he always——"

"Well, you shake a leg, my boy," Scott interrupted, "before your uncle hops it. And try and raise some chocolate, too," he added, as Merry disappeared.

He returned with the chocolate and cigarettes, and we lay in bed for another half-hour.

"Oh, it's a luvverly war," quoth Scott. "Send it down, John."

"It's going to be a sticky job getting off in this mud," I said.

"Don't be a pessimist, Vee. If we stick we stick, as the fly said when he dived into the jampot."

While we were dressing, Merry came for our valises.

"There's room in the mess lorry," he explained, "and you'll be sure of 'aving 'em to-night."

"Not if we stick here, in the mud," remarked Scott.

"Who's a pessimist now?"

"Oh, all right, quits!"

MORE GROUND-STRAFING

Captain Jackson was inspecting the machines and the mechanics were running up the engines when we walked over to the C Flight buses.

" They'll get us to Bertangles," he said, " and then we'll have them overhauled. By the way, I've bagged a tender to take C Flight into the village for lunch. Be in the road at one o'clock."

Shortly after lunch we took off. No. 22 slithered about as we taxied her out, but we got off safely and were soon back at Bertangles. It was a relief to see the Bristols being wheeled into hangars again. Then we went back to our former huts, and spent the rest of the afternoon playing bridge.

This was the first day, since the Push began, that we had not done a show. For the following two days we did nothing either, on account of the bad weather.

Griffin had found a pair of sheepskin thigh-boots in one of the huts and as he was no card-player he spent these dud days in cutting up the boots and making things to wear out of them. First, he made himself a pair of slippers putting the wool on the inside. Next he made a hat, and lastly, by joining up several bits he was able to make a sleeveless coat. He looked like Robinson Crusoe, when he had finished, but he was warmly clad on these cold days.

" Will you be getting another bed, sir ? " asked Merry, the morning after we returned to Bertangles.

" What's wrong with this one ? "

" Well, sir, it's like this. The bloke I borrowed it from is beginning to 'ave 'is suspicions that I got it——"

" Well, dash it all, take it back to him. I didn't know that you'd *pinched* it from anybody."

After breakfast I walked along to my rigger.

" Smeath, can you make me a bed ? " I asked him.

" I've got the very thing, sir," he said. " This kite-balloon covering. It'll be as easy as a spring-mattress."

That evening he brought it round to the hut, and it certainly was as comfortable a bed as I have ever slept on.

(vi)

On the 6th, towards midday, the weather cleared. At half-past twelve, Tomkins, Smiles and I were sent over as escort to two machines from A Flight who had to do a reconnaissance from Warfusee to Cerisy. Tomkins was leading us and we flew above the two reconnaissance machines, along the Somme, crossing the lines at 5,000 feet. We were heavily Archied when we crossed and to escape this we climbed up through a heavy patch of cloud. The bank was 1,000 feet thick and while we were climbing through it we were, of course, out of sight of each other. When Scott and I emerged at 6,000 feet we saw Tomkins' machine not far off, and presently the other three machines, one after the other, pushed their noses out of the bank. There was a good deal of white Archie high over Amiens, and we spotted four E.A. flying east at about 12,000 feet. Through gaps in the clouds we were able to pick up our bearings and we " formed formation " and flew towards Cerisy. High overhead we saw a formation of eleven E.A. flying west. As we approached Cerisy the clouds became more scattered and we descended to 3,000 feet. The A Flight machines went below us, and we escorted them up and down the valley while they did their reconnaissance. After half an hour I saw an enormous formation of triplanes coming towards us from the east, flying at about 1,000 feet above us. I pointed them out to Scott and we kept a watchful eye on them. There were eighteen machines in the formation. They came nearer and nearer and soon we made out that the leader was flying a scarlet triplane. It was probably von Richthofen[*] and his circus. Presently Scott tapped me on the shoulder and held up a red Very-pistol cartridge. I nodded and he slipped it into the breech. Before he could fire it a red light went up from Tomkins' machine. Tomkins' warning was acknowledged by a white light, the wash-out signal, from one of the

MORE GROUND-STRAFING

reconnaissance machines, and then we all showed our heels to the triplanes. I heaved a sigh of relief when our leader turned west. Bristols were better than any German machines, but five of them would hardly have stood much chance against eighteen triplanes, who had the advantage of height.

On the way back we dropped the bombs we were carrying, on some enemy trenches north-east of Villers Brettoneaux.

A few drops of rain were falling when we landed. These increased to a drizzle, which lasted most of the afternoon. After tea, Smiles, Tomkins, Parrish and I stoked up the fire in the little stove in our hut and drew up our stools or boxes round it. We were debating whether to play bridge or poker when Captain Jackson came in.

" If the rain eases off will you come with me, Parrish, to do some ground-strafing round Cerisy ? A Flight reported a lot of movement there, and the C.O. wants us to shoot 'em up a bit. The Boches seem to be flying in big formations these days so we'll need the other three of you as an escort. We'll go up about six. Now what about some poker till then ? "

We played poker till half-past five, and although it was still showery and misty then, Captain Jackson decided to go up.

Griffin went across to the mess to call our observers who were rehearsing for a concert that night.

There were some heavy, low clouds about as we took off, and we knew that it would be difficult to keep formation. It had been arranged that the wash-out signal, to be fired from the Flight-Commander's machine, was to be a green light followed by a white light. Tomkins led the escort and we flew above Captain Jackson and Parrish. It was a gloomy evening. The heavy clouds overhead made it unusually dark and we were frequently flying through patches of rain and through the lower-lying clouds, when we would lose sight of one another. We flew in loose formation, and when we reached Cerisy and the two Bristols went down to rake the roads, we sat above them and kept a sharp look-out for E.A. There was a surprising amount of activity in the air for such a wet evening. Several times small formations of our scouts passed by and also some lone machines. Occasionally we caught glimpses of E.A., but they disappeared behind clouds and we were not molested. Our skipper gradually worked south-west and we followed him down to Hangard, keeping him and Parrish in sight with difficulty. When we reached Hangard I saw a green light followed by a white light, fired from below us. This was the wash-out signal agreed upon so I turned westwards. I had barely started back when, looking over my shoulder to see where our other machines were, I noticed Tomkins and Smiles turning east again. Then I looked over the side and saw Captain Jackson and Parrish going east too. Naturally, I swung round at once and followed them but was some distance behind by this time. It turned out afterwards that the lights had not been fired from the Flight-Commander's machine at all. By a curious coincidence our wash-out signal had been fired from the ground.

The clouds were dropping lower now and we kept flying through dense patches of heavy grey mist. Several times I lost sight of the other Bristols, which were well ahead of us, and presently I lost them altogether. Once an S.E.5 dived straight at us out of a cloud overhead, and he missed us by a few yards. Presently Scott hit me hard on the shoulder, and then his gun began rat-tat-tatting. I shot a glance over my shoulder, saw a triplane on our tail, and swung the bus round in a vertical turn. After manœuvring for position I got in a burst of ten—when my gun jammed with a No. 4 stoppage. I had been so excited that I had not used the Aldis sight at all, but had been guided by tracer. I knew this was a useless thing to do and after clearing the stoppage had another go at him. As he flew across my line of flight I put him on the outer edge of the ring in the Aldis sight, and pressed the Bowden lever. After a very short burst from my gun he stalled up, fell over and plunged down vertically with black smoke streaming from his fuselage. Scott bent forward and yelled into my ear, " Good egg ! That got him ! " and we were both leaning over the side watching him go down, when we saw a group of holes appear in the left wing, just below us. On our tail was another triplane, with his gun flashing at us. Scott whipped his gun round on the Scarff mounting, gave him a good burst from it, and he sheered off into a cloud. It was very exciting work but it was all over in a few seconds. There was little hope of finding the other Bristols now as it was becoming dark. We were several miles beyond the lines and most of the time we were flying through rain, so I shouted to Scott, " Westward ho ? " and he nodded emphatically.

After crossing the lines we went down low and saw three Bristols ahead of us. They turned north before getting to Amiens and we guessed that they were the C Flight machines going home, but we could not catch up to them. We saw them land ahead of us at Bertangles.

" Have you seen anything of Smiles ? " asked Captain Jackson as soon as we taxied up.

" No," I said, " I saw him last following Tommy when you turned east at Hangard."

Tomkins said he had lost sight of Smiles just afterwards, in the mist, and had not seen him again.

Scott and I went along to the orderly room to put in our first combat-report, and then after changing out of flying-kit, hurried in to dinner. The concert had just started in the building adjoining the mess. The three C Flight pilots and their observers were still at dinner when we went in.

" The C.O.'s had a 'phone message," said Jackson, " that Smiles is down outside Amiens. He's been hit in the ankle. They're sending him to the —st C.C.S."

" How's Fitton ? "

"He's all right. A tender has gone off with Smiles' kit and it will bring Fitton back."

Scott was still busy with his soup when he was called to sing at the concert. He had a fine baritone voice and was always in demand on concert nights.

"'Od's teeth!" he exclaimed, as he walked off, "I'm famished!"

After dinner we walked across to the concert. At ten o'clock it ended and we were on our way back to the huts when the tender got back with Fitton, Smiles' observer.

Smiles, he said, was pretty cheerful but in a good deal of pain. They had lost sight of Tomkins after flying through some clouds. Then two triplanes had attacked them from below. Smiles had half-rolled on to them and after firing a good burst at one of them, the triplane, which was diving very steeply, had broken up in the air. In the meantime the other triplane had dived on them, hitting Smiles in the ankle and also hitting his engine. Smiles immediately turned west and got across the lines before the engine "conked" altogether. He brought the machine down safely in a field outside Amiens.

(vii)

For four consecutive days after this the rain came down steadily, without a break, and not a machine left the ground.

An order appeared about this time which gave rise to a good deal of discussion in the mess. The order stated that if an enemy observation balloon was attacked by a British machine and the observer forced to take to his parachute, the attacking machine was to shoot down the observer during his descent, if he could possibly do so.

"It simply isn't cricket," remarked Dickson in his rapid whisper, "and if my pilot attempted it I should crack him over the head."

MORE GROUND-STRAFING

"You don't seem to mind diving into the ground, Dicky," said Captain Jones, the Adjutant. "Look here, old lad," he went on, "the position is simply this. That observer has got information which may mean death to hundreds of our chaps in the trenches. Damn the balloon! Nobody cares two hoots about that. The Boches can easily afford another. The observer is the chap you're after."

"Jones, old Adge," drawled Scott, "if you don't mind my saying so you're talking bilge. The observer has got all his information written down neatly and methodically, in his little notebook, and even if you pot him his brother Fritzes on the ground are going to salvage that little book out of the mess. In addition to that the balloons on either side of him have probably got the same information that he has, so why not give the poor devil a sporting chance? He stands quite a good risk of breaking at least his leg, as it is. If he's jumped from a blazing balloon he surely deserves some small chance of saving his scurvy neck!"

Feeling was divided on the question, but the majority agreed with Scott and Dickson. In any case balloon-strafing was not a sport often indulged in by Bristol Fighters. Our S.E.5's and Camels were the machines that made a speciality of it.

When the clouds broke up on the fifth day I walked over to the hangar where No. 22 stood. The mechanics had been overhauling her and suggested that I should test her, so I asked the fitter to get into the back seat, and up we went. There was a pyramid of enormous cumulus clouds in the sky, and I climbed up towards it. It was a beautiful sight. There were no misty edges, the clouds were clear-cut and white, and they looked as solid as shining icebergs floating in the sky. When we reached 4,000 feet we were on a level with them and we picked our way through clefts and gorges between the great white mountains. The engine was running perfectly and we climbed up along a narrow ravine till we emerged above the highest peak of all. Then I picked out the biggest of the cloud-mountains, flew over it, and, shutting off the engine, threw the Bristol over into a spin. Down we whirled through the dense white mist, round and round giddily, till we suddenly shot out into clear air below. I was nearly intoxicated with the sheer joy of it! The experience, I am sure, would have set any lame poet on his legs again. However, the fitter tapped me on the shoulder and pointed to his wrist-watch, and I remembered that C Flight was due for a patrol at eleven o'clock.

From now on, for the next fortnight, we were put on high offensive patrols again, much to everybody's relief. During this time, Major Field returned to England and was replaced by Major Sparks. The new C.O. took a more active part in the life of the Squadron than Major Field had done, and on several occasions he led the patrols himself. He came to our Squadron after doing a spell of H.E. duty in England, but had been out to France before as a Flight-Commander, and had then been awarded the M.C., and a bar to it. He was soon voted a jolly good fellow by officers and Ack Emmas alike.

On moonlight nights we used to hear enemy bombing machines going over. They frequently crossed over Amiens on their westward journeys and then twenty or more searchlights would wave their long shining arms about the sky, groping for the bombers. One night we were watching this fascinating sight and we suddenly saw an aeroplane shining in one of the searchlight beams. Instantly all the beams converged on to it and the aeroplane was held in the focus. The pilot did everything he could to escape. He dived, zoomed, spun, but the searchlights held him inexorably at their meeting-point and he glowed like a firefly. Then tracer began streaming up at him and soon after he fell, erratically, like a leaf, and the crossing-point of the shafts of light followed him down.

Another night, while we were at dinner, a large bomb

MORE GROUND-STRAFING

suddenly fell, quite unexpectedly, 150 yards from the mess. The crash might have split the welkin. The bomb made a deep, wide hole in the earth, but damaged nothing.

On the other side of the aerodrome to us was a squadron of bombers. Late one afternoon, nine of them went over to bomb the railway junction at Chaulnes. For some unexplained reason they left without an escort. They had dropped their bombs and were on their way back when they were intercepted by a formation of twenty Fokker triplanes. The British machines attempted to fight their way through the formation, but they were not only heavily outnumbered, but were also out-manœuvred by the lighter triplanes. The leader's machine was set on fire and he was seen deliberately to ram a triplane, the two machines then crashing to earth. Of the nine bombers only two got back to Bertangles and these two were badly shot about, the observer of one machine and the pilot of the other being wounded. We heard that the observer died on the way to the C.C.S.

We did high patrols regularly when the weather permitted. At this time the Fokker triplanes usually went about in large formations, and occasionally we had skirmishes with the Baron von Richthofen's circus. That it was his patrol we could tell by the scarlet triplane that he favoured.

For several days, C Flight had no decisive combats. One afternoon when the five of us did see a smaller formation of seven E.A. and were expecting a dog-fight over Peronne, they spotted us while we were manœuvring for position between them and the sun, and they made off east.

It was after returning from one of these patrols, as we were getting out of our machines, that we saw a man make a parachute descent from one of our kite-balloons. It was a pretty sight. The parachute blew open and shone dazzlingly in the rays of the setting sun. Below it the man swung pendulum fashion two or three times and the parachute seemed scarcely to move. Then it floated gracefully down.

There is one case on record in which a balloon observer had a remarkably narrow escape. The balloon, at a height of 2,000 feet was attacked by E.A. and set ablaze. The observer jumped but his parachute failed to open. For 2,000 feet he fell like a stone and then crashed through the branches of a tree into a puddle of water. The tree and the puddle, between them, saved his life and he escaped with some broken bones.

Leave had been stopped for a while during the March retreat, but now officers were allowed to go off as their turns came round on the leave roll. There had been several casualties in the Squadron since the 21st March, and consequently all of us had moved up several pegs on the leave-list.

"Do you think, sir," said Anderson, my fitter, to me one morning, " that Mr. Scott would like another dog ? "

" I'm sure of it," I answered. " Do you know where one is to be had ? "

" Well, sir, a French lady in the village, with whom I am acquainted has two black-and-white pups that she is trying to sell."

" Well, let's have them both. I'll take the other, unless you want it ? "

" No, sir, I don't want it. I'll fetch them this evening."

That evening the two pups duly arrived. They were mongrel terriers, favouring no one strain more than another, but they were jolly little chaps. Since Susie had gone to the happy hunting grounds we had had no pet in the Squadron, with the exception of a small fox which we had bought for a few francs from a Frenchman. But it had not been a success and had refused to eat, so we had taken it to a wood and set it free.

Fellows returning from leave had been telling us of a show at one of the music-halls in London, in which one comedian said to another, " Do you know Arthur ? "

"Arthur who?" asked the second.

"Ahr thermometer," was the reply.

"Do you know Walter?"

"Walter who?"

"Wall ter lean against"—and so on for quite a while.

As a result of this, Scott called his pup Amos and I called mine Quito. They were cheerful little beggars and they slept on our feet every night.

(viii)

During April, the Royal Flying Corps and the Royal Naval Air Service were amalgamated into one flying service, the Royal Air Force. On the day of the amalgamation all "second-loots" in all squadrons became automatically entitled to put up two pips on each shoulder.

The German advance had been stopped for the time being, but it was expected that they would make another attack before long.

Machines were constantly being sent over on reconnaissance duty, and frequently they went over singly. The lone pre-dawn reconnaissance was the worst of them all and the souls of the pilot and observer would be engulfed in misery on this cold, cheerless flight before sparrow-chirp. The night before, the pilot and his brother officers would be sitting in front of a cheery fire, playing poker, and the world would seem merry and bright and full of good fellowship. Then the Skipper would come in, lay his hand regretfully on the pilot's shoulder and say, "Sorry, Smith, but you're for the high jump in the morning."

A little shiver would wriggle down Smith's spine, and he would answer, "Right-ho, Skipper," and go on playing. Every now and then the little shiver, lodged in his spine, would give another wriggle, to remind him that it was still there. He would not allow his mind to dwell on the morrow, but if he happened to glance across at his observer he might notice that his gaiety was perhaps slightly too loud to be natural. When the game broke up and he was back in his hut, he would see that his Sidcot, flying boots, goggles, helmet and gloves were handy, and then, putting the morrow out of his thoughts, creep into bed.

He has barely dropped off to sleep when someone, holding a lantern, shakes his arm and says, " Time to get up, sir." " Right-ho," he answers, and off goes the Ack Emma, leaving the world in darkness. He fumbles for the matches, lights the candle, and, shivering in the mean little draught, pulls on his cold clothes. A candle flickers at the other side of the hut and his observer too begins silently to dress. By this time his teeth are chattering with the cold. He gives one envious glance at his sleeping comrades, some of whom are snoring rhythmically, and out he goes into the bitter morning. It is almost pitch-dark outside, but there is a feeble light in the mess and he and his observer go across for the tea and bread and butter which they know is waiting for them. The mess waiter is very attentive and has a look of compassion in his eyes, and they feel that he will be glad to think afterwards how kind he was to them on their last morning. As they are finishing their tea they hear the engine start up outside the hangar, and putting their cups down, hurry through the chilly darkness towards the aerodrome.

Suddenly the observer speaks for the first time, " I expect von Richthofen and his circus are waiting for us over Peronne." This is exactly what the pilot has been thinking himself and he answers irritably, " Don't be a ruddy fool." They stumble on in silence through the darkness and the dawn breeze tweaks their cold noses.

" Morning, sir," says the mechanic. " Temperature's rising. She's ready to run up, sir." The observer clambers aboard and the pilot follows him. He settles himself in the seat, pushes his feet under the toe-straps of the rudder-bar, and with his numbed hand pushes forward the throttle.

MORE GROUND-STRAFING

The engine roars for a few seconds, and he throttles her back. Then he waves the chocks away and takes off into the darkness. In the east behind him, a faint streak of grey is beginning to show above the horizon. Up, up, he goes, gaining height as he flies towards Abbeville. Below him lies the sleeping world, and a tortuous ribbon of white mist marks the course of the Somme. At Abbeville he turns and flies east, still climbing steadily. When he crosses the lines the darkness below has given way to a greyish light, but no details can as yet be distinguished. Archie cannot see him, but hears him, and sends up a few aimless shells, hoping for the best. Mile after mile he flies steadily eastwards, getting farther and farther into enemy territory. All this time his observer is sitting huddled up in his cockpit. From time to time he pokes his head tentatively over the side, and then snuggles it back again between his shoulders.

After a while the day is sufficiently advanced for him to recognise objects on the earth and he pulls out his pad and begins to make notes of any movement on the roads or railways. All this time the pilot is keeping a very sharp look-out for enemy aircraft. If he is lucky there is none about yet, and when he has left the lines about twenty miles behind him he brings the nose round gradually and begins the return journey. It is broad daylight now, but bitterly cold. His face seems to be frozen, and he can feel no life in hands or feet. He wonders idly whether the observer's scrawl will be legible when he gets back to the aerodrome. Near the lines, Archie, who has been waiting for his return, and who can see him clearly now, greets him like a boisterous dog. Black bursts of smoke leap up at him but after some desperate dodging he wins through. He shuts off his engine, glides directly towards the aerodrome, and when he is above it he pushes the stick over and comes down in a graceful spiral—to land happily on the aerodrome. Shortly after, he and his observer are attacking with vigour a large and well-earned breakfast.

But this early reconnaissance does not always pass off so uneventfully. On the 21st April, Parrish and his observer Dickson went up, and on the return journey, as they passed over Estrees, seven E.A. dived on them out of a high cloud-belt. Parrish put the nose down and kicked on left and right rudder alternately to prevent the enemy machines from getting a bead on him. But they followed close on his heels, and Dickson kept firing short bursts into them. About two miles from the lines Dickson hit the petrol tank of one of them, and it went down in a flaming parabola. The remaining six still gave chase and about a mile from the lines Dickson was wounded in the knee, but he kept on firing till he had exhausted the drum. As he was trying to replace it with a full drum he fainted. Parrish was afraid to spin for fear of throwing Dickson out, so he continued to dive very steeply, zig-zagging as he went. The E.A. followed him down and shot away some of his control wires, so that his machine fell over into a side-slip. They were over the lines by this time and the Boches turned back, but do what he would, Parrish could not flatten out sufficiently to land the Bristol. When it crashed into the ground both he and Dickson were thrown out, but Parrish escaped with some severe bruises. Dickson's collar-bone was broken in the crash and as his knee had been shattered in the scrap he was packed straight off to a C.C.S. and, eventually, invalided back to England.

It was on the same day that the Baron von Richthofen in his scarlet triplane was brought down by Captain A. R. Brown,* flying a Camel. In the Royal Air Force Communiqué for the 21st April, there appeared the following paragraph:

"Captain M. von Richthofen, who is credited by the enemy as having brought down eighty Allied machines, was shot down and killed behind our lines near Corbie, by Captain A. R. Brown, No. 209 Squadron."

This was the end of one of the greatest of the German

fighting pilots, a man whose fame and prowess had become almost legendary.

The gallant airman was buried with full military honours.

Photographs were taken of his grave and dropped, by our aeroplanes, beyond the lines.

CHAPTER X

THE LAST BID FOR VICTORY

On the 24th April, the Germans attacked Villers Brettoneaux in another attempt to break through. At 5 a.m. we were called for a low strafe. A very heavy bombardment had been going on all night and when we took off there was a light mist over everything. We flew directly towards the lines, but as we got near them the mist became dense, and extended right to the ground. We could not get below it and it was useless to go above it so we were forced to return. We spent a miserable morning waiting for the fog to rise. The pessimists in the Squadron said that the Allies had no more reserves to bring up and that if the Germans broke through now, nothing could stop them.

At 12.30 the fog began to rise, but instead of breaking, it merely rose a few hundred feet and lay like a black blanket over everything. We left the ground again at ten minutes past one and flew towards the lines. The fog was low and we were flying at 500 feet most of the time. A great battle was raging on the ground below us. It was a horribly fascinating sight. Our infantry were crouching in shell-holes and bits of trenches, and a huge crater northwest of Villers Brettoneaux was full of our men. Our big guns were firing continuously. Everything was dark and gloomy under the impenetrable fog, and the gun flashes showed up vividly. It was impossible to see more than a few hundred feet and several times I got lost in patches of mist and had to fly south-west till I picked up the Abbé Wood and got my bearings again. Dead men

THE LAST BID FOR VICTORY

and horses were lying about everywhere. There were a few troops in advanced shell-holes just north of Villers Brettoneaux. There were also some men, mostly in pairs, mounted or on foot, on the roads in front of the trenches and shell-holes that were lined with our men. One man, on horseback, was in front of them all. East of this was no-man's-land. All the time, above the noise of the engine, could be heard the roar of the guns below and also the sharp crackling of rifles and machine-guns. Two or three fellows of our Squadron told me afterwards that they had actually seen shells in the air, and I daresay this was quite possible for I have heard gunners, too, say that they occasionally glimpsed a shell as it was leaving the muzzle, when they were directly behind the gun. I did not actually see any shells but several times, above the noise of the engine, I heard them whine as they went by.

We dived on the enemy trenches again and again and also dropped our bombs. Every time we got near the enemy lines tracer streamed up at us from machine-guns. There were a good many S.E.5's and Camels about, too, diving on the Boche trenches. Then a machine-gun gave Scott and me a particularly hot time and I zoomed up into the fog to escape it. When I came down I had lost my bearings completely, as it was impossible to see any distance in that queer, murky light. Presently we noticed a Camel in a field below us and landed next to him. Some Frenchmen gave us the direction of Amiens, almost due north, and we took off again. The Camel followed us as far as Amiens and then as we had nearly exhausted our ammunition we returned to our aerodrome. The other machines had returned too, and we heard that Tomkins had been hit in the leg. It was not a serious wound but was giving him a good deal of pain. Tomkins, however, was in high spirits at the thought of getting back to Blighty. After tea the ambulance took him off, grinning and groaning alternately, to the C.C.S. "Tommy" was a cheery fellow to have about the place and also a sound pilot, and everybody turned out to give him a good send-off.

In the evening, we had seven French officers, of the Alpine Chasseurs, to dinner in our mess. Only one or two of them spoke English and our French was deplorable, but we all got on famously together. Their regiment had just arrived in this sector, and they came full of enthusiasm. They were wonderfully cheerful and amusing fellows, and had a tonic influence on the mess. The Squadron was feeling a bit blue about the future. We knew what the previous attack had been like and were fearing a repetition of it, but they simply laughed the idea to scorn.

" Break sroo ! " cried the captain. " Zis is ze Boches' las' keeck and it ees not possible to keeck hard. Aftair zis he is fineesh ! "

There was a cinema show at the Squadron that night and after dinner we took the Frenchmen along to see it. They obviously enjoyed it hugely and laughed uproariously at the comic items. When the time came for them to return, and we were toasting one another in a final night-cap, we invited them to come over again, when they could, for joy rides in our Bristol Fighters, and they accepted with enthusiasm. Then they crowded into the big car which had brought them, and with much shouting, drove off. It was surprising and rather jolly to find that such a famous regiment should be composed of such volatile, cheery members.

Some very young and excited infantry subalterns passed through Bertangles the following day, and if all they told us was to be believed, the plight of the Allies was indeed rather desperate, and it was a toss-up whether or not the line could be held.

" Moroccan troops have been pushed into the line here," said one of the subalterns, " and they are bloodthirsty devils. They are never content with seeing a Boche drop from rifle-fire, but insist on cutting his head right off. They are very useful in attack, but no damned good

THE LAST BID FOR VICTORY 189

in defence. Well, we must be off. Thanks for the drinks."

"Cheerio!" we called after them. "Good luck!"

For some days we had to abandon all high patrols and revert to low ground-strafing shows. They were low, from our point of view in more senses than one. Reconnaissances also had to be carried out every day.

The following order, for instance, typical of such things, was handed to me one evening by the Flight-Commander:

"Information required—on 26-4-18. Reconnaissance of all roads between old front line and present front line, especially of roads running E. and W., South of Hamel in P 14, P 17, Valleys N. of Lamotte, South Wiencourt, E. of Hangard Wood and Valleys of Luce and Somme.

"It is anticipated that the enemy is likely to bring up reinforcements between the rivers Somme and Luce in view of the attack now proceeding on this front.

In the Field, R.R.S., *Major*.
    25-4-18.   O.C. No. A Squadron,
                                          Royal Air Force."

Scott and I had to go up at dawn. Directly we got back another machine would be sent up and so on during the day so that all developments could be closely watched.

One afternoon our friends of the Alpine Chasseurs arrived on the aerodrome for the joy rides to which we had invited them. B and C Flights were off duty, but A Flight was aloft. First, we adjourned to the mess for a few minutes and then led them across to the aerodrome where the Bristols were standing in line. A young officer, Lt. F——, went with me. Before getting into the bus he said to me, "Please be so good as to promees zat you weel not make stunts. I have onlee been marrayed for two weeks."

"All right," I said, "no stunts," and handed him a pair of goggles. Then I helped him to fasten the belt round his waist and we took off.

Lt. F—— had never been in an aeroplane before and when we turned and flew back over the aerodrome he gazed intently over the side at the hangars and huts below. Then we flew towards the lines so that he might get an idea of the appearance of the trench system from the air. He was immensely interested, and for some fifteen minutes we patrolled up and down the line. On the way back to the aerodrome he pointed out an R.E.8 to me, in the distance, so I gave chase and when we drew alongside I glanced back and he was shouting delightedly like a small boy. As we approached the aerodrome again, flying at 2,000 feet, I shut off the engine and pushed the stick right forward. The Bristol suddenly shot downwards in a very steep dive, and I was able to give the French officer a very considerable sensation without breaking my word about stunting. After flattening out gradually, we landed. The Frenchman was extremely excited and thrilled with his first flight. He talked and laughed and gesticulated, all very rapidly, and I could follow nothing for a while. When he had calmed down a bit he said to me, reproachfully, " But you did promees not to make a stunt. Was zat so ! " gesticulating, " not ze stunt ? "

" No one," I answered, " could possibly call that a stunt. It was merely a steep descent."

" Oh, zes," he replied, doubtfully. " But when you went—so ! " gesticulating again, " Oo-la-la ! my sto-mach."

Before leaving they invited us to dinner at their mess, two nights later, and drove off thanking us volubly for the entertainment.

In due course we dined with the Frenchmen. They gave us a topping dinner, but the order of serving it seemed curious to us. First we had soup. Then we had three vegetables, each served as a separate course. After this there was a pause and cigarettes were lit. I thought we had now come to the end of a vegetarian dinner, but presently the meat was served by itself. Following this again was a sweet, and finally coffee.

THE LAST BID FOR VICTORY

The Alpine Chasseurs were not the only officers whom we took up for joy-rides. Often, towards evening, English officers in the neighbourhood would walk over to the aerodrome and when we could we would take them up. There were Australian troops near Bertangles at this time too, and when the patrols were over for the day we gave many of the privates short " flips."

One evening six tanks from Amiens halted near our aerodrome and we walked across to see them. We got into conversation with the tank officers and one of them asked :

" Is there any chance of a ride in your aeroplanes this evening ? I have never even seen the inside of one before, and I don't think these other chaps have either."

So we led them across to the aerodrome and although it was fairly late we managed to give them each a short flight. Then we dined them and wined them and when they left they suggested that we should go across in the morning for a ride in their tanks. Early in the morning, several of us walked over to the road. The tank officers were waiting for us and as soon as we arrived, distributed us among the half-dozen tanks and set off.

" How would you like to exchange jobs with us ? " one of them asked me.

" Not at any price," I answered, decidedly.

" We're safe on Mother Earth, at any rate," he said with a grin.

" Are you ! If your engine conked on a raid you'd be caught like rats in a trap."

Every man always thought the other fellow had the more dangerous job.

A few hundred yards up the road the tanks halted and we got out.

" Good-bye—thanks awfully." " Same to you." " Cheerio ! "

We stood for a while watching those earth-bound monsters as they rumbled off on their way northwards.

CHAPTER XI

A RECONNAISSANCE AND AN O. PIP

(i)

"COMIC CUTS" was the inappropriate name commonly used for the official Royal Air Force Communiqués. These were posted periodically in the Squadron Office, and always made interesting reading. First a general account of aerial activities was given, and then some concise accounts of the outstanding combats which had taken place during the period under review. For instance, from 13th to the 19th May, 1918, inclusive :

"We have claimed officially 130 E.A. brought down and thirty-two driven down out of control. In addition, nine E.A. have been brought down by A.A. Fifty-two of our machines are missing. Approximately $193\frac{1}{4}$ tons of bombs were dropped and 13,964 photographs taken.

"May 13th. The weather was fine early, but later rain set in, making flying impossible.

"Fifteen reconnaissances were carried out and seven contact and counter-attack patrols.

"Eighty-five hostile batteries were successfully engaged for destruction with aeroplane observation (fifty-one by the 1st Brigade), and thirty-seven neutralised ; eight gun-pits were destroyed, eleven damaged, twenty-two explosions and nineteen fires caused. One hundred and eighty-six zone calls were sent down.

"On the 12th instant, nine balloons of the 1st Brigade carried out twenty-nine successful shoots ; four hostile batteries were successfully engaged for destruction and three neutralised. Two of the shoots were carried out in

A RECONNAISSANCE AND AN O. PIP

conjunction with aeroplanes. A great deal of general observation work was also done. Two balloons of the 5th Brigade carried out eight successful shoots; three of the targets were hostile batteries, which were successfully engaged for destruction.

"Twenty-one and three-quarter tons of bombs were dropped as follows:—"

Then followed some details of the activities of the bombing squadrons. This was followed by reports of aerial combats, and of the work of Artillery-Observation squadrons. For instance:

"Captain D—— and Lt. M——, No. 12 Squadron, ranged the 133rd Siege Battery on to a hostile battery. Sixteen observations were given, three O.K.s obtained, one pit damaged, and three large explosions caused. (The pilot ranged.)"

"May 14th. The sky was overcast, with occasional clear gaps." During the day, "Lt. W. H——, No. 3 Squadron, whilst flying through the clouds, almost collided with an E.A. two-seater which was crossing his front at the same height. He fired a long burst from both guns into it and saw the observer jump to his feet; at the same moment the E.A. banked steeply and began side-slipping. Lt. H—— then fired another burst at point-blank range which caused black smoke to issue from the pilot's seat, and the E.A. nose-dived and burst into flames. Lieut. H—— was then attacked by another E.A. two-seater which dived on him, but overshot him; he then got on the tail of the E.A. and fired a short burst into it. Immediately the right-hand lower plane folded back and came off and the E.A. went down completely out of control and was seen to crash near Vaux."

This was but one of many other combats on that day.

Each report always ended with, "E.A. were also brought down by the following:—" and then followed a list of the airmen and the squadrons to which they belonged.

Captain A. W. Beauchamp-Proctor, M.C., the South African, was frequently mentioned in the Communiqués. He was rapidly becoming recognised as one of the Aces among the Allied airmen. On one occasion, May 15th, " Captain A. W. B.-Proctor, No. 84 Squadron, left the ground at 3.25 a.m. to engage E.A. bombing Amiens. He decided to fly east in order to try and intercept the E.A. on their return to their aerodrome. He found the aerodrome by the landing-flares and glided down to 3,000 feet and then waited a few miles west of the aerodrome. At about 3.55 a.m. a twin-engined E.A. passed just above him, and Captain Proctor immediately got beneath the E.A.'s tail but was seen by the observer who opened fire. Captain Proctor then opened fire and the E.A. started to dive down, and the observer stopped firing and did not again fire during the combat. Captain Proctor's gun then jammed and on clearing the stoppage he again attacked the E.A., firing 150 rounds into it. The E.A. fired a red light, which was answered by another red light from the aerodrome. Captain Proctor was then subjected to very heavy fire from the ground, both by machine-guns and ' flaming onions,' and broke off the combat at 2,000 feet, having driven the E.A. some distance beyond its aerodrome. When last seen, the E.A. was still diving but probably under control. However, a considerable amount of ammunition had been fired into it and it was probably damaged."

On May 26th, Captain A. W. Beauchamp-Proctor was awarded a bar to the Military Cross.[1]

One of the great Aces who was taking steady toll of the enemy machines was the Canadian, Major Bishop,* V.C., D.S.O., M.C., of No. 85 Squadron. On May 27th, for instance :

" Major W. A. Bishop, No. 85 Squadron, dived on an

[1] See also Chapter XV.

A RECONNAISSANCE AND AN O. PIP

E.A. two-seater over Houthulst Forest. E.A. dived east with Major Bishop on its tail. The left top and bottom planes fell off, and a little later the right-hand planes and also the tail. E.A. crashed east of Passchendaele." On May 28th he shot down two more E.A. On May 30th, " Major W. A. Bishop, No. 85 Squadron, was attacked by two E.A. two-seaters. He zoomed and fired at one of them which fell in flames near Roulers. He then got on the tail of the second one, which, after several bursts had been fired, fell to pieces in the air. Major Bishop also destroyed an Albatros Scout later in the day."[1]

Captain E. Mannock,* M.C., was doing extraordinarily good work in No. 74 Squadron. On May 20th the Communiqués recorded that he had been awarded the D.S.O. He was accounting for a large number of E.A. On May 31st he was awarded a bar to his D.S.O. Shortly after, this officer, who had in the meantime been promoted to the rank of Major, Commanding 85 Squadron, received a second bar to his D.S.O.[2]

(ii)

" What's the matter ? " I asked Griffin, as he came into the hut one afternoon, pulling off his flying-cap. " You look pretty worried! "

C Flight had finished its patrols for the day and I was sitting alone in the hut writing letters. Most of the fellows were outside kicking a football about. Others had gone off to another hut to play cards.

---

[1] For further accounts of Major Bishop's fights, see Appendix.

[2] On July 26th, 1918, the Communiqués stated that " Lt. D. C. I—— and Major E. Mannock, No. 85 Squadron, attacked an enemy two-seater, which they shot down in flames. On returning at 200 feet, Lt. I—— saw Major Mannock's machine shot down from the ground, and his own machine was hit in the petrol tank, but he succeeded in landing five yards behind our front lines." Major Mannock was seen by others to go down in flames. He had destroyed altogether 73 enemy machines. Major Mannock was awarded a posthumous V.C., gazetted on July 18th, 1919. See Appendix for details of some of his fights.

"I've written-off my bus," said Griffin, " but I'm dashed if I can see that it was my fault."

"Have a gasper," I said, pushing across the tin. "What happened?"

He inhaled deeply, blew out a cloud of smoke and flicked the match across the room.

"My engine has been playing up lately and I asked the Ack Emmas this morning to have a look at it. I flew the new bus on both shows to-day. This afternoon the Flight-Sergeant told me mine was O.K. and I took it up to test it. There were patches of mist about and in diving through one of these I struck the cable of an observation balloon. I must have been doing at least two hundred when I hit it, and it sliced off my left wing-tips as clean as a whistle. I got the bus back to the aerodrome, but, of course, I crashed on landing, as the damn thing was side-slipping all the time."

"Anybody in the back seat?" I asked. He shook his head.

"Sandbags," he replied.

"Well, what the deuce is worrying you? You couldn't help it. Let's go and look at it."

"Incidentally," he went on, as we left the hut, "it's time you trained your dog not to chase machines. I missed him by inches when I crashed."

Scott's dog, Amos, had been "written-off" a week before this by a landing aeroplane. The pups would chase all aeroplanes, landing or taking off, and if a machine flew across the aerodrome they would chase its shadow, barking furiously. Scott had not been particularly upset when Amos went out, as the pup had never quite replaced Susie in his affections. Susie had definitely been a one-man dog, and Scott, for his part, was a one-dog man. Quito had fretted for a day or two, but then had shaken off his grief, like a sturdy pup should do, and was once more filled with the joy of life.

The crash looked worse than it was. The propeller had

been broken and both left wings completely smashed, but these could be replaced easily. The undercarriage had mysteriously escaped injury.

"We'll have her ready by the morning, sir," said the Flight-Sergeant.

Griffin looked more cheerful as we turned away.

"How about it ? " I asked, glancing up at the sun.

"I think so," he replied, and we adjourned to the mess.

(iii)

"Go up at eleven, Vee, will you, and watch the roads," said Captain Jackson to me one morning. "They're expecting movement along 'em to-day."

"Right-ho, skipper."

"Stay up for an hour and a half. Parrish will go up when you get back."

When Scott and I left the ground it was fairly cloudy. We climbed to 17,000 feet and then crossed over, following the Somme till we were over Peronne. We could see the ground pretty well, through openings in the clouds, up to this point, but where the Somme turns south at Peronne we lost sight of it. For an hour and a half we flew up and down above the straight road that runs west towards Amiens, watching all the roads below us. There was very little movement on any of them and the clouds gradually drew together. It was becoming difficult to see the roads below us so I flew north hoping to get a view of the Bapaume-Albert road. But the clouds soon closed up completely beneath us, and so we turned westwards. Very soon there was an unbroken sea of cloud below us, and with no landmarks to guide us we were lost completely. After flying about haphazardly for a while, looking for gaps in the clouds, I turned and flew west for a considerable time and then dived down through the clouds. The country below was all strange to us, so we looked about for a suitable landing-ground. Before long we found a large field near a village and came down in it. A crowd of villagers soon straggled out to the machine but to our surprise they stood about in groups and eyed us rather suspiciously.

" I believe the beggars think we're Boches, Vee," said Scott. "We'll have to do something about it." So, with his disarming smile, Scott pointed to the Bristol and said, " Il est—ah—Anglaise aeroplane," and after a pause, he added, for no reason at all, " Certainement."

Perhaps the peasants thought he did protest too much, or they may have thought no one but a Boche could speak French so badly, but whatever the reason, no one made any comment, and they stared at us in sullen silence.

" Damn it, they must tell us where we are," he said to me, and turning again to the peasants, " Où ? " he shouted, enquiringly, and waved his arm in a wide arc.

" Look here," I said, unbuttoning my Sidcot and showing them the khaki tunic underneath, " Anglaise."

The sight of the khaki may have reassured them, for when I asked " Où est Amiens ? " one of them pointed to the north-east.

After thanking them we got back into the bus.

" Suspicious blighters," said Scott, " thinking we were Boches ! They've hurt my feelings."

We had left the prop. ticking over, and, as there was practically no wind I turned the machine round and took off in the opposite direction to that in which we had landed. The ground was wet and soft, and the wheels sank rather deeply, but we managed to get off safely. I had had the bus up on a short test flight early that morning, and as the tank had not been filled after it I knew that we must be nearly out of petrol.

The country that we were flying over was wooded and hilly and bad for forced-landings, so I decided that our safest course was to come down in the first good field near a town and try to obtain petrol. We could then also find out exactly where we were. The country looked less and

A RECONNAISSANCE AND AN O. PIP

less promising as we went on, but after a while we came in sight of a small town, and to the north of it we saw a field which looked just about big enough to land in. I shut off the engine and glided down, but we had a little too much way on when our wheels touched and we ran into a hedge at the end of the field. This damaged our left lower wing and chipped the prop. slightly. Again a crowd soon gathered, but they seemed friendly enough.

We could not leave the machine to look for help, so Scott wrote a note on his observation pad, and addressed it to the O.C. English troops, Forges-les-Aux, for this, the people told us, was the name of the town. We singled out an alert-looking youngster from the crowd and Scott said to him, " Anglaise Commandant." The youngster grinned and nodded and set off at a trot for the town.

At the edge of the field, beyond a small gate, was a farmhouse, and while we were waiting for a reply to the note a dear old lady, who had been watching proceedings from an upstairs window, came out to us with some bread and cheese and cider. As we stood at the little gate consuming this we carried on a rather halting conversation with her. Between us Scott and I had just managed to understand that the name of her farm was Compainville, and that she had a son a prisoner of war in Germany, when a car drew up with the English O.C., Major Brown, the French Commandant, and two privates with stakes and barbed wire.

Major Brown shook hands very cordially with us, presented us to the French Commandant, and then ordered the two privates to put up the stakes and barbed wire round the Bristol and to mount guard over it. Then he bustled us into the car and we drove in to Forges-les-Aux.

On the way Scott gave him an account of what had happened and when we got to his office I asked him if he would be good enough to send off a wire to the Squadron for us.

"Certainly, certainly," he said. "How would you like it worded?"

"I think, sir, it would be sufficient if you just said, 'No movement on roads this morning. Forced-landed at Forges-les-Aux. Left bottom wing damaged. Propeller chipped.'"

He went out to see that the wire was sent off immediately and when he returned he said to us:

"I'm afraid I can't offer you hospitality as my quarters are very cramped, but there's the Hôtel du Lion d'Or in the village where I think you'll be fairly comfortable. Can I lend you any money?"

"Thank you, sir. It's very good of you. But we happen to have enough between us."

Before we left the French Commandant invited us to dine with him and Major Brown that night, and then we were taken to the Hôtel du Lion d'Or in his car.

"Well," remarked Scott as we drove off, "those are a decent couple of birds."

"They couldn't possibly have done more for us."

"My idea of it," went on Scott, "is that the Major feels a bit out of it, stationed in this hole, miles from the line, and he is jolly pleased with this little incident. It gives him something definite to do, and he's making the most of it. Putting up those stakes and barbed wire round No. 22 was almost a pathetic touch, wasn't it?"

We dined with the O.C. and the Commandant that evening, but we had to apologise for appearing in our thigh-boots. We had been able, of course, to shed our Sidcot suits, but we had no other shoes with us.

The next morning we went for a stroll in our clumsy flying-boots and soon had a pack of urchins on our heels yelling "Les aviateurs!" so we dodged into a barber shop where we each had a shave. We also managed to procure some Woodbines there, and then to escape the unwelcome publicity occasioned by the small boys we returned to the hotel.

I was lying on the bed smoking a Woodbine, and Scott was leaning out of the window, when a young girl and her mother stopped in the street and the girl said to Scott in perfect English, " Excuse me, but can you tell me when you are going up, as my mother and I should like to see you take off ? "

When Scott had recovered from his surprise, he explained to her that the bus was broken and that our departure would depend upon when the repair-lorry arrived from the Squadron. They chatted for a few minutes and then the girl and her mother invited us to spend the evening at their home. After dinner that night we went to them, still in our wretched thigh-boots.

The girl, Miss Petit, had been educated in England. She sang and played several pretty things to us and then turning round on her stool, said, " But perhaps one of you will sing now ? "

She had addressed me, and I answered, firmly, " I'm sorry, Ma'm'selle. But I think you could coax Mr. Scott to sing."

" And how must I coax you ? " she asked, folding her hands on her lap, and smiling demurely at him.

" Vee, you're an ass," said Scott, rising and walking over to the piano. " Do you know this old ballad, Ma'm'selle ? " he asked, and picked out an air on the keys with one hand.

" But of course," said the girl, " it is Robin Adair," and she swung round on her stool and played the accompaniment by ear. Scott sang that and several other songs in his rich baritone, and he and the girl also sang several duets together.

When we were bidding them good night, they invited us to tea the following afternoon.

At ten o'clock the next morning a tender from the Squadron drew up at the hotel. Our own two Ack Emmas had come down and they had repaired the bus and refilled her the previous evening. So after taking them and the driver to the bar and telling the landlord to see to their wants, we went off to say good-bye to Madame Petit and her pretty daughter, and to Major Brown and the Commandant.

Then we drove out to the field in the tender, and, everything being in order, we took off. Three times we circled over Forges-les-Aux, diving down low and waving to the people who were crowding the streets, and then we turned her nose homewards.

" Aha ! you fellows," said Scott, smiling, and wagging his finger as we entered the hut, " you thought you were two-up on the leave list, didn't you ? "

(iv)

When Jackson walked in to lunch that day I noticed that he was wearing an M.C. ribbon next to the other two decorations under his wings.

" Hullo, Skipper, when did that arrive ? "

" Oh, turned up with the rations yesterday morning."

When I congratulated him the curious fellow glanced down at it casually.

" Thanks, Vee. There's only one decoration worth having and that's the V.C. I shall be satisfied when I get that."

Parrish, who sat opposite me, was drinking ale when the Skipper made this appalling remark, and he promptly choked. It was certainly a bit unnerving. And yet it was not mere swank in Jackson's case, but only a statement of fact. The man was simply without fear. Remarks of this sort, however, made openly in the presence of a number of fellows, occasion awkward silences and people are inclined to feel a grievance against the speaker. Jackson never hesitated to say things like this and, as a result, he was not so popular in the Squadron as his predecessor, Pitts, had been, who had always been the soul of modesty.

"Get 'em to fill up your tanks, Vee," said Jackson to me. "C Flight is doing a patrol at 2 p.m."

"Oh, well," remarked Scott, "we've had our little holiday so I suppose we mustn't grouse."

A new pilot, Gregory, was to do his first patrol with us that afternoon. We were five strong when we left the ground. Jackson was leading, Parrish flew inside right and I flew inside left, Griffin outside right and the new man Gregory, outside left. It was to be a high-offensive patrol. When we had "formed formation" in the air, instead of flying west to climb, Jackson made for the lines, and flew up and down in front of them gaining height. I felt a bit uneasy as we rose. Glancing round once at Scott I saw him gazing rather grimly eastwards. It was not usually considered good policy to climb in view of the lines, as the Boches could see the patrol coming and could accordingly lay any traps they wanted to for it. Eventually, we crossed over, to the north of Albert, at 17,000 feet. Archie greeted us with a great salvo. He placed some of his bursts unpleasantly close, but we flew steadily southeast and soon left the worst of it behind.

Then, a thousand feet below us, we saw a formation of seven E.A. flying south-west.

At the beginning of a patrol I always felt as jumpy as a cat on hot bricks, and the first sight of triplanes would send a shiver down my spine. A formation of E.A. gave one a strong impression of deadly insects crawling through the sky. Because of their "balanced" controls they moved jerkily, with none of the graceful swing of the British machines.

The jerky movements of this enemy patrol as it turned south, somehow increased its sinister, malevolent appearance. I found myself longing for and yet dreading the red light, the attacking signal, to flare up from our leader's machine. Anything to end the suspense! I knew that once I heard and felt my own gun hammering, this cowardice would leave me.

From what other pilots have told me I know that they have often experienced the same sensations. Before going into action they, too, would be nervous and filled with dark forebodings, but once the action began, fear would utterly leave them and their minds would be swamped with the one desire to kill and kill. War is rather a bestial affair.

The leader of the E.A. below us was flying a triplane with a scarlet body and black wings. White-edged Maltese crosses showed up vividly on the latter. The machines on either side of him were triplanes too. The one on his left had a pale-green body with yellow wings, and the other was striped black-and-white. The four remaining machines were black D.V.s. We were only a thousand feet above them, and they must have seen us, but they made no attempt to get away. They turned south and then flew steadily on and we kept on our course till we were behind and above them. Then a red light went up from Jackson's bus and the five Bristols dipped their noses and roared down at the Boches.

Jackson was diving on the leader, and I went down after the green triplane with my Bowden lever pressed hard. The air was filled with the roaring of the engines and the rattling of the guns. After a few seconds, Jackson pulled out of the dive, climbing up to the left, over my machine. But I was close on the green triplane's tail, firing hard, and I kept on till he suddenly zoomed up and fell over on his back. I did a climbing turn then and, looking over the side, I saw him shearing sideways and plunging erratically and thought he was out of control. But I had no time to watch him. Then a Bristol spun slowly past me. Black smoke was streaming from it and almost immediately it burst into flame. This must have been Jackson's bus for it started spinning from somewhere to the left of and above me, just where Jackson would have been. When we turned, the E.A. were on our level and had been reinforced by about six more triplanes. The

A RECONNAISSANCE AND AN O. PIP

sky seemed full of black Maltese crosses. This was a quite unexpected development as we had not seen them before we attacked and they must have been waiting for us against the sun. A regular dog-fight now took place. I dived on a triplane but triplanes have a colossal zoom at 16,000 feet, and he climbed up out of reach. Then I dived on another, firing short bursts at him, but he got away, split-assing downwards from side to side and I could not afford to lose height by following him down. As I zoomed up I saw an extraordinary sight. A Bristol was attacking a D.V. To escape him the D.V. side-slipped steeply and crashed into a triplane, and the two of them fell, interlocked, to earth. I shot a glance over the side and, far below them, caught a glimpse of a blazing ball of fire which I supposed was Jackson's Bristol. Several of the E.A. were going down now out of the fight, quite possibly to entice us down. Then Scott hit me on the shoulder and pointed to a green Very light which had gone up from a Bristol. A short distance below I saw three E.A., one of them the red-bodied triplane, close on the Bristol's tail, so I pushed forward the stick and shot down to his assistance. Three or four triplanes at once got on to our tail and followed us down, and they were so near that I could hear the rattle of their machine-guns. Scott's gun kept firing in short bursts and one of the triplanes, pulling off slightly to one side, suddenly went down in a vertical dive. Scott thought the pilot fell forward but could not be sure. For a second or two he watched the triplane speeding downwards, but he was hard pressed and had to give all his attention to the remaining E.A. The Bristol below was having a bad time. He was diving westwards, kicking on left and right rudder alternately, and the three triplanes were close on his heels. As soon as I could I opened fire on the nearest Boche, but almost at once my gun jammed. Immediately after this the observer in the Bristol hit one of the triplanes and it swung off to the right, bursting into flames. Then began a gruelling race for the lines. The E.A. were close on us and firing hard. Our wings were badly shot about. The fabric showed several gashes and two or three wires were cut. Then Scott's gun stopped. I almost dreaded to look round. When I did glance over my shoulder I saw him viciously throwing his empty drums at our pursuers! After that he fired off all the coloured lights at them from his Very pistol. The last few seconds of this running fight were the worst of all for we were flying at about 5,000 feet as we approached the lines, and Archie was waiting grimly for us. When we reached them, he put up a deadly barrage in front of us, and we had no option but to go through it. One shell after another crashed in front of us, on either side and below us, and we were enveloped in the choking fumes. But at last we shot clear of the barrage, and were safely across the lines. The E.A. had turned back at the fringe of the barrage, and our troubles were over. But this was not the case with the other Bristol. He was side-slipping badly, and was beginning a slow spiral. I dived down near him and recognised Parrish's machine. Then Scott and I saw his observer, Lockwood, climb out of his cockpit and work his way outwards along the wing till the Bristol was flying on a nearly even keel again. Owing to the slow spiral she had got into, she was pointing almost back to the lines by this time, but Parrish pulled her round gradually and set off, on half-throttle, for the aerodrome. He did not have her under complete control and when he got back and was gliding down to land, without warning she side-slipped right down to the ground and when she struck it turned over on her back. Lockwood was thrown clear and escaped with a few bruises. Parrish was held in by his belt and suffered no injury at all.

The machine had been badly shot about by the pursuing E.A., but the chief damage had been caused by Archie just as Parrish crossed the line. A large bit of the wing had been blown away by one of the final bursts. Some of the control-wires had been cut earlier in the fight, and because of this, Parrish had fired the green light and turned back.

Griffin landed just after we did, but there was no sign of Gregory. None of us had seen him go down during the scrap. But he never came back.

We had lost two Bristols during the fight, but, on the other hand, had accounted for at least four and possibly six E.A. Griffin had attacked the D.V. which had sideslipped into the triplane. These two had definitely been destroyed. Parrish had shot down the striped triplane when the Flight first dived with Jackson. Lockwood had seen the triplane break up in the air, and had later brought down in flames one of the pursuing triplanes. This I had seen and could confirm. It was possible that Scott had killed the pilot of one of the triplanes which followed us down, and I felt reasonably sure that I had put the green-bodied triplane out of commission.

This was the last patrol that I did with A Squadron. For some time boils had been appearing on my legs, causing me a good deal of discomfort. At last, in desperation, the morning after the patrol, I asked our M.O. for some ointment to put on them. When he had examined me he told me that I should have to go to hospital. The boils, he said, were due to lack of green vegetables. I protested strongly and pointed out that I was nearly due for leave.

"Surely, Doc, you can give me something to tide me over till then!"

But he was an obstinate old chap.

"Get your kit together, my boy. You are leaving for the —st C.C.S. this evening. You'll be back again in about ten days."

I felt unhappy about this and regretted having spoken to him. I felt, too, that I would be letting Parrish down. Parrish would almost certainly be given command of the Flight, and, when the gaps in it were filled, his Flight would be composed almost entirely of new men. Even

Griffin, who would now be senior pilot after Parrish, had done very little war-flying as yet.

However, there was no help for it. That afternoon I put my kit into the tender, pulled Quito's ear and commended him to Scott, and was driven off to the —st C.C.S.

CHAPTER XII

CASUALTY CLEARING STATIONS, HOSPITALS, AND A NEW SQUADRON

(i)

THERE were some half-dozen officers in the ward when I arrived. I was shown my bed, slung my haversack and cap on to it, and lit a cigarette. The fellow in the bed just opposite mine in the long narrow ward, was smoking too, and he beckoned to me.

I sat at the foot of his bed, talking to him till an orderly came along to tell me that my bath was ready.

At the Squadron we used to clean ourselves in collapsible canvas baths but they were so small that the bathing had to be done in sections. It was delightful to be able to submerge completely in a real bath again. After the bath I was told to get into bed and it was a further delight to crawl between sheets once more.

" This is top-hole, sister ! " I said as she came over to my bed. She smiled faintly but made no reply. She was a tall, silent woman with a serene, pure face, such as one associates with nuns. The beds on either side of me were empty, but towards evening, when the light was going, a tall powerfully-built gunner-officer arrived and was given the bed on my right. He had walked down the ward unaided and I wondered what could be wrong with him.

When the orderly had removed the screens round his bed I proffered him my tin of Gold Flakes. " Have a coffin nail," I said.

He accepted one without a word. Once or twice when I spoke to him he jumped. After the orderly had taken away our dinner trays, I got out of bed and strolled across to my friend opposite. He told me that most of the ward had been emptied into a hospital train for the base at noon that day.

We yarned for a bit, till the sister came into the ward and ordered me back to my own bed.

It was a calm, moonlight night. "A good night for a raid," I thought. For a while I read, but the light was bad and I put my book away. I lay wondering what the fellows were doing at the Squadron, and whether Parrish would get the Flight. The man in the bed next to me seemed to be asleep and I was becoming drowsy myself, when I heard the far-off drone of night-flying aeroplanes. They were coming our way and soon there was no mistaking the throbbing noise peculiar to the Boche raiders. Soon distant Archie-batteries opened fire and then nearer ones commenced to clatter. The man next to me began trembling and once or twice he whimpered a bit. A night sister had come on duty but presently I saw our day sister coming down the ward. She came straight to the big fellow and tried to pacify him. The night-fliers had passed overhead by this time and before long one of them dropped an " egg." It went off with a terrific bang, not very far off, and, like a flash, the big gunner had thrown himself on to the floor between our two beds. At once the sister put a blanket over him, stretching it from one bed to the other. " There, there," she said, soothingly, " you'll be quite safe now." It was pitiful. He stayed there for half an hour, till the raiders had returned and Archie was silent once more. Then the sister coaxed the poor shell-shocked fellow back to his bed. The raiders had started some big conflagration over Abbeville way, and the western sky was filled with the glow of it.

I spent four days at the C.C.S. Several wounded officers were admitted each day. There was a gramophone in the ward, but only a few records. The favourite among these was a song called " Parted." It must have been

CASUALTY CLEARING STATIONS

played a dozen times a day. One evening I had put my book aside and was lying with my eyes shut when I heard the tall sister stop at the foot of my bed and say: " Tired ? "

" No, sister," I answered, " of course not. But you've been hard at it all day and I expect you're dead-beat."

" No, but I take off my hat to you for thinking of it," she answered quaintly, and walked on.

On the fifth day most of us were sent off in a hospital train to Rouen. To my great annoyance and embarrassment I was not allowed to walk into the hospital when we got there, but had to be carried in on a stretcher ! I felt an awful fraud and lost no time in asking the M.O. when I should be allowed to go back to my Squadron. He did not answer my question but told me that in a day or two I should be sent from this hospital, No. M. General, to No. N. Stationary on the outskirts of Rouen.

The ward was a large one and it was crammed with beds, all of them occupied. In the bed next to mine was a fellow who seemed to be very popular with all the nurses. They all addressed him as Jock, and they seldom passed his bed without stopping to exchange a few words or a joke with him. I was told that a bullet had passed clean through his chest, emerging between the shoulder-blades. He had already been in hospital for several weeks. On the other side of me was a burly fellow whom I judged to be an Australian. In a bed across the ward a little man was lying reading. He was almost hidden by a cage-like erection over his bed. His pale face, with a little sandy moustache, made him look like a city clerk.

During the night it was pitiful to hear the moaning from some of the beds. Now and again a soft-footed sister would flit silently from one to another of them. The moaning went on all night. In the morning the dressings began.

When the sister arrived at the Australian's bed she laid her hand on his forehead and asked :

"How do you feel this morning, Captain?"

"Dandy, sister," he answered in a gruff voice.

"Come along now," she said, and helped him to roll over on to his stomach. When she took away the bandages I saw that all his back was criss-crossed with deep, ugly-looking cuts. Some of the last bandages stuck as she removed them, but not once did he utter a sound. When she had finished with him she went across to the little man opposite. The poor little chap screamed with pain while she was dressing his wounds.

That afternoon I was sent off to No. N. Stationary.

Here I met a number of fellows also down with boils and other minor ailments. There were three or four flying officers among them. One of them, Tim O'Rourke, had been with the Dublin Fusiliers before joining the Air Force as an observer, and was known as "Whizzbang" in the ward. He used to give a very good, but objectionable imitation of a "Whizzbang," to the annoyance of all who had experience of such things.

We were allowed a good deal of freedom and Tim O'Rourke and I used to go into Rouen practically every day. One afternoon we climbed the Cathedral spire together. The last stage of the ascent had to be made up ladders placed vertically in the open framework of the spire. Both of us had done a great deal of flying, at altitudes vastly greater than that of the spire, and yet we were both nearly ill with dizziness when we reached the top. The descent was even worse. We clawed our way down painfully from rung to rung and were both in a cold sweat when we reached the bottom of the ladders! It is a curious thing that a fellow with no head whatsoever for heights never experiences any dizziness in an aeroplane.

After I had been at No. N. Stationary for eight days, Tim O'Rourke and I were sent to the Cyclist Base Depot, also in Rouen. We were here for another four days.

After this Tim and I were sent off to Marquise. We just

CASUALTY CLEARING STATIONS

escaped having to take charge of a draft of men. Our first-class compartment had only one other occupant, a Frenchman. Tim could speak the language well and he was soon chattering away rapidly to our fellow-traveller. I could make nothing of what they said, but I noticed that the Frenchman was looking across interestedly at me. I knew that Tim was an artistic liar and I wondered what he was telling him. He whispered to me later that he had told the Frenchman that he was my observer and that I had already brought down eleven enemy machines, but he himself had so far only accounted for seven. I may mention that Tim was an observer in an Artillery Observation Squadron and had never had occasion to bring down a single Boche machine.

After a twenty-hour journey, we reached Marquise, only to find that we should have been sent to the Pilots' Pool at Setques. We had three hours to wait for a train and so went for a long walk. Neither of us had ever seen " blimps " at close quarters before and we spent an hour watching one of them trying to land. It came in slowly over the hangars and then a weight at the end of a long rope was dropped from it on to the aerodrome. But whoever dropped it, misjudged the height, for the rope was too short to reach the ground, where a crowd of men were waiting to catch it. The weight snapped off and immediately the little airship rose rapidly. The pilot took her round in a wide circuit till he got to the rear of the aerodrome again. Then he tried to force her down by means of the elevator planes, but she would not descend. With her tail up and nose down she merely moved forward at a constant altitude. Eventually they must have released some of the gas for she began to sink gently, and when she was fairly low she flew slowly over the crowd of mechanics on the aerodrome and the end of the rope, which was still dangling from her, was seized and she was pulled in.

" Many thanks," said Tim, as we turned away. " That

helped to pass the time very nicely. What do we do next?"

We strolled slowly on till we came to a low stone wall. Here we sat down and lit cigarettes. Across the road was a small millinery shop and just inside the doorway two pretty girls were sitting sewing. They looked up and smiled at us and went on with their talking and sewing.

"C'm'on," said Tim, and led the way over.

I bought a lace collar in the shop, and Tim a pair of very ornate garters. We chatted to the girls till it was time to go to the railway station.

We reached Boulogne that same evening. The following day we left for Lumbres, the nearest village on the railway line to Setques, our destination.

We spent a pleasant nine days at Setques. Everybody had to put in five hours a day on the range. After that we were free to do as we liked. Tim O'Rourke and I swam in the river every day, and we frequently went for long walks. One evening, while out on a walk, we came to a small dilapidated *estaminet* and went in for a glass of wine. While we were inside eight ragged French labourers came in and ordered beer. When it arrived they all stood up and ceremoniously clinked glasses together before drinking. When they had finished we asked Madame to fill their glasses again. They marched solemnly, carrying their glasses, across to our table and we at once rose and raising our glasses, said, " Vive la France ! " Then we all clinked glasses and drank the toast standing.

Twice Tim and I went in to Boulogne, lorry-hopping there and back. On the second occasion we met a number of American officers at the hotel where we had dinner, and we spent a convivial evening together. They had just arrived in France. One of them, who addressed me all evening as "lootenant," came from Baltimore, Maryland, a city which I knew well. It must have been near midnight when we left the hotel, rather the worse for wear.

CASUALTY CLEARING STATIONS

The Americans took us in their car as far as Harlettes, and from there Tim and I began marching back, singing, to Setques. But weariness overtook us and we turned aside into an old barn at the side of the road, and, finding some straw in it, we lay down and slept. Very early in the morning an old Frenchman found us there and the good fellow brought us some coffee. Then we set off again for Setques. We had barely left the barn when a Belgian car pulled up and offered us a lift. It took us all the way to the Pool which we reached in time to have a wash and a shave before parade.

Lorry-hopping was quite the recognised way of getting about France in those war-days. One simply waited till Emma Toc came along the road, in the right direction, and the driver would almost invariably pull up and give one a lift. Tim told me that he once stopped a car and, to his horror, saw a full-blown general inside. But the general merely smiled at his dismay and said, " Where can I take you, my boy ? "

There was little red-tape about the range-work. We used to get in a fair amount of practice with machine-guns. We also potted clay pigeons with shot-guns, for small wagers. Ten-franc notes used to change hands, too, at the revolver range. The targets were bottles suspended by strings, " like a row of Armenians," said one fellow, showing me a photograph of six of them hanging by the necks, side by side, from a long gallows.

One morning I awoke feeling desperately ill. I tried to get up but could not, and sent a batman for the M.O.

" Spanish 'flu," he said, and sent me off to a hospital outside St. Omer. I was there for two days and was then sent to Wimereux, near Boulogne, for a week. From there I went to St. Martin's Camp in Boulogne for a further two days.

At the Officers' Club in Boulogne I met Ransley, one of the pilots from A Squadron. He had just finished lunch and came across to my table. " I don't mind if you eat while I smoke," he said, and sat down. He was on his way back to England on H.E. He told me that the Squadron had been having a bad time and that there were only half a dozen fellows left of the crowd that had been there when I went to hospital. Parrish had got his Flight. Scott, my observer, was wounded and back in England. Hendry, the A Flight-Commander, was down in flames. His observer, Davidson, had been seen to fire a white light, the wash-out signal, as the machine went down. Foord, a very good chap, in B Flight, was also down in flames. Several others were wounded. It was depressing news and I felt again that I was malingering in hospital. But it was not for want of trying that I had not yet got back to the Squadron. The military machine grinds slowly.

When I got back to the Pool, Tim O'Rourke was still there, but he left the following day for his R.E.8 Squadron.

Then at last one morning I was told to be ready to leave, after lunch, for M Squadron at Dunkerque. I pleaded to be sent back to A Squadron, but, in Army fashion, my protests were completely ignored and to Dunkerque I went.

(ii)

I joined M Squadron on the 12th July. When I reported at the orderly room I found that Major Wood was the Commanding Officer. I remembered him visiting A Squadron, some months before, and said so. He was the man who had spent a fortnight with us at Guizancourt, learning the ropes, before bringing the new squadron out from England. He told me they had been out three months. He questioned me about A Squadron and asked after Major Field. I told him he had been replaced by Major Sparks.

" How many Huns have you brought down ? " was his next question.

"Only one, sir. I claimed another but it was not confirmed."

"Well, Vee," he said eventually, "you've done more war-flying than most of my men. I'm glad to have you as a new pilot. Will you report to Captain Hepworth, A Flight."

I was pleasantly surprised at his friendliness. He had not struck any of us as being a very likeable person when he was mooning about the aerodrome at Guizancourt.

Outside the orderly room, a very youthful observer was chatting to the Recording Officer. I enquired of them where Captain Hepworth was to be found.

"You the new pilot?" asked the observer. "I'll take you across to him. By the way, this bloke here is Captain Long, our R.O., commonly known as Daddy."

I grinned and shook hands, and then we walked across to a long iron building.

"So you're in A Flight? I'm in A Flight too, and I'll very likely fly with you as I'm unattached at present."

The observer, whose name was Heath, led the way down a corridor, off which rooms opened on either side.

"You seem to be comfortably housed here."

"Not too bad," he answered. "That's Hep's room."

"Thanks."

I knocked and a high-pitched voice shouted, "Stay out!"

So I opened the door and went in.

Captain Hepworth was a sturdily-built, rather aggressive-looking Australian, with a curiously high voice. I said I had been told to report to him. He questioned me about my previous flying experience, and said he would assign me a bus later. I was given a room in the long hut.

For two or three days I did no flying, then one afternoon Captain Hepworth asked me to take up a machine, with an Ack Emma as a passenger. It was about six weeks since I had been up, so to "get my hand in" again, I did a bit of stunting and ended up with a succession of half-rolls. After a few of these the Ack Emma touched my shoulder and when I looked round he pointed to the ground. His face was a greyish-green. The half-rolls had been too much for him. I felt sorry for my thoughtlessness and landed immediately. During the next couple of days I did a good deal of flying, taking note of the principal landmarks in the neighbourhood. Most of the Bristols in this Squadron were fitted with long exhaust pipes, which terminated behind the observer's cockpit. They were thus not so noisy as those carrying short exhausts.

It was a week before I went up with A Flight on a warshow. It was the morning patrol and six machines left the ground. In A Squadron we had always left the ground singly and picked up formation in the air, but Captain Hepworth insisted on his Flight always taxi-ing into position on the ground, and taking off in formation. I disliked this very much at first, as one got into the backwash of the machine in front and this occasioned some nasty bumps very near the ground.

The patrol was uneventful as regards E.A. but I found it interesting as this was all new country to me. It was a bright day, with good visibility, and we could see England clearly. The sea sparkling below us was a pretty sight, with a few small boats dotted here and there, possibly destroyers or trawlers. Near Ostend we were Archied for a few minutes but our leader made a detour out to sea and we were soon beyond the range of the batteries. We continued flying along the coast till we were near Zeebrugge and I was immensely interested in seeing for the first time the two sunken ships lying across the entrance to the harbour. Numerous craters in the neighbourhood gave evidence of the bombing raids that had been carried out. At Zeebrugge we turned south and flew along the canal to Bruges. As we neared the town we saw two fish-tailed E.A. a good distance below us, and dived on them. Each of them promptly showed a clean pair of heels, split-assing downwards at break-neck speed, so after following them down a short distance we left them and zoomed up again.

We had been Archied from time to time during this patrol but never very severely. On our return journey we ran into the most vicious attack from Archie that I had ever known. After three or four ranging bursts the Boche gunners suddenly put up a terrific barrage right in front of us. We did all we could to dodge it but it followed us round with amazing accuracy. If one bears in mind that we were flying at 20,000 feet, approximately four miles above the battery, the excellence of the shooting may be appreciated. When we eventually left Archie behind us I saw a fairly big hole in the centre of my left lower wing. As we crossed the lines, Captain Hepworth dipped his nose and dived very steeply with his engine full-on. No wash-out signal was fired so we all dived, in formation, with him. Down, down we went from 20,000 feet to sea-level, at a speed of well over 200 miles per hour, and when we landed, my ears were singing and my head throbbing with the rapid change in pressure. When we had taxied up to the hangars we found that each of the six machines had been hit by Archie. And that at 20,000 feet! Archie had certainly worried us a good bit along the Somme but he had never shown accuracy like this.

"Oh, he often hits three or four of us," said young Heath.

"Yes, it's good shootin'. They say he uses twelve-inch naval guns up here. He's never brought any machines down, though."

"Does your Skipper always come home at such a lick?" I asked.

"Yes, always. Your head buzzin'? Yes, it's one of his little failin's. The first time I went up on a war-show we landed at ten ack emma and I spent the rest of the day on my back—splittin' head and ear-drums nearly bust. You soon get used to it."

During my first few days with M Squadron I often felt a home-sickness for the old one and cursed my luck at not having been sent back to it. Just as a new boy at school requires some time to find his proper place in the general scheme of things, so I had not yet settled down among my new comrades, and the events of the following day certainly did not help matters along. It was no fault of my own but simply a piece of bad luck. A Flight was due for an O. Pip at 1.30 pip emma. After an early lunch we walked over to the aerodrome, ran up our engines, taxied into formation position, and took off. I was flying outside left. My engine had run up perfectly on the ground, but just after we got up, when we had barely reached a height of 100 feet, it sputtered, and cut out completely. The aerodrome was a large one but we had reached the opposite side of it, and were almost over the hangars of a bombing squadron by this time. I was too low to attempt to turn back into the aerodrome. Also, the old warning flashed through my mind, "Never attempt to turn back, but land straight ahead, if necessary into a brick wall." I shot a glance round, and spotted the only possible field, a small one to the left and in front of us. Immediately ahead of us were the hangars and huts of the bombing squadron, and between my machine and the field was a huge marquee.

I tried to lift the nose over the top of the marquee. Now a Bristol Fighter is a heavy machine and, also, we were travelling at a good pace. When the undercarriage hit the top of the marquee it ripped it off the ground, exposing a crowd of Ack Emmas at lunch. It was like kicking the top off an antheap. The tail swung up and over went the Bristol in a half-somersault, crashing down on its back. My belt held and I was pinned underneath the machine. Mechanics came running along and peered underneath to where I was trapped and I asked them where Heath was. They told me he had been thrown clear. Then they extricated me and a tender took me across the aerodrome to M Squadron. Heath, who had not been strapped in, had been catapulted through the air and had broken a collar-bone. He was also suffering from slight concussion. I was helped along to my room, and lay down on my bed. After a few minutes the C.O. came in.

"I want to congratulate you, Vee, on doing the best thing possible under the circumstances," he said. "I was on the aerodrome and saw the whole episode from start to finish."

He chatted on for a few minutes and when he left I felt very pleased that he took so sporting a view of the accident.

I was not much hurt, but was pretty badly shaken, so I stayed where I was for the time. The remaining five machines of the Flight had, of course, carried on with the patrol.

After about an hour the C.O. came in again with a ground officer, from an inspection of the crash. I could feel the temperature drop several degrees as they entered, and wondered what the trouble could be.

"Your petrol was not turned on properly," snapped the C.O.

I remembered distinctly turning the dial till the arrow on it pointed exactly to the arrow below "Front Tank." I had not been able to do so as easily as usual because the belt in the machine had been slightly too tight and had prevented me from leaning right forward. I told the C.O. this. He was in a bad temper.

"That's no test. You did not turn the dial till it clicked into the groove near the arrow."

"What groove?" I asked.

Now the C.O. was right about this. The groove, however, was so shallow that it had to be felt for very carefully and if the dial were at all stiff it could easily be missed entirely. Strange though it may seem, I had never before even known of the existence of this groove although I had been flying Bristols for several months. I had always brought the two arrows into alignment and in ninety-nine cases out of one hundred this was all that was necessary.

But I had now had the misfortune to strike the hundredth case, where the arrow on the dial was not quite correctly placed.

For four days I did no flying. I had become stiff and sore and whenever I moved I felt a sharp stab of pain. It was several days before this disappeared.

This accident did not increase my popularity in the Squadron.

Heath was the youngest officer in the Squadron, and well liked by everybody, and I, a newcomer, had put him out of action.

After tea, a few days later, I heard Captain Hepworth say that he and some others were getting a tender to take them to the hospital where Heath was lying, and I asked him if I might go with them. We found the youngster having the time of his life in hospital and being fussed over and petted by the nurses. Heath greeted me very cordially and he, at any rate, bore me no grudge. He expected to leave within a few days for England.

On the fifth day after the crash I went up again and from now on Sergeant Antler flew with me as observer. He was a good chap, and capable, and I was glad to have him in the rear cockpit. It was bad luck for a pilot to be saddled with a timid observer. A machine was badly handicapped in which there was not mutual confidence between the pilot and the observer.

For several days we did high O. Pips from Dunkerque. On these patrols we seldom came across triplanes, but we met Fokker biplanes in ever-increasing numbers. As flying-machines they were very good. They were fast, could manœuvre rapidly, and could dive far more steeply than the less robust triplanes. Archie continued to worry us on these O. Pips but he did no serious damage to the machines of our squadron.

We heard, about this time, of a unique adventure which befell a scout pilot returning from a patrol. The Flight was being heavily Archied some four or five miles beyond

CASUALTY CLEARING STATIONS

the German lines. A near burst blew the tail off one of the scouts, tossed the machine about like a feather, and, during the upheaval the pilot was flung out. A second later, by some miracle, he found himself astride the fuselage. The machine was upside down, and pointing to our lines. The pilot slid himself back gradually, nearer the tail, till the machine picked up a gentle gliding angle. The inverted scout sailed slowly down till it finally crashed well inside our lines. The pilot escaped with a broken ankle.

One evening a flight of bombers returned to the aerodrome at Dunkerque after dark. Flares were put out for them and five of them got down safely. The sixth was flown by a new pilot who had never before landed in the dark. As he was gliding down to land his nerve forsook him and he opened up and flew round again. This happened time after time and he made one circuit after the other. Eventually his petrol gave out and he made a perfect landing.

During these patrols which we did from Dunkerque, I learned to appreciate Captain Hepworth's qualities as a leader. It is no easy matter to spot distant machines against the unlimited sky but Hepworth never seemed to miss one of them. When the red light went up from his machine and we attacked E.A. no one ever felt that we might be diving into a trap.

On one of the last patrols which we did from Dunkerque, we were flying above high-lying clouds. Some miles beyond Ostend, Hepworth decided to investigate below the layer as there was not a machine of any description to be seen above it. We glided down gently into the clouds and in a very short time emerged below them to find ourselves over the sea. To the right, a few hundred feet below us, was an unfortunate solitary two-seater. It was a straw-coloured machine, with the black crosses showing vividly on its wings. In a flash Hepworth had swung round on it, and lines of tracer were streaking in front of him as he dived. He must have hit the German pilot with his first burst for the machine reared up vertically, hung for a second, and fell over to the left. Down it went in a wild swoop, swung up again and stalled, sheered away to the right, stalled again and flopped sickeningly forward in another long nose-dive. From time to time Antler and I glanced over the side, watching the doomed two-seater in its erratic downward course, till at last it plunged into the blue sea thousands of feet below us.

(iii)

A day or two after this patrol, the Squadron got orders to move south to Drionville. It was raining when we left and it rained frequently during the next fortnight. The landing-field was large but uneven, and several propellers were broken during our short stay at Drionville by machines turning up on their noses while landing or taxi-ing over the sodden, rough surface. Canvas hangars had been erected for our Bristols, and there were bell-tents for us to sleep in. The latter were in a sad state of repair. There were four of us to a tent and the rain came in freely through splits and tears in the ancient canvas.

On our second evening at Drionville A Flight was sent up on reconnaissance duty. My observer, Sergeant Antler, was flying with Captain Hepworth on this show and I had in the rear cockpit, Second-Lt. Whitley. This man had come to the Squadron as a pilot, but after carelessly crashing three Bristols, the C.O. had offered him the choice of remaining on as an observer, or being sent back to England. Whitley had chosen the former alternative.

It was 7.30 p.m. when five of us, led by Hepworth, left the ground. It was a misty evening, with many low-lying clouds about, and we frequently ran into patches of rain. We crossed the lines at 10,000 feet and began the reconnaissance. Up and down we flew over the prescribed area, taking note of all transport on the roads

CASUALTY CLEARING STATIONS 225

below us and of all movements of troops. All the time we were subjected to fire from Ack Ack batteries. As time went on I think we all became impatient to turn back, but whatever Hepworth did he did well, and he kept us out on this reconnaissance till it was nearly dark.

At last he turned westwards and we began the return journey. We soon found ourselves over a heavy cloudbank, which seemed to have no end, and after a few minutes, Hepworth dived down into it. The rest of us followed him. But if one is not used to it, it is no easy matter to keep a straight course in clouds, and when Whitley and I emerged below the bank there was no sign of the other Bristols. It was fairly dark now and there were many low-lying clouds about. The other machines could easily have been hidden behind these. We were pointing south when we got through the clouds so I turned north-west and kept a sharp look-out for Very lights from the skipper's machine. He would naturally fire some to collect us. But neither Whitley nor I saw any lights. I yelled to Whitley now to try to pick up our position on the map. I also tried feverishly to locate it but without success. The country below was entirely new to us, and it was becoming less distinct every minute in the deepening twilight, so very soon we gave up the attempt to find out our whereabouts and began looking for a possible field to come down in. We were flying at 3,000 feet now. It got steadily darker and I shouted to Whitley to fire some Very lights, hoping that they might attract a signal from some aerodrome, but all that our Very lights did was to evoke a vicious fusillade from Belgian Archie batteries. Fortunately their firing was as inaccurate as it was unwelcome. With this hope of locating an aerodrome removed, we had to find a suitable field as soon as possible to come down in, before the light went entirely. I could no longer read the instruments in my cockpit and there were no lights fitted in this bus. Soon I spotted a large field directly below us and I shut off the engine and glided round in a wide arc

P

to land in it. As we approached it, coming back, it appeared to be quite clear. I landed the Bristol as slowly as I could and she was rapidly losing way, when I saw a wire fence right in front of us. We were too near it to swing round so I pushed on the throttle and tried to jump it. But we had lost too much speed for this and the machine stalled and crashed. We picked ourselves up and were examining the wreck in some dismay when a British sergeant and some Belgian soldiers came running along. We enquired our whereabouts of them and found that we were near Houtem. We had come down at ten minutes to ten. The Belgians offered to lead us to their station, so after telling the sergeant to put a guard over the machine we followed them. Their officers treated us well. They rang up the British Mission which was not far off, and a car was sent off for us. While we were awaiting this, the Belgian officers gave us some wine and some very good cigarettes. One of them produced some salve which he put on my cheek, which had been cut against the cowling when we hit the ground. Whitley had been thrown clear of the crash. I told these Belgian officers how we had been fired at by their Archie batteries, and they were profuse in their apologies. German machines, they said, had on two or three occasions fired Very lights at night to draw signals from Belgian aerodromes, and had then bombed these aerodromes.

It was nearly midnight when Whitley and I reached the British Mission.

In the morning a Staff Captain sent off a wire for us to M Squadron. It was two days before the lorry arrived from the Squadron, and in the meantime Whitley and I slouched round in our ungainly thigh-boots. Time hung heavily on our hands. There seemed to be a dearth of reading matter at the B.M. and we could not even go for walks because of our clumsy boots. We messed with a General wearing three rows of ribbons on his chest, a Staff Major (Lord V——), and the Staff Captain. The

CASUALTY CLEARING STATIONS

latter was anxious to see our crash and drove us across to it in a comfortable car. Two British privates were on guard, and just after we drove up the Sergeant whom we had met before arrived on the scene. While Whitley and the Captain were inspecting the crash I took the opportunity of drawing the Sergeant aside.

"What the devil is this British Mission, Sergeant? Trying to convert the heathen in Belgium?"

"I'm none too sure, sir," he answered, grinning, "but I believe it's a sort of *liaison* station between the British and Belgian armies."

Eventually the lorry from the Squadron arrived with the Flight Sergeant and several mechanics. The Bristol was too badly damaged for immediate repair so the Ack Emmas dismantled the wings and attached the tail of the machine to the rear of the lorry. It was towed back in this way to Drionville.

This was the second Bristol I had crashed in M Squadron and I expected Major Wood to be peevish about it. He was in a good humour, however, when we reported at the Squadron Office, and remarked that we were lucky not to have broken our necks. Of the other machines, Captain Hepworth's alone had been brought back to Drionville on the evening of the reconnaissance, Eastwood had landed his on the old aerodrome at Dunkerque, while Farrell and Venter had reached the coast and had landed their buses safely on the sands.

We had a good deal of rain while we were at Drionville, living in the ancient tents. Often at night our bedding would be soaked. None of us came to any harm, probably because the life we were leading was such a healthy one.

We carried out some exciting O. Pips from Drionville, in between showers. On one occasion we had four separate scraps in the course of an hour and a half. We seldom saw triplanes now, but often the air would be full of Fokker biplanes. Most evenings, when the patrols were over for the day, and if the weather permitted, we would sit about outside the tents, smoking a pipe or two before dinner. Then Simkins would bring out his gramophone, a portable Decca, and play us, " That Saucy Little Bird on Nellie's Hat," a martial air or two, some jazz, and " Humoreske," played by Miss Marie Hall to the subdued accompaniment of "Swanee River." This record was a prime favourite and great was our wrath when two observers, indulging in some horseplay near the gramophone one evening, upset it and broke the record in half.

Captain Simkins, the owner of the Decca, was a pilot in A Flight, and had obtained his captaincy in an infantry regiment before transferring to the Air Force.

One evening A Flight landed just before dinner and as we taxied up to the hangars there were seven strange Bristols drawn up in front of them. I stayed behind for a few minutes to tell my rigger to tighten up certain controls.

" Hul-*lo* !" said a familiar voice as I turned away.

" Why, hullo, Griffin ! Where have you sprung from ? " and we shook hands vigorously.

" Your C.O. has invited us to spend the night here."

" That's the stuff to gi'e 'em. But what's it all about ? "

" We got bombed out last night—but I'll tell you about it later," he said, as we began to walk towards the mess.

" Why, hullo," I said, noticing his sleeve for the first time, " three pips ! So you've got your Flight, now ? Congratulations, old man."

" Thanks," he replied, " yes, I got C Flight when Parrish stopped one."

" Put out ? "

" No, only a Blighty."

" You'll have to tell me about that, too. Well, here we are."

After dinner when Griffin and I were comfortably ensconced in deck-chairs in a corner of the room, each with a long drink beside him on the floor, he gave me an account of the happenings in A Squadron, from the time I had left up to the bombing raid of the night before.

CASUALTY CLEARING STATIONS

"Major Sparks thinks the Boches were bent on reprisals for a daylight raid carried out by two squadrons near us a few days ago. They set every Boche hangar ablaze on that show."

The bombing raid of the previous evening had been a bad affair. Shortly before eleven o'clock the Boche machines were heard approaching. No one paid much attention, as the night fliers came over whenever there was a moon. When they were directly over the aerodrome there was a whine, followed by a deafening crash. The first bomb had fallen in the men's quarters. For a moment people were stunned by the unexpectedness of the attack. Then the night was made hideous by the cries of the wounded and the shattering explosions of successive bombs. Several fell among the officers' quarters, three hangars were hit and several fires started. The C.O., Major Sparks, was blown clean out of his hut.

"The C.O. behaved magnificently," said Griffin. "He was badly cut about but he at once began organising the rescue work. He himself carried several fellows out from the blazing huts. All the wounded were got out in time. Ack Emmas were sent to pull the machines out of the hangars. The raid lasted about twenty minutes. Two officers were killed outright and thirteen wounded, some of them badly. Eleven men were hit.

"They were severely knocked about," said Griffin. "One of them died this morning before we could get them off to a C.C.S. We've got just seven machines left. All the others were 'written off.'"

Griffin and I sat till late discussing the raid, and also old times at the Squadron. Since I had left, Griffin had brought down five enemy machines, all of them two-seaters. Major Sparks, he said, often led a patrol himself, and had over a dozen E.A. to his credit since joining the Squadron.

"Does your C.O. lead you on many shows?"

"Well—er—not very often," I answered. "By the way, tell me about Parrish."

Before we turned in that night, Griffin urged me to apply for a transfer to A Squadron.

"We were sorry you didn't get back to us. You'd have had your Flight for a certainty if you'd come back, and of course you lose your seniority by coming to a new squadron."

"It's no good," I replied. "I broached the matter of a transfer as soon as I arrived, but the C.O. wouldn't look at it."

"Oh well, look here, you come over and visit us at Boisdinghem. Our C.O. will apply for you if he knows you want to get back."

The upshot of it was that I did fly over to Boisdinghem a couple of days later. Most of the original Ack Emmas were still there, but I knew hardly any of the flying-officers. Major Sparks was very cordial and he offered to try and arrange a transfer for me.

The following morning Murray and I were reading " Comic Cuts " in the room adjoining the Squadron Office, when the telephone bell rang. There was only a wooden partition between the rooms and we could hear everything the C.O. was saying. I gathered immediately that he was talking to Major Sparks, about me, so I left the room and wandered back to my tent. The same scruples about eavesdropping did not worry Murray, as his name was not involved, and he walked over to my tent a few minutes later and told me that Major Wood had refused point blank to let me go, as he did not approve of his officers trying to wangle these transfers behind his back.

"Oh, the purple idiot," I groaned. "I spoke to the feller himself about it as soon as I got here. What more does he want ? "

I made no more attempts to get back to A Squadron.

After visiting them at Boisdinghem I was not really sorry at having to remain with M Squadron. Our C.O.

was not in the same class with Major Sparks, but the rest of the officers were a thoroughly good crowd. To have gone back to the changed A at this stage would have been like going to a new squadron.

Two days later I went on leave.

CHAPTER XIII

DOG-FIGHTS AND RUNNING FIGHTS

(i)

On the day I left the Squadron a tender was going to Boulogne for certain supplies so I went in on that. It was a tempestuous day with frequent squalls of rain. But I enjoyed the drive for I was going on leave, my first leave from France. The clouds had broken up when the transport left Boulogne, but it was blowing great guns in the Channel and there was a high sea running. The boat was crowded and a great many of us remained on deck. We were pitching and rolling horribly, and frequently the destroyers accompanying us would disappear for several seconds in great troughs in the sea. Sometimes it seemed as though they must have been swallowed up by the great waves. I was thoroughly enjoying our boisterous passage but some of my fellow-voyagers were not. Glancing round I noticed two of them sitting near the rail, clasping it. Green misery was in their faces. The man in front would be violently sick, and the wind howling past would sweep the result right over the rear man, who was much too ill even to notice it. I am the happy possessor of a very stable tummy, but this sight was nearly too much for it, and I moved to another part of the deck.

Many of the passengers were more dead than alive when we reached Folkestone.

The fortnight passed all too quickly. The first week of it I spent in London. I stayed at the South African Officers' Club in Grosvenor Square. There I ran across several South Africans whom I knew. One morning I was

DOG-FIGHTS AND RUNNING FIGHTS

sitting chatting to an amusing old chap, Captain B——, from Johannesburg, when a lady came in and very kindly offered us tickets to a matinée performance of " The Luck of the Navy." We both accepted and after lunch went to the theatre together. After the performance, as we were strolling back, we passed a fruit shop, in the window of which we saw some fine bunches of grapes.

" B'gad, Vee, that makes me homesick," said Captain B——. " Let's go in and get some."

We entered the shop.

" How much are your grapes ? "

" Fifteen shillings a pound."

Without a word he turned on his heel and walked out again.

As we walked off I glanced at him and smiled.

" Vee," he said, solemnly, " I hope all his grapes go bad, to-night."

Before leaving London I searched the music shops for another violin record of "Humoreske," exactly like the one we had lost, for Simkins' gramophone. A condition was that it had to be played to the accompaniment of " Swanee River." At last I ran one to earth and this, and three other records, I got the shop assistant to post out to the Squadron for me. The imbecile merely wrapped them up in brown paper. They arrived at the Squadron in tiny fragments.

At the end of the week I took the night train up to Stranraer and early the next morning, crossed over to Larne. It was a bright sunshiny morning, and the sea looked beautiful. Just after the boat left Stranraer, breakfast was served, and what a breakfast it was ! There was no war-time lack of butter, and a great bowl of sugar stood on each table. People in England had seen nothing like this for many a long day.

The day after I arrived in Belfast we left for my cousins' seaside cottage at Island Magee, and the rest of my leave was spent in that utterly peaceful spot.

I was told of an amusing incident which had occurred on the railway along which we had travelled from Belfast. Tickets were never inspected along this line, but were collected at the gates of the stations at which travellers left the train. A certain traveller entered a first-class carriage in which there were two other passengers. He was filling his pipe when one of the men objected, pointing out that they were in a non-smoker.

"Do you object to smoking?" asked the newcomer of the other passenger. "No," was the reply.

"Then the majority rules," said he, and lit his pipe.

When they reached the next station the first traveller called the guard and lodged a complaint against the smoker.

"I'm sorry, sir," said the guard, "but this is a non-smoker and you'll have to put away your pipe."

"One moment, Guard," he replied, unperturbed, "just you have a look at that man's ticket."

The guard asked the objector to show his ticket, found that it was a third-class one, and ejected him forthwith.

"That was a smart bit of work on your part," said the other passenger as the train moved off again. "What made you think he had a third-class ticket?"

"I saw it peeping out of his pocket," was the reply, "and it was the same colour as my own."

On my return I crossed over by the night boat from Kingston to Holyhead. Directly the boat left, everyone in uniform was given a lifebelt and compelled to put it on. There was a number of civilians on board, including many women and children, but they were not given lifebelts.

(ii)

When I got back to France I found that the Squadron had moved to Serny. On arriving at Serny the first thing I heard was that Major Wood had returned to England. His successor, Major the Honourable Stanley Wells-

DOG-FIGHTS AND RUNNING FIGHTS 235

Smythe, M.C., had been with the artillery in the earlier part of the war. He had already, in the five days since his arrival, won the goodwill of everyone in the Squadron.

" Not one of your strong, silent men," said Eastwood, when I asked him what the new C.O. was like, " but a good chap. Happy-go-lucky—never stands on his dignity, if he has any, and quite willing to join in a game of poker."

Captain Hepworth introduced me to him just before dinner.

" Ah, Hepworth, your other pilot, what ? Have a good leave, Vee ? Tell me, have they put on the new show yet at the ' Gaiety ' ? "

He was a very tall, slight man and I thought then, and afterwards, that Eastwood's description fitted him well. It was he who had known Captain Pitts, M.C., my former Flight-Commander in A Squadron, and who questioned me about him shortly after my arrival, as I have related earlier in the book.

After dinner I joined a group round the new C.O.

" So the guv'nor sent me along," he was saying, " to see to it. I walked up rather nervously to the Battery-Commander, a short, hard-bitten Australian, and I said to him, ' My father wants those guns withdrawn immediately.' ' Oh, indeed,' said he, looking up at me, and compressing his lips, ' and what does mother say ? ' " The C.O. joined very heartily in the laugh which followed.

A new pilot had arrived in A Flight during my absence, a South African, Ian Fraser. He was slight, very straight, and had a pleasant face. I liked the look of him from the first. There were now six South Africans in the Squadron. Three of us were in A Flight, Eastwood, Fraser and myself, and the other three in B Flight, Captain Venter, Andrews and Prinsloo. Venter had been a pilot in A Flight. The former commander of B Flight had returned to England on H.E. I found, too, that we had acquired a new Equipment Officer, Second Lt. Griffith. Griffith had quartermaster-sergeant written all over him. He was a big fat chap and was always in trouble with his aitches. After listening to the C.O.'s story I had strolled across to a table on which some papers were lying and was looking at an old *Sketch* when the new E.O. sank with a grunt into a chair next to me. We got into conversation and in no time he was telling me 'ow a pal of 'is, 'oo had got commissioned rank at the same time as 'imself, was now a major, and of the series of mishaps which had prevented himself from also reaching that exalted state. Then Eastwood, who was talking to the new pilot Fraser, beckoned to me and, excusing myself, I left Griffith and joined them.

" You haven't met Fraser yet have you ? Has Griffith been explaining to you why he is still only a second loot ? We've all heard all about it."

" Coffin-nail ? " asked Fraser, profferring his tin.

" Thanks. When did you arrive ? "

We lit our cigarettes, Eastwood was hauled off to a rubber of bridge, and Fraser and I found a couple of chairs in a corner and settled down for a yarn.

" Ek hoor jy is ook een van die Boertjies ? "[1] I remarked.

" Net soos jy,"[2] he replied, smiling.

Whenever South Africans met overseas they always made a point of exchanging a few words in Afrikaans. Even fellows like Eastwood whose Afrikaans was of the poorest, and whose whole vocabulary consisted of about ten words, insisted on using these whenever they ran across fellow-countrymen. The language formed some kind of bond between us. For the same reason no doubt we addressed one another as " Boetie," which means " little brother."

Fraser had been out to France before as an observer in an Artillery Observation Squadron. This was his first time out as a pilot. He told me of an unhappy coincidence which had occurred when he was on his way back to England to train as a pilot. It had happened in an

[1] " I hear you are also one of the little Boers ? "
[2] " Just like you."

DOG-FIGHTS AND RUNNING FIGHTS

estaminet in a small village, in which his train was held up for a couple of hours. He was sitting alone at a table next to three French soldiers. He could understand the language pretty well and gathered that they had just come up from the south. One of them said he had not seen his home at M——, near B——, for three years. He was consumed with excitement at the thought of seeing it again within a few days. Fraser recognised the spot mentioned. Up to a month before it had been in German hands, and a position of strategic importance. During a shoot carried out some months previously, he himself had registered a siege battery on to it and blown it to bits.

In a corner of the room six or seven fellows were playing some card game. Presently Captain Simpson rose from the table and they tried to pull him back. " Come back, Simmy," " Have one more round."

"No, no, I'm through," he said and strolled over towards us. " Gad, that's a wicked game ! I've lost fifteen quid since dinner."

" You've usually got a pretty good poker face. What's gone wrong to-night ? "

" It's not poker. It's an invention of the devil called Slippery Sam. Don't you know it ? Well, take my advice and don't learn it."

" What's this I hear about wireless telephones being fitted in the buses ? "

" Oh, of course, you haven't seen them yet. Yes, we've all got 'em. The skipper's is the only bus that has a sending set. All the others have only receiving sets. Hep usually sings comic songs to us while we're climbing."

" Do you have to trail aerials ? "

" Yes."

" Isn't it a bit risky getting into a scrap with an aerial out that's likely to get tangled in somebody else's prop. ? "

" Rather ! We pull 'em in as soon as we've got our height."

"What's the good of them, then?"
"Not much. But orders is orders."

(iii)

While I had been away the Squadron had taken part in company with three other squadrons, in two raids on neighbouring Boche aerodromes near Lille. "Comic Cuts" for August 16th and 17th made the following mention of these:

"A raid was carried out on Haubourdin Aerodrome by Nos. — and — Squadrons and —nd and —th Squadrons A.F.C. Sixty-five machines in all took part, dropping 136 thirty-five pound and six forty-pound bombs, and firing a large number of rounds from a height varying from 400 to 500 feet. Three large hangars containing machines were completely burnt, and two machines standing outside were set on fire. Several fires were also started in huts, and what is believed to be the officers' mess was blown up and burnt. Several other hangars in addition to those burnt received direct hits. The station at Haubourdin was also attacked with machine-gun fire from a low height, causing confusion among the troops. Two staff cars were fired at, one of which upset in a ditch and another ran up a steep bank; the occupants were not observed to leave. A train was also shot at, which stopped. Considerable casualties were caused among the personnel at the aerodrome who were seen rushing to take refuge in a hospital. All our machines returned."

"A bomb raid was carried out on Lomme Aerodrome by —nd and —th Squadrons A.F.C. and Nos. — and — Squadrons, led by O.C. —th Wing. 104 twenty-five pound and two forty-pound bombs were dropped from an average height of 200 feet. Some pilots, who dropped them from 50 feet, had their machines damaged by their

THE RAID ON HAUBOURDIN AERODROME ON AUGUST 16TH, 1918.

[*Royal Air Force Official—Crown Copyright Reserved*

DOG-FIGHTS AND RUNNING FIGHTS 239

own bombs. Many direct hits were observed on sheds, hangars and huts. From photographs taken during the raid two sheds can be seen burning fiercely, and from the strength of the wind it is probable that others also caught fire, but the sheds to the leeward were obscured by smoke. Several other fires can also be seen among the huts and workshops. A large number of rounds were also fired and casualties inflicted on the personnel on the aerodrome, and on a party of mounted troops who made for Lille at full gallop. Two hostile machines dived down to Haubourdin aerodrome on the approach of our machines and crashed without a shot having been fired at them. The aerodrome defences were much stronger than on the previous day's raid on Haubourdin. One of our machines did not return."

We were quartered in Nissen huts at Serny. After the dilapidated tents at Drionville these seemed the acme of comfort. When A Flight was not due for the early patrol we would lie a-bed as late as we could. This meant that we stayed in bed as long as Hepworth did. Once he was up he would start pulling the rest of us out. He would dash round the hut pulling the bed-clothes off the fellows and if anyone objected there would be a wrestling match. As Hepworth was a sturdily built fellow he always ended on top. But if we hated him before breakfast, we loved him after it. Alan Hepworth was the perfect Flight-Commander. Any unpleasant duties, such as lone reconnaissances, were apportioned impartially among the pilots of the Flight, and Hepworth himself never shirked his own share of these. A certain amount of risk was part of the day's work but never, through mismanagement, did he land his Flight in difficulties, or through misjudgment lead them into a trap. When he really looked for trouble, however, was when he was alone, without the Flight in tow. One evening, for instance, as the Flight was coming back from an O. Pip, Hepworth noticed a new

German aerodrome some ten miles behind the lines. The next morning he and his observer went over before breakfast and raided it. From a height of 200 feet he " shot up " all the hangars and several machines which were drawn up outside them, sprayed the huts next to the aerodrome with his Vickers gun and dropped his four bombs on them. Then his observer was hit by rifle-fire from the ground and Hepworth came back. When he landed, his machine had a great many bullet holes in it, and his observer had a " Blighty " wound in the shoulder.

As time went on it became more and more noticeable, on this part of the front at any rate, that the Boche airmen were playing for safety. Our patrols never met them west of the lines. East of the lines they usually only attacked us if their numbers greatly exceeded ours. Of course, there were exceptions. Occasionally a small patrol of Fokkers would turn and scrap fiercely when we attacked, but in most cases the encounters were of the hit-and-run variety. Sometimes days would pass without our really getting to grips with the enemy machines.

One morning A Flight did the dawn patrol. That, as it happened, finished our duties for the morning, so after breakfast we sat about making derisive noises as we watched the C Flight men don flying-suits. When they had gone we settled down to a game of poker, which lasted till lunch-time. Then B Flight went up. C Flight on their return reported very little activity behind the lines. They had seen one small formation of E.A. but had not been able to get near it. When the B Flight machines got back they reported considerable activity in the air. They had had two minor scraps with Fokker biplanes, with no decisive results, and, towards the end of their O. Pip, had had to run from a very large formation. This was to have been the last patrol of the day.

I was standing next to my machine in front of the hangar, talking to the fitter, after watching the B Flight machines come in, when an orderly came up. " Captain

DOG-FIGHTS AND RUNNING FIGHTS 241

Hepworth's compliments, sir. A Flight machines to go up in half an hour."

"Right, Fulton. Warn Sergeant Antler, please."

I walked over to the mess and as I got near it met Captain Simkins strolling across very leisurely. As Orderly Officer for the day he was excused flying.

"Hello Vee," he called out cheerily, "I hear A Flight's doing another show? Coming in for your last cup of tea I suppose?"

"Don't be tactless, Simmy."

"Well, anyway, it looks as though you'll have a bit of fun, unless the B Flight birds have been talking through their hats."

I drank my tea and was leaving to collect my flying-kit when at the door I ran into Captain Hepworth.

"Seen Simmy?" he asked.

"Inside, skipper," I replied.

"Please tell him I want him to fly on this show. You'll have to hurry," he added glancing at his wrist watch.

I turned back into the mess. "Still guzzling tea, Simmy? You'd better shake a leg."

"Why should I shake a leg?" he asked with dignity. "Surely not for your beastly patrol. You seem to forget that I'm Orderly Officer."

"Sorry, Simmy, but you're the exception to the rule. The skipper has sent me to tell you that you do fly this evening."

Outside the hangars our machines were waiting, filled up with petrol and ready for us. There were five machines going up on this show and after we had run up our engines we taxied out into position and took off in formation.

Eastwood was flying inside right and Farrell outside right, Simkins inside left and I outside left. Directly we we got up we let out our aerials. We were wearing special flying-caps which had earphones fitted in them. Presently we heard Hepworth's high-pitched voice singing:

"' Oh, there *was* a little hen, and she had a wooden leg,
The best little hen that ever laid an egg,
And she laid more eggs than any on the farm,
And another little drink wouldn't *do* us any harm.
Another little drink, another little drink——'

Farrell! close up there, you'll be left behind soon——

' Another little drink wouldn't *do* us any harm,
Another little drink, another little drink,
Oh, another little drink wouldn't *do* us any harm.
Umpty, oompty, umpty, oomp. Oh-h-h,

" ' There *was* a little Spad !——'

Farrell, blast you, get into place. I'll kick your jacksie when we get down! Cripes, it's cold!

' Then I set my sails and sail away,
No pilot e'er was tighter!
For where e'er I go I fear no foe
On the good bus, dear old Bristol Fighter!'

B'gad it's freezing! I hope you chaps are as cold as I am.

' Some other ti-i-ime
I flew a Monosoupape,
You-know-the-kind-that-always-catches-fi-i-re,
Some other ti-i-ime
I flew a Spad——'

What the hell's happened to Farrell now?"

I looked round and at first could see no sign of him. Then thousands of feet beneath us I saw his Bristol gliding down in spirals towards the aerodrome. Engine-trouble, as we found later, had prevented him from keeping in position and had eventually forced him to return.

We were at 19,000 feet by this time, flying towards the lines, and the aerodrome was almost below us. There was a west wind blowing and in a very short time we had crossed

THE RAID ON LOMME AERODROME, AUGUST 17TH, 1918.

[*Royal Air Force Official—Crown Copyright Reserved*

DOG-FIGHTS AND RUNNING FIGHTS

the lines. The visibility was good. Far below us the little fields, close-set, stretched like a patchwork quilt.

"Oh boys, oh boys, it's cold," said Hepworth. "Yank in your aerials."

As I wound mine in I noticed a few black puffs from Archie appearing below us. Then a few more nearer our level. Something glinting away to the left caught my eye. It was a small bluish balloon, a considerable distance below us, and it shone so brightly in the rays of the evening sun that it seemed almost incandescent. It was a propaganda balloon and while I was watching it, it discharged its cargo of leaflets over the German lines. They resembled snowflakes as they tumbled gently down. It was a pretty sight. We flew eastwards steadily for fifteen minutes. As soon as we got within range of the batteries in the citadel of Lille we were, as usual, heavily Archied. They always gave us a bad time when we got anywhere near them. Then Hepworth made a wide turn to the south. We were flying at 21,000 feet now. It was as we neared Douai that I noticed six Fokker biplanes a couple of thousand feet below us. We were approaching Douai from the east so we could not get "into the sun." Our skipper, therefore, went straight at them. We dived down at great speed, with our engines full on, but they saw us coming and promptly lost height. I got the Aldis sight on one and put several long-range bursts after him, but my own speed was becoming excessive and I had to pull out of the dive. As we came out I glanced at the "Pitot" and saw it begin to unwind. We must have been doing about 300 miles per hour.

Hepworth now led us north for a while and then swung north-west towards Armentières. With his amazing eyesight he had been the first to spot a scrap going on between Camels and Fokker biplanes. As we flew towards it a stream of Dolphins and S.E.5's came streaking down from the north-west, and another stream of Fokker biplanes from the north-east. The two streams looked for all the world like swarms of flies. They were converging towards a point directly over Armentières. The original scrap was still going on fiercely and we saw one machine fall away hopelessly out of control. The Dolphins, about twenty of them, were the first to arrive. For a moment they circled round the fight, and then the rest of the machines came up—S.E.5's, Fokker biplanes, triplanes, Pfalz scouts, and I even noticed one old, fish-tailed D.F.W. Our four Bristols were the last to arrive, and promptly kicked up their heels and plunged into the biggest dogfight I had ever been in.

It would be impossible for anyone who took part in it to describe the whole fight which now took place. I saw the black-crossed machines tackle the Dolphins, to be attacked in their turn by the S.E.5's. I dived on the nearest Boche, a Fokker biplane crossing our line of flight below us, but he turned under me and I lost him. Then I got in a shot burst at another who was circling round an S.E.5. There must have been at least sixty machines taking part in the scrap. Above, below, and all round us, were the British circular markings and the German crosses. A short distance to the right a crippled S.E.5, with one wing at a grotesque angle to the fuselage, was going down in a slow spin. A triplane sheered past in a great curve with black smoke streaming from it. In the fading light flickering lines of tracer could be seen on all sides, going in all directions. I dived on a triplane and had got in a short burst when I had to swerve violently to avoid a Dolphin. We seemed to miss one another by inches. Sergeant Antler now pulled my arm, and as I glanced back he pointed to his gun and waggled his hand. That was one of our guns out of action. My own, thank goodness, was behaving splendidly. Then right in front of me I saw a Fokker biplane coloured a greyish-green, diving straight for a Dolphin. I pushed the stick forward, adjusted the rudder-bar and in less than a second had him right in the centre of the Aldis sight. I was very close to him when I

DOG-FIGHTS AND RUNNING FIGHTS 245

pressed the Bowden lever. At once the Fokker swung off to the left. I was right on his tail and just behind him. I could see the Boche pilot clearly, crouching over his joystick. I simply sprayed him with machine-gun bullets. Tracer streamed into his cockpit. I saw him jerk forward and knew that I had killed him. Down went the Fokker completely out of control.

Before I could release the Bowden control, my gun jammed. At once I pulled out and flew off to cure the stoppage, for with both guns out of action we were helpless. With a dud gun Antler could do nothing, so watched the Fokker all the way down till he saw it crash to the north of Armentières.

We had been losing height rapidly for some time and were now at 6,000 feet. As we left the scrap, a Fokker horribly painted in green, yellow and black, flew past below us. It was a sitting shot for Antler's gun or mine, but we could do nothing but watch it fly away.

I had a bad No. 3 stoppage and it took me a minute or two to clear it. Then I turned back to the scrap. Two machines were dropping rapidly to earth, one of them in flames. The fight was still going on fiercely. Twice more I dived on E.A. and got in short bursts. It was tantalisingly difficult to hit a Fokker in the air!

Then quite suddenly the fight broke up. A Pfalz scout half-rolled and shot off eastwards. Another tucked his tail between his legs and followed the first. A third followed them. One could almost hear them yelping. Then panic descended upon the rest. They stood not upon the order of their going. Fokker triplanes, biplanes, Pfalz scouts, jostled one another in a mad race eastwards, with the fish-tailed D.F.W. panting close behind them.

We followed for a short distance, firing a few last bursts after them, but it was becoming late and we turned homewards.

I had long before this lost all touch with the other three

Bristols, but we came together again near the aerodrome. It was nearly dark when we taxied up to the hangars.

(iv)

One morning, when I was Orderly Officer for the day, I accompanied the Sergeant-Major on some of his early rounds, and looked in at the Ack Emmas at breakfast to ask if there were any complaints. The answer being in the negative, I said, " Carry on, Sergeant-Major ! " and adjourned to my own breakfast.

Half an hour later I was stamping a few letters in the Office when our portly E.O., Second Lt. Griffith, looked in. " 'Ullo, Vee, 'ow about comin' in the tender with me to collect some supplies ? "

" A sound scheme," I replied. " I'm with you."

Leave of absence was readily granted and four of us set off. Griffith was a cheerful fellow and good company on a jaunt of this sort. We visited St. Omer first, and then went on to Calais. At Calais we had lunch and did some shopping. I managed to get a few English novels in Calais, among them *The Little Iliad*, one of Maurice Hewlitt's books which was new to me. From Calais we went to Boulogne, where each of us had a hot bath at the Officers' Club. After this we assembled in the lounge and sank into easy-chairs, with our skins tingling from an unwonted sensation of cleanliness, which became akin to godliness when a waiter placed a large bottle of Bass in front of each of us. We devoted a quarter of an hour to these, and then with a feeling of great contentment we returned, with a well-laden tender, to the Squadron.

Griffith had a large and varied acquaintance. I accompanied him occasionally on some of his foraging expeditions and at every port of call he met three or four old cronies, some of them N.C.O.s, others " second loots "

"FAR BELOW . . . THE LITTLE FIELDS . . . LIKE A PATCHWORK QUILT."

Royal Air Force Official—Crown Copyright Reserved

DOG-FIGHTS AND RUNNING FIGHTS 247

like himself. As long as we were within reach of the Base there was no trouble about obtaining solid or liquid supplies, but later, when the Squadron moved farther east it became more difficult to replenish our stocks. Then Griffith's hordes of friends became useful. We might enter a canteen together, and pause inside the doorway. Griffith's eyes, slipping about freely in their fat casings, would dart here and there and come to rest upon some figure behind the counter. He would stride forward, beaming,

" 'Ul-*lo !* And 'ow is Corporal Smith this mornin' ? "

Corporal Smith would be delighted to see him and their voices would drop to a confidential whisper.

" Well, Alf," Griffith would say, " and 'ow's things, old boy ? "

" Not too bad, 'Arry, and 'ow's yourself ? "

For a time I would leave the two of them to " swop " reminiscences while I bought cigarettes, or examined pipes or pocket-torches along the counter. Then I would hear Griffith say, " 'Ave a drink, old boy ? "

" I don't mind if I do, 'Arry. Come this way. 'Ow about your friend ? "

Griffith would beckon me, and we would adjourn to a less public spot. After this it would be easy for Griffith to broach the question of a couple of cases of beer, and not so easy for Alf to get out of it—though to be just the Alfs whom he met always seemed very willing to help him.

Shortly after I first met Griffith, and before he had included me in his large circle of friends, I had had the misfortune to lose the Colt Automatic from the holster in my cockpit. There was one in every cockpit. It was put there in case of a forced landing beyond the lines. Griffith discovered the loss one morning on a tour of inspection, and spoke to me about it. We had an argument and he wanted me to make good the loss.

" Dash it, man ! " I expostulated, " you don't expect me to sleep in the bally bus, do you ? Anyone who fancied it could nip into the hangar and take it, so how the devil can you hold *me* responsible for it."

Griffith was a garrulous old chap, with an endless flow of back-chat, and as, after several minutes, the argument showed no signs of coming to an end, I closed it by saying, " Well, little Willie isn't paying for the Colt," and walked off.

" Big Willie isn't paying for it either," he called after me.

That evening I borrowed a leaf out of his own book. After dinner I stood him a drink and we chatted amicably for a while. Then, " What about the automatic ? " I asked him. " Surely, Griffith, a man of your experience should have no difficulty about a trifle like that. Why, most old soldiers could think straight off of half a dozen ways of getting out of it."

" Leave it to me, Vee," he said, putting his finger to his nose and shutting his left eye solemnly, " leave it to me."

A few days later there was a minor crash on the aerodrome. The following morning I noticed a Colt back in my holster. As we were going in to lunch Griffith stopped me and winked. I returned the wink. " Funny thing," he said, " Marshall's revolver disappeared in 'is crash, and I've 'ad to write it off."

We remained at Serny till the middle of October. Often we would walk across to one of the coalmines for a bath. There were excellent baths there for the miners and, for a trifle, we were allowed to use them. Each man would tie his clothes in a bundle and hoist them up to the ceiling on a rope passing over a high pulley. A spliced loop in the rope would be secured by a padlock to a ring in the floor. These baths were a godsend to us.

Our patrols were developing into rather strenuous affairs owing to the Boches' increasing shyness of the line. Hepworth was determined that our Offensive Patrols should justify their name. At twenty to thirty miles inside enemy territory, we would meet German patrols, and, if the odds were not too great, engage them, but we

DOG-FIGHTS AND RUNNING FIGHTS 249

could not afford to run into traps at that distance from the lines. It was now that Hepworth's qualities as a leader became very evident. The strain on him was greater than on us, for he had the responsibility for the whole Flight in his rudder-bar, whereas we had only to follow blindly where he led.

One afternoon, when a patrol of five of us were some thirty miles beyond the lines, we spotted a patrol of seven Fokker biplanes some distance to the south. They were below our level and we dipped our noses to overtake them. In a few minutes we were within striking distance of them. The leader was flying a black machine with bright yellow wing-tips and a yellow tail. I was in a fever of excitement waiting for Hepworth to dive, and had picked out my Fokker—black-and-white chequered wings, and black-and-white stripes running the length of the fuselage. I wondered frantically why ever Hepworth did not dive. The Fokkers were sailing along steadily below us, perfect targets, and at any moment they might scatter, or spin down, and we should lose an almost unique opportunity. Suddenly, to my amazement, Hepworth swung to the right and with his nose well down streaked for the lines. Instinctively we all swung after him but as we did so I cursed him bitterly. My mind had been so completely focussed on the imminent attack on the Fokker patrol that I had not given a single thought to the possibility of a trap. But we had missed one by the narrowest of margins. Down they came out of the sun and from behind high cloud-banks, till the air was thick with them. We scattered, and roared west with our noses well down. It was a thrilling race to the lines. I dared not fly straight or I should be offering a perfect target to the pursuing Fokkers, and sooner or later they would be bound to get us. Every couple of seconds I kicked on right or left rudder. Once we got near a solitary cloud and I shot into it, but it was much too small to be of any use and in a flash we were through it. I glanced back and saw half a dozen Fokkers popping out of it. Instantly their guns began flashing again. Antler's gun was firing in short bursts all the way back, but owing to our zig-zag course, it was difficult for him to get a bead on any of the Boches. The other Bristols were in as bad a case as we were and I could see them some distance off going hell-for-leather for the lines, each with a pack of Fokkers on his tail. Goodness knows their shooting must have been bad for we all got through. At the line they turned back. When it was all over I felt suddenly weak at the knees. The five Bristols drew together and made their way back to the aerodrome. When we landed and examined our buses we found that they had all been considerably shot about, but no one had been hit.

"Skipper," I said, laughing, "I feel like apologising to you for what I thought when you turned away from those seven sitters."

"It was a close thing," he replied. "I only saw them just before we ran. There must have been quite sixty of them over the spot when we did a bunk."

(v)

Captain Hepworth's qualities of leadership were recognised not only by the fellows of his own Flight but by everyone in the Squadron. He was the C.O.'s right-hand man and even the Wing-Commander, Colonel Napier, kept a fatherly eye on him. After pilots had been in France for about six months, they could usually get back to England for a spell of H.E. duty if they wished to do so. Hepworth had never taken H.E., although he had been flying with another squadron in France long before his transfer as Flight-Commander to M Squadron on its arrival from England. Colonel Napier knew the strenuous time that Hepworth was having and suggested that he should go back on H.E. for a rest. Hepworth refused the offer

DOG-FIGHTS AND RUNNING FIGHTS

point-blank. Then Brigade took a hand. The Boches were beginning to move back fairly rapidly and a reliable officer would be needed to select new aerodromes as the line advanced. Hepworth was offered this duty. It was shortly after lunch, on a very dud day, that Hepworth came back to the hut, from the Squadron Office, with a face like thunder.

"I'll teach the b——rs to put me on the retired list," he muttered fiercely. "Dillon, get your flying-kit and come with me." He grabbed his own leather coat, helmet, gloves and goggles, and stalked out of the hut.

"You're for the high-jump, Dillon," someone remarked.

"Crikey!" said Dillon, "we can't fly on a day like this! It's bloody madness."

He followed Hepworth to the hangar. The soft, grey clouds were nearly on the ground. Occasionally a wisp of them would obscure the top of a hangar.

Hepworth had his bus taken out and the tanks filled. He had four twenty-five pound bombs put in the rack of the undercarriage and he got the photographic mechanic to fit a camera into its housing in the rear cockpit. While this was being done he studied a map. While the mechanics were running up the engine for him he continued poring over the map, and making some calculations.

"Get in!" he said to Dillon.

Then he climbed in himself, adjusted his goggles, and opened the throttle. They were in the clouds almost at once. We saw him dip below them, and go hedge-hopping in the direction of the lines.

The news quickly went round that Hepworth had flown off, in a blazing temper, eastwards into the mist. Hepworth was an outstanding personality in the Squadron and his action gave rise to a good deal of speculation and excitement that afternoon. A good many fellows agreed with what Dillon had said, that it was simply madness to fly at all with the clouds bouncing the ground. The A Flight men, however, stood solidly behind their skipper.

Simkins expressed our feelings when he said, " Hepworth might have been absolutely cock-eyed with rage when he pushed off, but he's too good a pilot to foozle any job that he puts his hand to. He'll come back as sure as hell."

At tea-time he had been gone for two hours. A Flight pilots and observers admitted to one another that they were beginning to feel a bit worried, but they were cocky enough in front of B and C Flights. His tanks had been filled and he had petrol enough to keep him up for three and a quarter hours. The time dragged on slowly, but at last the three and a quarter hours were up.

"It looks as though he's down in Hun-land," said Conway, of C Flight.

"Hun-land my foot," retorted Farrell, angrily. "How could you expect anyone to find his way home in this bleeding mist? He's down safely in some field nearby."

Farrell happened to be right. The following morning, before breakfast, Hepworth and Dillon landed on the aerodrome.

Hepworth had hedge-hopped all the way to the lines. When he reached them he zoomed up into the clouds. It is no easy matter to keep a straight course and an even keel in clouds, but Hepworth managed it. He was at 11,000 feet when he emerged from the clouds. Then he flew by compass and clock till he judged that he was near Tournai, which was then some twenty miles behind the lines. He now throttled back and glided down into the clouds. The last stages of this descent were full of hazard for he stood a remarkably good chance of flying straight into the ground, with the mist as low as it was. His luck held, however, and he came out over a small village, which was quite near to Tournai. Hundreds of German soldiers were drilling in a field near the railway station, and in the station itself a troop-train was standing. He dived on the soldiers, raking the field with his Vickers gun, and he also attacked the train. He obtained direct

DOG-FIGHTS AND RUNNING FIGHTS 253

hits on this, and Dillon took photographs with his aeroplane camera, of everything that occurred. The photographs were taken from a height of 50 to 100 feet. Owing to the unfavourable conditions under which they were taken, the photographs were blurred but they showed enough detail to enable the place to be identified, and two of them showed the splintering due to direct bomb-hits on the train. Naturally no E.A. were about during the attack, but the Bristol drew a great deal of rifle-fire from the ground, and the machine was hit in several places. Hepworth actually stayed there for forty minutes, and did a great deal of damage during this time. Then he zoomed up once more into the clouds and made for home.

No one could, short of a miracle, come out exactly over the aerodrome under such adverse weather conditions. Hepworth actually came through the clouds at a spot some twenty miles from Serny. His engine refused to pick up when he emerged from the clouds and he scraped over some trees and landed his Bristol safely in a field.

He and Dillon spent the night with some French peasants, and flew back the following morning.

The Squadron C.O., the Wing-Commander, and the Brigadier were all impressed with this effort, and Hepworth was recommended for the Distinguished Flying Cross, which in due course he received.

This was the first decoration which Hepworth had ever been awarded. His " bag " of enemy machines up to date was eighteen. By the time the Armistice was declared the number had risen to twenty-four, but Hepworth received no recognition for this. Once, much to his indignation, a rumour got about that he was to be given an O.B.E. Rightly or wrongly, this award was regarded in France as being suitable solely for distribution among non-combatants. A friend of ours in a neighbouring squadron had been awarded an O.B.E., which he refused to wear. He used to carry it about in his pocket and whenever he met a kindred spirit he would produce it, flaunt it under his friend's nose, and exclaim, " See what I did in the Great War, Daddy ! "

It seems a pity that bravery and unfailing devotion to duty, such as Hepworth's, should have received such inadequate recognition, while people in officers' uniforms, holding " cushy " jobs at the Base, should so often have been the ones to collect the decorations which had originally been intended only as rewards for gallantry in the field.

CHAPTER XIV

CLOUD-FLYING AND LOW RECONNAISSANCES

(i)

OUR Wing-Commander, Colonel Napier, was interested in the possibilities which Captain Hepworth's " voluntary " raid had opened up. The German retreat was beginning and daily reconnaissances behind the lines would soon become of first-rate importance. Cloud-flying was such a difficult matter that it had been generally accepted that no flying could be done on rainy or very cloudy days. Hepworth's performance had thrown a different complexion on the matter and, eventually, after the Wing-Commander had discussed the question with Major Wells-Smythe and with Captain Hepworth, A Flight was formed into a " Special Reconnaissance " Flight.

But before this happened some of the members of A Flight tried some cloud-flying on their own account. After lunch on the same day that Hepworth and Dillon got back to Serny, Ian Fraser walked across the hut to where I was lying reading, helped himself from my tin of Gold Flakes and said, " Wot abaht it ? "

" Wot abaht wot ? " I asked.

" Do you think it's up to us to carry on the good work with a cloud-show like the skipper's ? Or would it seem apish, or look like stealing some of his thunder ? "

" Imitation is the sincerest form of flattery," I remarked sententiously.

" I'll toss you for it," said Fraser. " Heads you go first, tails I do."

" You fellers, Ian, are too heroic for my simple tastes. All right, let her rip ! "

The penny came down with the head on top. The weather had been dud for three or four days and I had not seen Sergeant Antler during this time. I walked across to the N.C.O. quarters to rout him out, and found him "off duty" with a bad dose of frostbite. His fingers were puffed up out of all recognition and it made me positively squeamish to look at them. I returned to our huts and sounded two of the other observers, but they both made excuses for not going with me. Then I spotted Lindsay, Farrell's observer, reading a novel, and tackled him. He raised one objection after another. I dangled a possible decoration as convincingly as I could in front of his eyes, but he was "not having any," and finally refused point-blank to go. This left only Fraser's observer, Redfern, and I could not with a clear conscience try to entice him. The upshot of it was that my chance lapsed, and Fraser and Redfern set off. But cloud-flying is no easy game. They hedge-hopped up to the lines, started climbing into the clouds then, and after about two minutes got into a spin with their engine full-on. They were both nearly thrown out. Fraser righted the bus as they emerged from the clouds, directly over the Boche lines. A good many shots were fired after him as he sped homewards, and he decided to postpone his show until he had been able to practise cloud-flying on a day when the clouds were farther from the ground.

For the next three days we carried on our normal patrols, in clear weather. A new observer, Alec Trent, flew with me. He was a little Scotsman, not much more than five feet six inches high, but a pugnacious little devil with the makings of a good observer in him.

On the fourth day, Antler was declared fit for duty. The sky was overcast and it rained early in the day. Shortly after breakfast the rain eased off and with the clouds at 800 feet Antler and I set off on a "cloud reconnaissance." We flew below the clouds to Lille, through which the line passed at this time, and then zoomed up

CLOUD-FLYING

into them. This was my first experience of any continuous cloud-flying. I had read somewhere that in each ear there is a compartment containing some fluid, by means of which one is enabled to tell when one's balance is disturbed. I am not disputing this. I soon discovered, however, that this indicator was not nearly sensitive enough to enable one to correct any small change from the horizontal position before such change became dangerous. After flying in dense mist for a few seconds I noticed that the bubble on the level was moving over to one side, and that our speed was increasing. I eased the stick over to the same side to which the bubble was moving and also pulled it back slightly. This should have righted the Bristol, but, instead, the speed increased and the compass started spinning. It was an eerie feeling when the bus did not respond as it should have done to the controls. To right matters I pulled back the throttle, put the rudder-bar central, and pushed the stick forward. Immediately I regained control of the Bristol. Then, turning slowly till the compass pointed due east, I slowly opened the throttle. This happened three or four times and I soon found that if I shut off the engine and put the controls central directly the bubble and compass began wandering, I could regain control without losing height appreciably.

The Bristol pushed its nose through the clouds at 6,000 feet. It is difficult to convey the sense of utter and glorious freedom that comes over you when you escape from the dull grey weather below the clouds to the bright sunshine above them. The under surface of the clouds may be leaden-grey, but the upper surface, lying below a clear blue sky, is like pure snow. A beautiful effect can be seen, too, on the cloud surface. If you look in the direction of your shadow you see a bright, circular rainbow, and always in the centre of it a black silhouette of your machine, riding over the cloud-waves after you.

We flew east for a few minutes, and then, with the engine off, glided down slowly into the clouds. From time

R

to time during the descent I opened the throttle for a second or two to keep the engine warm and to make sure that it would pick up when we got below the clouds. We came through to find ourselves over Antoing, a short distance south-east of Tournai. The layer of clouds was not so thick here as it had been over Lille, and we turned north at a height of nearly 3,000 feet. Within a second or two Archie spotted us and we were soon busy dodging his bursts. As we flew on Antler alternately craned his head over the side, or wrote busily in his notebook. It suddenly struck me how ludicrous it was for the pair of us to duck whenever one of the " Cr-r-umphs " came particularly close to us. As though the flimsy aeroplane fabric could afford any protection against Archibald! This gentleman became very objectionable when we neared Tournai. I flew an erratic course to upset his aim, but we offered a good target at 3,000 feet. All around us black oily blobs of smoke were unrolling themselves, accompanied by deafening crashes. To make matters worse the clouds were beginning to break up. When we turned west over Tournai we had a clear gap above us. Then we raced for the lines. We had sixteen miles to go. At times Archie became so intense that I zoomed up into a cloud-patch to escape him. But the cloud-patches were not very big now and we had to dodge from one to another. When we shot into a cloud we could see nothing of the explosions but we could hear them crashing near us. Antler kept his head over the side most of the way back, making notes of the transport and troop movements along the roads below us. When we reached the lines I glanced back and the sky seemed to be covered with black patches of smoke. It was cheering to think of the amount of ammunition that brother Fritz had simply wasted on us. There were two or three small holes in our wings, but the damage done was of no consequence.

(ii)

When A Flight was formed into a " Special Reconnaissance Flight," dud days lost their appeal. They had been generally looked upon as legitimate holidays, but now they became periods of anxious activity. It was seldom that any pilot did more than one reconnaissance a day, but any of us would willingly have chosen two offensive patrols in preference to one " low-show." No doubt the weather had something to do with it. To fight in the open, with the sun shining, is one thing ; to skulk along blindly in clouds, on a grey day, to emerge finally all alone above sodden fields and dripping hedgerows, is quite another. It is a trying game. You stand a fair chance of getting lost if you are not thoroughly familiar with the lie of the land behind the lines. If after nosing about for landmarks when you emerge, you succeed in locating your position, you have to fly below the clouds all the way back because you are on reconnaissance duty, and you are subjected to a good deal of rifle and machine-gun fire from below. If your engine lets you down, or is hit from the ground, well, then you are " for it." When your luck is really out, you fly over a flaming-onion battery, and you think what a hard world it is.

Cloud-flying caused most of us some trouble to begin with. My second effort, a " duty " show, was less successful than my first trial one had been. The Boches were retreating every day and Farrell and I were told to find out whether the bridges over the Scheldt at Tournai were still standing. It was a gloomy day and the clouds were at 1,000 feet. The two machines left together and we flew just below the clouds as far as Lille. Here we ran into a heavy fog which reached to the ground, and so I swung round and flew back a few miles to Armentières. Farrell turned back, too, but at Armentières he made off and neither Antler nor I saw him again on that show. We now glided down almost to the ground and, turning once more towards Lille, hedge-hopped along till we came to the fog and then climbed up into it. I had considerable difficulty in maintaining an even keel in the fog and several times had to shut off the engine, and glide down with rudder-bar and joystick central, to regain control. We got through finally, flew above the clouds for a while and then glided down once more. We were clear of the fog when we dipped below the clouds but we had wandered considerably in it and now found ourselves near Courtrai, about fifteen miles north of Tournai. We climbed up once more. When I judged that we were near Tournai I went down again with the engine half-on. As we dropped lower and lower I kept an uneasy eye on the altimeter. When we passed the 1,000 foot mark there was still nothing to be seen but dense, swirling mist all around us. We had got back into the fog-belt again. Lower she went and lower. Antler was leaning over my shoulder watching the altimeter. It showed three hundred feet, two hundred, one hundred.

"Climb!" he shouted, "climb!"

A streak of stupid obstinacy made me keep on. Suddenly at fifty feet I saw the river below us. We were crossing it from east to west, and the next instant a château loomed through the fog directly in front of us. The engine was half-on and the wires were whining with the speed. I jerked back the stick and we shot up over the château, missing it by a narrow margin. I knew now that it was not worth while trying to reach Tournai, as we should almost certainly fly into a house before we got there, so I began climbing, for the third time, through the fog. We got through it at 10,000 feet and then flew west till we judged that we were near Serny. Our guess was a lucky one. At 1,000 feet we emerged from the clouds, over Aire, and so were able to find our way to the aerodrome.

CLOUD-FLYING

(iii)

From Serny we moved to Floringhem. The aerodrome was good but small. We only stayed a few days here and the weather was foul. We did several cloud-shows from Floringhem and gradually all of the A Flight pilots got better at cloud-flying.

From Floringhem we moved to Ascq, near Lille. This was a long hop and it was two or three days before our heavy transport arrived. In the meantime we ferried the essentials of life across in our machines. Several bottles were packed in the rear cockpit of each Bristol, and also some tins of bully-beef and some "dog biscuits." We supped off this the first night, in one of the hangars. The following morning, for breakfast our Ack Emmas managed to produce some porridge. We sat at two long tables in the hangar. A plate of oatmeal porridge was placed in front of each of us, but then the mess orderlies could find no spoons. They scattered in a search for them and came back at last with two for each table. Then began a relay race. The two fellows facing each other at the top of our table started off as hard as they could go and then handed on the spoons to the next two. We, farther down, urged them to greater efforts and laid small bets on our respective sides.

"Swallow, man, swallow! Jimmy's licking you." "Don't stop to chew—swallow!" "Oh, well done, Jimmy! Now Farrell, buck into it!" "Come along, our side!"

I was near the bottom of the table, and by the time the spoon reached me my porridge was stone-cold, but I dashed through it and handed on the spoon to my neighbour.

Our side lost by two plates, and I had to pay Fraser ten francs.

At Ascq, for the first time, we were billeted. Ian Fraser, Alec Trent and I were in the same house.

The Germans had only evacuated the village three days before we arrived. The old people to whom the house belonged had been saddened by the war and by the hardships they had suffered, and they were pitifully poor, and yet whenever we entered the house they always offered us coffee. They had no milk, but they produced some fine snow-white lump sugar which they had buried during the German occupation. There could not have been much of this. The first time it happened Ian Fraser looked at me. The old people could not understand a word of English. " Do we prefer it without sugar ? " he asked.

" Absolutely," I replied.

" It is a national failing to take it unsweetened," said Alec. " God-damn it," he added, after sipping it.

The line was close to Ascq and the guns were thundering all the time.

Usually after a move our messing arrangements would be upset for a day or two, but after this move they did not return to normal till after the Armistice. Our food was of the plainest, but bully-beef and hard tack were always on hand if we got too hungry. Our P.M.C., Griffith, frequently went out on foraging expeditions and would usually return with some loot. But even Griffith found it difficult to get figs from thistles, though in justice to him, if anybody could have done it he could. At table in the mornings we used to make one another's mouths water with descriptions of the breakfasts we would order when we went on leave. Griffith would snort derisively. " Mphm! If we 'ad some 'am we'd 'ave 'am and eggs, if we 'ad the eggs," he would quote. Then he took to cutting breakfast. Knowing what a great trencherman he was it was difficult to understand this—till the Orderly Officer discovered him one morning with three N.C.O.s behind a shed, with a pan of sizzling bacon and fried bread between them.

After three days at Ascq we moved to Gondecourt. Here we had comfortable quarters in a large building which had been a hospital. There was a verandah in front

CLOUD-FLYING

of it, where for three sunny days we drowsed pleasantly, read, or played cards when off duty.

Ian Fraser, Alec Trent and I as usual shared a room. In it Alec and Ian put up their stretchers. A new one which I had brought back with me from leave had disappeared in our previous move, but after rummaging about, we discovered an old iron bedstead which we hauled off to our room, and on this I stretched my valise.

We were comfortable in Gondecourt but we did not care much for the inhabitants of the place. They spoke too favourably, we thought, of the Germans. One of them in particular, an elderly white-haired lady, was always at the hospital, trying to engage the officers in conversation. She was evidently an educated woman and she spoke English very well. She never tired of telling us how generously the Germans had treated the people of Gondecourt during the occupation, and altogether, she pleaded their cause too well. Those were suspicious days and we thought she might be a spy, so we decided to have nothing to do with her.

On our third morning at Gondecourt, Hepworth asked me to lead a patrol of five machines. Our duties were, primarily, to act as escort to some D.H.9's who were going over to bomb Grand Metz Aerodrome, and also we had to photograph Grand Metz and Wattines Capelle, next to it. This was the first time I had deputised for Hepworth. The show passed off uneventfully. The bombers dropped their eggs, and we obtained good photographs of both aerodromes. Far below us, over Leuze, we saw four Fokkers making off east, but we met none near enough to attack.

On the following morning the Squadron moved farther east to Bersée. Five machines of A Flight were to do an O. Pip from Gondecourt, and land on the new aerodrome at Bersée. Near Renaix we met a patrol of eight Fokker biplanes, and attacked. Hepworth shot down the leader during the first dive. The Fokker was seen to crash and burst into flames on hitting the ground. I missed my man and was pulling out of the dive when I saw a Fokker streaking down on Hepworth's tail. I dived and he turned off to the left. With the Bowden lever hard pressed and the Vickers rattling I went after him, but he seemed to bear a charmed life. We were losing too much height so I pulled out in a climbing turn and as I did so Antler let him have it with his Lewis gun. The Fokker continued to dive very steeply, zig-zagging downwards, but evidently under control, and at last Antler saw him land in a field. The fight broke up now and we followed Hepworth back to Bersée. On landing, we found that Farrell had been shot through the thigh. Fraser had brought down a Boche, his first one, in flames, and was very delighted about it. The patrol had thus destroyed two Fokkers and damaged a third.

At Bersée we were billeted again. Fraser, Trent and I contrived to be in the same house. Fraser and I shared a large room and Trent had a smaller one next to it. Every evening we sat talking to Madame Olivier and her daughter, in the kitchen. They told us many interesting things. When the Boches got near Bersée in 1914, M. Olivier, who seems to have been a mechanic, was advised by his brothers to go to Paris so as not to have to work for the Germans. Madame and her daughter stayed on in Bersée. German troops were billeted with them nearly all the time. The German privates, according to Madame, were heartily sick of the war, and they hated their officers. How far Madame's love for truth was tempered by a desire to please us it would be hard to say. The Boche flying-men, she said, were considered to be poor pilots. On an average one machine crashed per day on the aerodrome. This, incidentally, was told us too at practically all the aerodromes we went to. When a solitary British machine came over, presumably on reconnaissance or photographic duty, the soldiers would become very angry because thirty or forty German pilots would remain on the ground watching him. Soldiers billeted with her would tell her of military operations. On one occasion one hundred of them worked steadily for a week on a big-gun emplacement. Then an English airman flew over and dropped a bomb on it, wiping it all out.

Madame showed us an interesting photograph of Hindenburg, standing in front of her house.

One day Madame took the three of us down into the basement of the house. There we saw stacks of German Mausers, some rusty, others in a remarkably good state of preservation. There must have been several hundreds of them.

" Are you responsible for these, Madame ? " Ian asked her.

" No, no ! " she protested in her rapid French. " These rifles were abandoned when the Boches left. No English officers but you know they are here. I am not responsible, no ! " she replied.

" Do you mind if I take one, Madame ? " I asked.

" But certainly ! Take two, take six ! " she replied.

I searched among them and selected one, in perfect condition. Later I got an Ack Emma to cut the stock for me so that, when taken apart, the rifle would fit into my valise. Neither Fraser nor Trent bothered about the Mausers as each of them had already obtained a German revolver as a souvenir.

(iv)

Hepworth came away from the Squadron Office one morning in a bad temper.

" We're doing a reconnaissance in relays this morning," he barked, as he sat down to breakfast.

" Cripes ! In this rain, Skipper ? " asked Simkins, cocking an ear to the steady tattoo on the roof.

" D'you think this is a bloody tea-fight ? " snapped

Hepworth. "I'll kick off at nine. Simmy, you'll follow at ten. Eastwood, go up at eleven. Vee, twelve."

He discussed details with us.

By twelve o'clock no reconnaissance had yet been done, and the rain was still coming down steadily. The first three pilots had returned and had reported weather conditions too unfavourable to warrant their crossing the line. Alec Trent was to fly with me and he was in pugnacious mood that morning.

"Gad! we simply must pull this off," he said, as we walked across to the hangars. "I've always wanted a strip of blue and white ribbon on my chest and here's our chance. Even the Skipper didn't cross over."

I did not feel as enthusiastic about it as he did. The actual flying difficulties would be considerable in such weather. Alec climbed into his cockpit, the mechanics pulled the prop. over a few times, and when they yelled "Contact!" I turned rapidly the little starting handle on the side of the bus. When she was ticking over smoothly, I turned away to smoke a cigarette in the shelter of the hangars, while the engine warmed up. As I turned a shot rang out, and a bullet hit the ground at my feet. I swung round and saw Alec, with blanched face, goggling at me. He had been toying with the Colt Automatic, let it off by accident, and nearly put an end to our reconnaissance. A few minutes later we took off. It was unpleasant flying in such weather. The drops stung one's face and obscured one's vision. As we flew north-east towards Tournai I had to keep dragging a gauntlet over my streaming goggles. Before reaching Tournai I zoomed up into the clouds.

We had flown east for a while before I remembered that I had not noted the time when we entered the clouds. One's sense of the passage of time can easily be upset. We were flying due east into enemy territory, and I simply had not the vaguest idea whether we were half a mile, or twenty, beyond the lines. After what seemed an eternity,

CLOUD-FLYING

I decided that it was quite time we came down, so shutting off the engine, I turned west and glided down and soon the ground reappeared below us. For a moment I could not locate our position and then, glancing around, saw a large town a short distance ahead of us. To my dismay I recognised Tournai! Almost at the same instant Archie blazed at us. Of course, he had heard our engine and had simply been waiting for us to pop through. He gave us a rough passage back, but we were soon out of his reach. Then I turned again and, pulling Alec toward me, bawled into his ear " Want to go back ? " and I pointed a glove towards the lines. He nodded his cocky little head determinedly and shook his fist towards the east. So up we went into the clouds again and this time, as we entered them, I looked at the clock in the bus. The clouds were thin and we were above them at 4,000 feet. The Bristol fully opened was doing 110 miles per hour and for twelve minutes we flew due east. It seemed an eternity. Once or twice I felt quite sure the clock had stopped. When the time was up I turned west and shut off the throttle. At 800 feet we were below the clouds and in plain sight of our objective, the railway junction at Ath. Alec made notes of the rolling stock in Ath, and we began the return journey. As we were so low we could see the ground clearly and Alec alternately made notes of, and fired at the German soldiers, lorries and cars on the road. As we passed over Leuze, we saw six lorries passing through the village and I dived on these, giving them a short burst from the Vickers. Alec continued the good work with the Lewis gun and they all pulled up, though whether they were damaged or not we could not tell. All this time we were being fired at continuously from the ground. The regular ta-ta-ta-ta of the machine-guns was interspersed with the irregular crackling of rifles. After leaving Leuze we flew over a flaming-onion battery and he sent up one after another of the dreaded cones of greenish tracer. I dodged desperately, sometimes above and sometimes below them, and all the time Alec fired bursts from the Lewis gun at the battery. Near the line Archie took up the tale with shrapnel. The bursts were close, and as we had finished the reconnaissance now, I shot up into the clouds. Half a dozen bangs followed us into the mist, and then we were free.

Before returning to the aerodrome we landed, as we always did after these reconnaissances, at Ronchin, to report to the Brigade Intelligence Officer. While he was noting details I pin-pointed the flaming-onion battery for him but he merely grinned and ignored it. When we got back to Bersée we were examining the bus for bullet-holes when the C.O. and Captain Hepworth passed the hangar. They stopped on seeing us and the C.O. called out:

"Show washed out, I suppose?"

"No, sir, we got over to Ath."

"Oh, stout effort!"

He questioned us about the reconnaissance and then joined us in an inspection of the machine. The Constantinesco oil-cup below the propeller had been smashed by a bullet and there was a small hole in one of the wings. This was the only damage done by enemy fire.

"Hullo! You've missed this one," remarked the C.O., pointing to a hole in Alec's cockpit. "B' Gad! It's the most serious of the three. It's gone through a longeron!"

Alec began fiddling with a shoe-lace, and I replied, "Why, yes, sir, so it has!"

(v)

At regular intervals the South Africans in the Squadron would get parcels from the South African Gifts and Comforts Committee in London. In each parcel there would be a couple of bags of Springbok tobacco, several packets of cigarettes, and occasionally a woollen sweater or a pair of socks. The arrival of these parcels always caused excitement among the Scotsmen in the Squadron.

The English fellows could not acquire a taste for the South African tobacco, but the Scotsmen took to it like a duck takes to water. Shortly after Alec Trent arrived in the Squadron I received a parcel and handed him one of the little yellow bags of Springbok. He filled his pipe, took a few puffs and declared that it was great stuff. Always after this when a fresh supply came in I would give him a bag.

" Does the stuff really please your palate, Alec, or only your Scots instincts because it is free ? "

" Awa' wi' ye, laddie ! It's a *mon's* tobahco ! "

Letters and parcels from South Africa were often months in transit. I heard once, from Pretoria, that a cake had been sent off to me. I told my friends the good news and for several days we kept a look-out for it. But the weeks went by and no cake arrived. One dud afternoon half a dozen of us were sitting round the fire, yarning, when a parcel from South Africa arrived for me.

" Gad ! It must be the cake at last."

When the package was opened, sure enough it contained the long-looked-for cake, a large iced one. I carved it into several slices and passed it round. The Skipper pulled out a slice, buried his teeth in it—and made a rush for the nearest window. The cake was hairy with mildew.

One afternoon, Simkins took the village priest up for a joy-ride. Practically the whole village turned out to see him take off. He was a jovial old fellow and marched up at the head of his flock with a small flag of France in his hands. Two of us gave him a leg-up into the observer's cockpit and adjusted the belt round his ample middle. Then he waved to his people and clasped the flagstick firmly in both hands, Simkins opened the throttle and the villagers raised a cheer. But before the Bristol had left the ground the wind-blast had ripped the tricolour off the stick. Simkins flew him round for twenty minutes and when they landed, the old chap was still holding on like grim death to the bare stick.

As the days wore on we did a good many low reconnaissances. The B.I.O. at Ronchin was pleased with the information these gave him, but the work was trying. Even the cheerful Simkins showed signs of strain.

"These low-shows," he remarked wearily one evening, on landing, "are making an old man of me."

Flying could be very unpleasant if one were not physically fit. On one of the few occasions at this time on which we did a high patrol I was feeling anything but fit. I had eaten nothing all day, and at no time is it good to fly on an empty stomach. There was a cold wind blowing, towards evening, when we took off. At 21,000 feet the cold was intense. To make matters worse we ran into a snowstorm at this altitude. Some yellowish liquid oozing slowly from the side of the engine congealed as it came out. I watched this yellowish mass growing, till the vibration or the wind pressure broke it away. My head was throbbing and I could hardly see a thing, certainly not the eight Fokkers on which Hepworth dived towards the end of the patrol. I went down with the Flight but simply could not take any part in the scrap which followed. An extraordinary thing happened to Fraser during this encounter. After the first dive, as Fraser zoomed up, he collided with a Fokker diving across him. His undercarriage crashed into the Fokker's upper plane, carrying it away, and sending the E.A. down in an uncontrollable spin. After a short fight the remaining enemy machines made off. When we got back to Bersée I had to apologise for my behaviour to the pugnacious Trent, who had been flying with me, and who wanted to know what the purple blazes had gone wrong with me. Fraser's undercarriage collapsed when he landed.

Ian Fraser was doing good work in cloud reconnaissances and he had quite redeemed the "break" he had made on his first war-show with the Squadron. It had been a high O. Pip and Fraser, who had never been above 15,000 feet before had gradually found the cold becoming

CLOUD-FLYING

unbearable. At last he could stand it no longer, so he broke away from the patrol and returned to the aerodrome. On landing he went straight up to the C.O. and told him what had happened. Major Wells-Smythe's sense of humour saved the situation for Fraser. He burst into a shout of laughter and turning to Captain Long, asked him what he was to do with the young lead-swinger. "Daddy" smiled sympathetically and replied:

"I think, sir, he'll get all, and more, than he deserves when Captain Hepworth gets back."

When the patrol landed, Hepworth got the story direct from Fraser. He listened without saying a word and without blinking an eyelid.

"Right," he said, when he had finished. "Get sandbags into your bus and take her up. Get up to 20,000 and stay there for half an hour. And, by God, if you come down before that I'll skin you alive."

One afternoon two machines were sent up on reconnaissance duty. Ian Fraser was flying the one and Jimmy Gale the other. They were to get what information they could of movements behind the lines. It was late afternoon when they left and the clouds were at 5,000 feet. There were many open patches in the layer of clouds, and Jimmy Gale realised that it would be a risky proceeding to go far behind the lines in these circumstances. If he flew at 18,000 feet he would not be able to see the ground sufficiently well through the broken clouds, whereas if he flew below them he would not only offer a good target to Archie, but he would quite probably run into enemy patrols for it was by no means a "dud" day. So Jimmy flew up and down the lines at 5,000 feet for an hour, and both he and his observer jotted down full details of all Boche activities within their range of vision. Their separate notes combined to form a useful report and they were congratulated by the B.I.O. on their afternoon's work.

Fraser, on the other hand, on reaching the lines plunged

straight across them, climbed through the clouds, and flew east above them for twenty miles. He must have wandered a bit, or the wind may have drifted him out of his course, for when he came through the clouds he was hopelessly lost. He started back, flying westwards by compass, and as he was not Archied at first he dropped to 2,000 feet. There was a fair amount of movement on the roads but Redfern and he did not think it was worth recording as they did not know its whereabouts on the map. So they contented themselves with doing it as much damage as they could with their fore and aft guns. Soon after they started back, Archie opened up and heaved things into the sky at them. They were too low now to get back into the clouds and had to split-ass up and down and sideways all the way back. About half-way home a flaming-onion battery made things very hot for them. Instead of avoiding it, Fraser flew straight at it and tried to bomb it with the last of his twenty-five pounders. He missed it and had to re-double his split-assing tactics till he was out of its range. He was most fortunate not to meet any large formations of E.A. but once two Pfalz scouts dived on him quite unexpectedly out of a cloud. Redfern was studying his map, which was mounted on a bit of three-ply, at the time—when to his utter astonishment it was shot to pieces between his two hands. He dropped it like a hot potato and made a lunge for the Lewis as the two Boches zoomed upwards. He got in a burst at them at the top of their zoom and they both turned off eastwards. The shoulder of Redfern's flying-coat had been pierced but he himself had not been touched.

At the aerodrome, Trent and I were becoming more and more worried as time went on and Fraser did not come back. When it was nearly dark we went across to the mess for a drink and as we were hurrying back heard a machine taxi-ing in. It was a relief to see Fraser and Redfern climb out of it. They were worn out when they landed after a plucky but apparently useless show.

After dinner there was some discussion as to which of the two reconnaissances, Gale's or Fraser's, was the more meritorious. The fellows who defended Jimmy Gale's effort put up sensible, matter-of-fact arguments. If information could be obtained without danger, so much the better. By crossing the lines on a day when there was every likelihood of running into a Boche circus a fellow would be needlessly risking a valuable machine, his observer's life, and his own. If he did cross the lines and then lost himself, he might just as well have stayed at home. The net result of the afternoon's work, said Jimmy's advocates, was that Jimmy had brought back useful information and Ian had not. There was nothing more to be said.

"There's a hell of a lot more to be said," retorted Simkins. "If Jimmy decided it was too unhealthy to cross the lines he might just as well have come home and left the reconnaissance to the balloon-merchants."

"Come off it, Simmy! In the first place no balloon can sail up and down the lines——"

"Oh, I know all that! What I'm getting at is that it's not a Bristol's job to do contact patrols. Bristols are supposed to go farther afield, like Fraser did. The fact that he got lost was a bit of bad luck. But he showed that it was possible to carry out the reconnaissance. Also you can't neglect the moral effect on Mister bally Boche. We've seen often enough, lately, that their pilots are getting a bit jumpy. It's bound to add to their windiness and that of the troops when they see a Bristol, absolutely alone, sailing along twenty miles behind their lines."

CHAPTER XV

THE LAST DAYS BEFORE THE ARMISTICE

(i)

THE young South African, Captain A. W. Beauchamp-Proctor, was doing remarkably fine work on his S.E.5. The R.A.F. Communiqués announced on April 10th, 1918, that he had been awarded the Military Cross. On May 26th he received a bar to the M.C. The award of the Distinguished Flying Cross followed on June 30th and of the Distinguished Service Order on September 15th. Captain Proctor also received numerous French and Belgian decorations. Finally he was awarded the highest honour which it is possible for a British officer to receive, the Victoria Cross.

The *London Gazette*, in which the award was announced, on November 30th, 1918, after giving some details of Captain Beauchamp-Proctor's gallant exploits, concluded the account as follows: " In all he has proved himself conqueror over fifty-four foes, destroying twenty-two enemy machines, sixteen enemy kite balloons, and driving down sixteen enemy aircraft completely out of control.

"Captain Beauchamp-Proctor's work in attacking enemy troops on the ground and in reconnaissance during the withdrawal following on the Battle of St. Quentin from March 21st, 1918, and during the victorious advance of our armies commencing on August 8th, has been almost unsurpassed in its brilliancy, and as such has made an impression on those serving in his squadron and those around him that will not easily be forgotten."

(ii)

Half a dozen of us, one wintry afternoon, were sitting round a small stove in one of the huts. Pipes were going and we were talking the endless " shop " of flying-men. Captain Long was the only ground-officer among us. Gradually the talk veered round to the question of German atrocities, of which there were some lurid accounts in a newspaper which had been received that day by one of the observers. "Daddy," puffing away quietly at his pipe, had taken little part in the conversation. Presently someone asked him for his opinion on the matter.

"Where there's smoke there's usually a bit of fire," he replied, " but I think it's mostly smoke. In time of war some newspapers deliberately try to foster a feeling of hatred against the enemy. Look at the stuff that was written about the Boer atrocities during the Anglo-Boer War—rubbish, most of it. Our pots were as black as any of their kettles. But there's one case that I'm sure of in which Mr. Fritz has behaved damned badly, and that was when he asked us not to bomb the Rhine Towns during one of the religious festivals—and the same day he shelled Paris with Big Bertha, and bombed one of our hospitals, killing some of the nurses. That'll take some explaining."

"Daddy" always had a steadying influence on the young firebrands in the Squadron. His judgment was always sound, and he never got things out of focus. Mob-psychology simply did not apply to "Daddy." Most of us, I am afraid, were only too willing to think evil things of " our friend the enemy." The present occasion was the only one on which I had known " Daddy " to lay an indictment against the Boches.

A new arrival once remarked in Ian Fraser's presence that Captain Long seemed to be a bit of a pacifist. Ian swung round on him.

"How the hell do you think he got his M.C. ? "

The newcomer looked uncomfortable and murmured

something about its being not unknown for decorations to be " dished out to non-combatant staff-wallers."

" Non-combatant grandmothers ! " snorted Ian. " He got it for a damned fine bit of work in the trenches on the Somme, young feller, and if you'll take my advice you won't go making funny remarks about Captain Long in this Squadron."

During the evenings, when we were not playing cards, we used to collect round the small stove and talk of shoes and ships and sealing-wax, and cabbages and kings. One evening the talk turned on the future of the British Empire. Now most of the youngsters there, although they wore wings, were only fledglings, and their views are not worth recording. Dumas, a French Canadian, made some gloomy predictions on the subject and one Englishman was equally pessimistic. " Daddy," puffing at his pipe, smiled faintly but made no comment. The following day, " Daddy," Dumas and I happened to meet in the Squadron Office and while we were there a new " Comic Cuts " was posted. This was what we read :

" Major Barker*, who was on a refresher course from England with No. 201 Squadron, while on patrol on a Sopwith Snipe, attacked an E.A. two-seater at 21,000 feet over the Forêt de Mormal, and the E.A. broke up in the air. He was then fired at from below and wounded by a Fokker biplane, and fell into a spin, from which he pulled out in the middle of a formation of 15 Fokkers, two of which he attacked indecisively. He then got on the tail of a third, which he shot down in flames, from a range of ten yards. He was again wounded and fainted ; on recovering he regained control of his machine and was attacked by a large formation of E.A., one of which he shot down in flames from close range. He was then hit in the left elbow, which was shattered, and he again fainted, his machine falling to 12,000 feet before he recovered. Another large formation of E.A. then attacked him and, noticing heavy smoke coming from his

THE AMMUNITION TRAIN AT ENGHIEN SHOWING TRUCK ON WHICH DIRECT HIT WAS OBTAINED, BLOWN OFF THE LINE.

[*Royal Air Force Official—Crown Copyright Reserved*

LAST DAYS BEFORE THE ARMISTICE

machine, he believed it to be on fire, so tried to ram a Fokker. He opened fire on it from close range, and the E.A. fell in flames. Major Barker then dived to within a few thousand feet of the ground, but found his retreat cut off by eight E.A., at which he fired a few bursts and succeeded in shaking them off, returning to our lines at a few feet from the ground, when he finally crashed near our balloons. During the latter part of this combat, Major Barker was without the use of both legs, and one arm, and brought his machine back with the thumb switch."

"By God," said "Daddy," stirred out of his usual placidity, "I should think that after a fellow had been hit once he would be justified in thinking only of how he could get down without writing himself off, but to attack, be wounded, attack again—and fainting—three times——" Then he turned to Dumas, "As long as England can breed men of this calibre, Dumas, you need have no sleepless nights about her future."

(iii)

Squadron raids, in which every machine in the Squadron took part, were not unheard-of events, and even Wing raids were occasionally carried out. But both of these were regarded rather in the nature of "stunts," than as orthodox R.A.F. duties. During the last phase, before the Armistice, when the Germans were retreating rapidly, our Wing-Commander, Colonel Napier, instituted "Wing-shows," as regular features of the day's work, and he would lead these shows in person, in his Camel. Eighteen Bristols would take the air at a given time, and fly in three close formations. Over a pre-arranged spot we would meet the other squadrons of the Wing. Then this imposing array of bombers, scouts, and Bristols would cross the lines together. The bombers would fly below the other squadrons. Above them went the S.E.5's and Camels. Higher up came the Bristols, and they usually crossed the lines at about 9,000 feet. Above us all flew the Snipes.

On reaching the objective the bombers would glide down low and " lay their eggs." After this every machine in the Wing would go down and begin " ground strafing." Each Bristol carried its complement of twenty-five pound bombs, and these would add materially to the confusion and havoc on the roads below. Great damage would be done, too, by raking the roads with machine-guns from the air.

Undoubtedly these raids were of considerable value at this time. Not only did they cause a heavy death-roll among the enemy, but the Germans were also materially hampered in their retreat as a result of them. Special attention was paid to railway junctions, and on more than one occasion direct hits were scored, by the bombers, on ammunition trains. The Wing carried out many raids on Enghien, an important junction, and during one of these raids a D.H.9 dropped a bomb right on to an ammunition train standing in the station. I was flying, at some 2,000 feet, directly over the train at the time and as I glanced over the side a gigantic column of smoke rushed upwards, and then spread out like a huge mushroom. It was a most impressive sight. The explosion I could hear distinctly above the roar of my engine. The damage done was considerable. The line was badly torn up, and as fire and explosions spread along the train the greater portion of it was gutted completely.

Many trains west of Enghien would have to be abandoned as a result of this explosion.

(iv)

When the dawn came one morning there was not a cloud to be seen in the sky. The opportunity was at once

LAST DAYS BEFORE THE ARMISTICE 279

seized of carrying out a high O. Pip, and soon orderlies were struggling with the sleepy pilots and observers of A and B Flights. Those of us sleeping in the same hut as Hepworth had no chance to struggle. His methods were crude but simple. He merely ran through the hut jerking the bed-clothes off us.

In the mess we scalded our throats with hot tea, and then away to the aerodrome where our mechanics had already taken out the machines. Five Bristols were available in each Flight, and after running up the engines the ten of us left the ground.

It was a glorious morning. The earth below us looked beautiful in the sunshine. It was a great relief, after the low-shows we had been doing, to go up on an offensive patrol once more. As we climbed, with aerials out, Hepworth sang cheerily to us. But before long, to my great disgust, my engine began to give trouble and I had to drop out of my position of inside left, to the rear. I decided to sacrifice height for position, and remained directly under the formation. The line still ran through Tournai and directly after crossing it, Hepworth dived on some white Archie to the north of us. White Archie, fired by our people, frequently warned us of the presence of E.A. During this dive I got left far behind and could not see what was happening, but before long, Hepworth turned west to regain height and then turned back to the lines, still climbing. We crossed again at about 10,000 feet. B Flight was a short distance north-west of us and slightly above us. Soon after crossing the lines a patrol of ten Fokkers, flying north-west passed overhead, about 500 feet above us. They passed us by and attacked B Flight. Hepworth immediately turned, and, supported by his three Bristols, went to their assistance. I turned too, but was considerably below them and had to await developments. Then things happened quickly. The Fokkers meant business and the scrap up above was a fierce one. After a minute or two a Fokker came tumbling downwards like a wounded pigeon. Then another streaked past us with a Bristol on his tail following him down. Hard on the Bristol's heels was another Fokker. They were diving very steeply and they simply flashed past us. I caught a glimpse of Fraser's number as the Bristol streaked by, and immediately I dived. I was close behind them but dared not fire for fear of hitting the Bristol. Then Fraser zoomed up to the right and at once I pressed the Bowden lever. The Fokker climbed up to the left and I followed him. Then three Fokkers dived on us. I heard Antler's gun rattling and, glancing back, saw them coming at us with their guns blazing. I left them to Antler and kept after the green and yellow fellow in front. After getting in three long bursts my gun jammed with a bad double feed. I tried desperately to rectify this but could do nothing with it. Then the Fokker in front half-rolled and came at us. In a fraction of a second he was up to us, swung up to the left in a climbing turn, half-rolled again and was on our tail. I could do nothing now but prevent him from getting a bead on us. I had never before flung a Bristol about so violently as I did then. Antler was nearly thrown out. Once his leg was over the Scarff-mounting. The Boche was a good pilot. Every time I glanced back I saw the yellow and green Fokker above us. I like to think that my faulty engine had something to do with it, but, whatever the reason, I could not out-manœuvre him. And then suddenly Antler got him. He must have killed the pilot, for the Fokker went down quite out of control. The other three Fokkers, after the first dive, had left us. Probably they had been engaged by other Bristols. I could do nothing with my gun, and turned back to the aerodrome. Antler had kept his eyes fixed on the falling Fokker and he pointed him out to me. We watched him all the way down till he finally crashed into the ground.

When we left the line there were still two or three isolated scraps going on but the main fight had broken up.

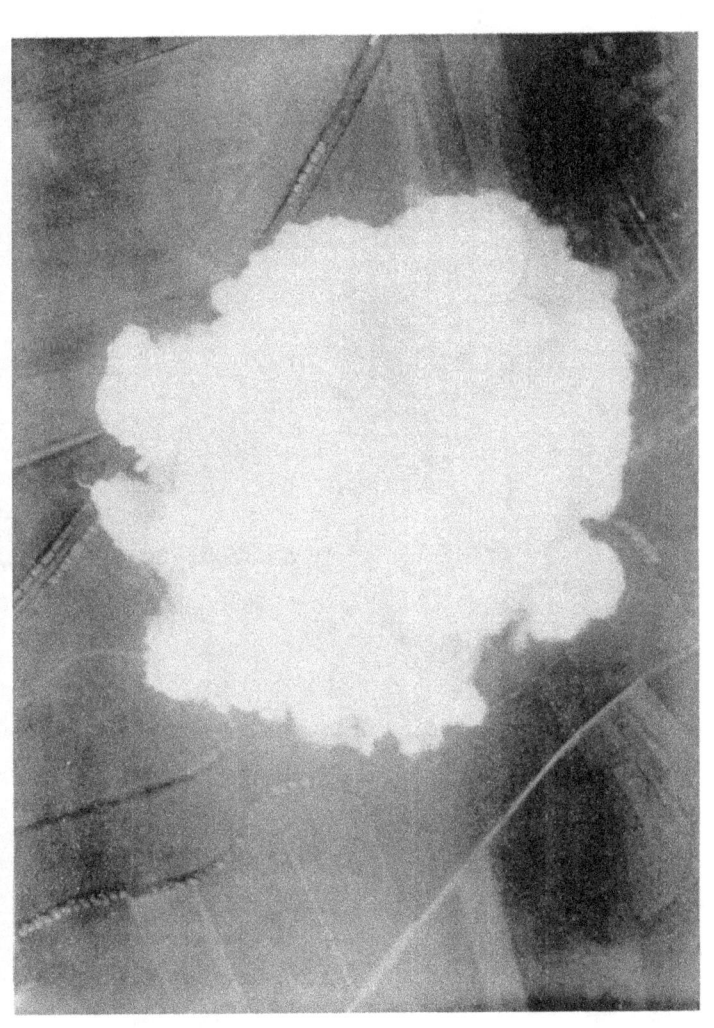

THE DIRECT HIT ON AMMUNITION TRAIN AT ENGHIEN, ANOTHER VIEW FROM A DIFFERENT ANGLE AND FROM A LOWER ALTITUDE.

[*Royal Air Force Official—Crown Copyright Reserved*

LAST DAYS BEFORE THE ARMISTICE

There was great excitement on the aerodrome when the machines began to come in. Hepworth had come back some time before with a jammed gun, but as soon as it had been cleared, had returned to the lines. After the first fight had broken up and the Bristols were drawing together again, fully twenty Fokkers came swooping down on them out of the sun. After a great fight these Fokkers, too, were routed. The Squadron had given a good account of itself that day. One after another the machines came in till they were all back with the exception of Prinsloo, the South African in B Flight. Half an hour later the C.O. received a 'phone message that Prinsloo had landed in the balloon lines. Both he and his observer, Jeffreys, were wounded.

Altogether the Squadron claimed sixteen Fokkers. Of these eleven were confirmed by our Archie batteries. Prinsloo himself had shot down a Boche in flames during the first attack. Both he and Jeffreys had been wounded when the Fokker circus dived on them out of the sun, but each of them, after this, had succeeded in shooting down another Fokker. Their machine was badly shot about but they managed to glide back across the lines. Prinsloo was later awarded a D.F.C. for the morning's work.

(v)

Our time was mostly taken up now with Wing-shows. We raided the aerodrome at Grandmetz and set most of the hangars ablaze. We visited Ath and caused havoc on a road crowded with mechanical transport, all going east. We carried out several raids over Enghien and on one occasion attacked the aerodrome there from a height of a few hundred feet, pouring tracer into the hangars and into all the machines standing outside them.

It was on this occasion that we witnessed a comical incident. As we got near the aerodrome a Fokker, all unsuspecting, taxied out and took off. Then the pilot must have glanced up and seen the air filled with British machines. In nightmare panic he dived for the nearest field, landed his bus, and scuttled away from it as fast as his little legs could carry him.

On these low-shows the dread of engine-failure was always with us. On a high patrol there was always a chance of gliding back to safety. But when we flew low the firing from the ground was sometimes intense, and if the engine were hit there could be no chance of getting back. Ian Fraser and I made a compact that if one of us were forced down, the other would land near him and endeavour to take him and his observer off. On one of these raids I was flying with sandbags as the B Flight Commander had borrowed my observer. On the way back my engine began to give trouble and I gradually dropped lower and lower. Fraser saw this and he followed me down. As it happened, after descending from 3,000 to 1,000 feet my engine picked up again, and got me safely across the lines but it was comforting to know that one had a pal at hand who was prepared to come down in Boche-land if necessary, to take one off.

One afternoon as we were returning from a raid we spotted four Pfalz scouts flying north, some distance below us. The wash-out light had been fired and so three Bristols turned off to give chase. The Pfalz scouts had a good start and they got away from us. On the way back we were attacked by ten Fokkers. Three Bristol pilots with but a single thought dived for the lines. In the back cockpit I had a new observer, Haslitt. As we split-assed away he fired repeatedly, and particularly at a Fokker with a scarlet tail who clung to us like a leech. Some of the straggling raiders, tailing along behind the others, who were over the lines by this time, saw our predicament and came to help us. The Fokkers immediately made off. We climbed towards the lines now and as we got near them I dived on a German observation balloon. I had got in a long burst and had pulled out preparatory to making another dive, when Haslitt hit me on the shoulder and pointed to our tail-plane. It had been shot nearly to ribbons! On seeing this I flew straight to the aerodrome. On landing, we found that one of the elevator wires had been cut as well. The red-tailed Fokker may have caused some of the damage, but, from an inspection of the tail-plane, it looked uncommonly as though Haslitt had done most of it with his Lewis gun.

(vi)

Guest nights at Bersée were, as always, occasions for glorious rough-houses. We could not offer our visitors much in the way of food, but thanks to Griffith's genius, there was never any lack of drink. On one of the last guest nights before the Armistice we had a great padre to dinner. He stood six foot six if an inch, and he was broad in proportion. He was a cheerful fellow, seemed thoroughly to enjoy the hash he got at dinner, and drank lemonade with it. He cracked jokes with everyone and from time to time his deep laugh would boom through the mess like a foghorn. After dinner we played Rugby for a while with a rolled-up Sidcot suit as a football. The game was rapidly becoming too expensive, so those of us who were sober enough, stopped it. Then Simkins began thumping the piano and we gathered round and sang Squadron songs. Most of them were local productions, sung to well-known airs. We began with a vainglorious song which dealt with the exploits of the Squadron in the great fight which had taken place a few days before. Some of the verses were as follows:

> " Twelve young pilots from (Squadron M),
> Took the air one morn at eight,
> They met fifty Huns, they say,
> Over the middle of Tournai.

Chorus : So early in the morning,
So early in the morning,
So early in the mor-r-r-ning,
Before the break of day.

Hep was leading A Flight then,
(Murray) followed with B Flight men,
There were eight old Fokkers in the sun,
That is the way of the wily Hun.

Chorus : So early in the morning, etc.

Hep got a Hun right on his tail,
He did a half-roll without fail,
Then his gun went dud they say,
So he came home and left the fray.

Chorus : So early in the morning, etc.

A Flight followed back to the lines,
And there we met some D.H.9's,
They didn't see any Huns about,
Soon they went like a bloody scout.

Chorus : So early in the morning, etc.

The wily Fokkers climbed aloft,
And thought ha ! ha ! here's something soft,
But we four Bristols came out of the sun,
And that soon stopped the b(e)ggars' fun.

Chorus : So early in the morning, etc.

The P.B.O.s shot well that day,
And every gun got its Hun, they say,
(Trent) fired and kept them away,
While (Grant's) Very lights frightened them away.

Chorus : So early in the morning, etc.

Practically everyone who had taken part in the scrap had contributed some verses to this epic. All the verses, as can be seen from the samples quoted, were crude and a number of them we omitted altogether out of deference to the jovial padre. No one knew all the verses, but each man knew some of them, and the solo was carried on by different members as the song progressed. But at the end of each verse we all, including the padre and half a dozen other guests, roared out the chorus with vast enjoyment.

This song was followed by another, sung to a popular air:

> " What do I *have* to do a low reconn. for,
>   It's the second time to-day,
>   It makes me sad,
>   It makes me *mad*
>   To think of all the bolo jobs I might have had!
>   What do I *have* to fly below the clouds for,
>   A thousand feet is quite too bally low!
>   But never mind, we'll go up again some day,
>   At eighteen thou' we'll gambol about in play.
>   If I do another show like the last one,
>   Why, I won't need next month's pay!"

The singing was thirsty work and before long there was a yell of " Drinks all round, on the C.O.! "

Our good-natured C.O. promptly gave his consent, and Bobby Westcott climbed on to a table, with his glass in his hand, to make the C.O. a speech of thanks. Bobby was a comical fellow and he made an extraordinarily good speech. To keep him there, and to keep him going, he was plied with drinks, and it was not long before Bobby began to feel uncertain of his ground. Points which he had made in his speech reminded him of certain anecdotes which he told very wittily at first, and less securely afterwards.

" Have you heard this one, padre? " he asked, and stopped short. " I say, Hep," he appealed to the skipper who was sitting on the edge of the table, next to him.

"D'you think it would be all right to ask him that one about the neat little girl and the Irishman ? "

" Of course not, you fool," replied Hepworth, in a stage-whisper. " Do you want to disgrace the whole bloody lot of us ? "

" Oh, all right. Well, what about this one——" and so Hepworth acted as censor, and saved the padre's blushes. That big man hugely enjoyed his evening, and towards the end of it won our admiration for the presence of mind that he showed in an emergency. Bobby Westcott had pleaded in vain with Hepworth. " But it's a good story, Hep, a *damn* good story ! "

" You try and tell it," said the skipper, " and I'll kick your jacksie ! "

Bobby then announced that according to his prudish friend Hepworth, he had reached the end of his parlour stories, and would now sing us a song. Waving the leg of a chair as a baton, to keep time for himself, he began

> " Our Maggie's got eyes of blue,
> Blue is her beautiful language, too——"

At this point the padre, who either knew or could guess what was coming, let out a great " Whoop ! " and jumping to his feet, lifted Bobby over his shoulder and rushed him out of the room. Which was really an extraordinarily tactful way of saving the situation.

(vii)

Our Rolls-Royce engines and our Vickers guns seldom let us down, but when they did it usually spelt trouble. When the former occurred the pilot was forced to turn back, and when the latter occurred it was considered advisable for him to do so. Through a neglect of the latter precept I got into serious difficulties during one of out last raids over Enghien.

A RAID ON MARCQ AERODROME (CANVAS HANGARS) OUTSIDE ENGHIEN.

[*Royal Air Force Official—Crown Copyright Reserved*]

LAST DAYS BEFORE THE ARMISTICE 287

The whole Wing crossed over at eight-thirty ack emma, dodged Archie who was very active near the lines, and proceeded towards Enghien. Just after we left the lines I tested my gun. There was a sharp rat-tat-tat-tat— and the gun stopped. On examining it I found that the cartridge belt had slipped out. This was a fault which could not be rectified in the air. Had we been going out on an offensive patrol I should have returned to the aerodrome at this stage, but we were out for a ground raid and I considered that with Antler's Lewis gun and our four bombs we could still do useful work by remaining with the Wing. When we neared our objective we dropped to 1,000 feet while the bombers did their work.

Then we all scattered, dropped still lower and began to punish the roads.

Not a Boche machine was to be seen in the sky. I had dropped two of my bomblets on troops below when I noticed a procession of lorries on a road some distance off, and flew off to attack them with my remaining two bombs. Twice I dived on them, each time dropping a bomb, and each time as we rose, Antler sprayed the road with his Lewis gun. We had gradually been drifting farther away from the rest of the Wing and as we rose the second time I noticed some machines overhead but paid no attention to them as I thought they were S.E.5's. The Bristol was nearly under them when I happened to glance up, and to my horror saw the black crosses under their wings. At the same moment they dived. Four of them came down on our tail and Antler's gun blazed out at them. The fifth streaked right across, over us, and I watched him closely as I dived. When he was above us and to the left, he half-rolled, and I immediately kicked on left rudder and shot under him. But this did not deter him, for he came down vertically on us and I saw tracer flashing past, directly in front of my face. I was amazed that he did not ram us, for he was exceedingly close when he half-rolled. As we dived for the lines Antler's gun was firing almost continuously. Then, glancing over my shoulder, I saw a Bristol attack one of the Fokkers on our tail. The Fokker swung off, and then to our great relief, two of our scouts came up and engaged the remaining Fokkers.

The engine was making a frightful row and I saw now that the Fokker who had half-rolled on us had perforated one of the long exhaust pipes in a number of places. The upper right wing was badly cut about, and there were gaping holes in the tank carrying the cartridge-belt, eighteen inches in front of my face. We were still a long way from the lines but we got back without further incident if one can except the attentions of the ever-watchful Archie.

When we landed at Bersée, Antler's ammunition drums were nearly empty. Our Bristol was in a sorry state. It was badly shot about in a number of places and the right upper wing had to be replaced. The Fokker who had half-rolled on to us had hit my ammunition-belt and a large portion of this had blown up, causing the holes in the tank which housed it.

When the rest of the Squadron returned we found that it was Harmer, a B Flight pilot, who had seen our plight and come to our assistance. The Fokker whom he had attacked had gone down out of control and had crashed into the ground, but another had got on to Harmer's tail and had actually shot a close group of holes through the seat of his Sidcot suit without touching him.

Eastwood was the only casualty on this raid. He received a nasty wound in the side from a machine-gun on the ground, but managed to bring his machine back safely to the aerodrome.

The days wore on, each bringing us nearer to the Armistice. When the dawn was breaking Ack Emmas with lanterns used to go through the huts waking the sleeping flying-officers. Quickly and profanely they would tumble into their clothes, hurry across to the mess for

LAST DAYS BEFORE THE ARMISTICE 289

bread-and-butter and a hot drink of tea, and then assemble in front of the hangars. The Bristols would be out, and the bitter morning air filled with the clop-clopping of the propellers as they ticked over.

It was very cold now in the mornings, when we took off for the first raid. Sometimes the Squadron would go over alone to the objective, but usually we would meet the other squadrons of the Wing near the lines, and all go over together, led by the little Camel of the Wing C.O.

One morning we were standing by, at seven o'clock, for a Wing raid over Hal. The engines were ticking over and the observers were in their cockpits stowing away the ammunition drums for their Lewis guns. Already two or three Rolls engines had roared as they were run up, when the tall figure of our C.O. was seen hurrying from the Squadron Office. His long arms were swinging and the ends of his scarf flapping as he came striding across to the hangars.

" Morning, Major ! " several voices greeted him as he approached.

" Mornin', lads ! " he called out and waved both arms. " Wash-out, everybody. The war's over. Hostilities cease at eleven ack emma to-day ! "

The engines were speedily switched off. For a moment there was silence, then someone raised a cheer and we all joined in. After that we talked in excited groups for a short while, and then, feeling rather lost, wandered back to our huts.

T

CHAPTER XVI

APRÈS LA GUERRE

(i)

" Après la guerre
There'll be a good time ev'rywhere——"

So sang the concert parties in France.

The Squadron began its search for the good time, in Lille, on the morning on which the Armistice was declared. Just after breakfast practically the whole Squadron went in, by tender and lorry, to the ancient city. And here we celebrated right royally the coming of Peace. The demonstrations of joy were not confined only to the streets of Lille. In the air overhead, Snipes, Camels, S.E.5's, Dolphins, Bristols, were careering back and forth like a flight of swallows gone mad. A stately Handley-Page came sailing majestically over Lille, and when it reached the centre of the city it was caught up in the general enthusiasm and began performing the most outrageous feats. They would have turned to water the blood of its designer, could he have witnessed them.

The members of the Squadron had scattered far and wide throughout the city, and it was late that night before the last of them, weary and frayed, came straggling back to Bersée.

During the last few days before the Armistice was signed, the Wing had lost a good many machines. I heard, too, that my friend Captain Cameron, who had been made a Flight-Commander in his Ack-W Squadron, had been shot down in flames two or three days before the end of the war. During one of the raids a D.H.9 had been forced

APRÈS LA GUERRE

down just east of the lines, and the pilot and observer had made a run for some ruins at the edge of a shattered village. There they remained in hiding for two days, when they heard English voices and emerged to find themselves on the right side of the line once more.

During one of the last of the Wing raids we had noticed several tanks outside a small village, near Ath. One morning, about the middle of November, some of our flying-officers visited the place by tender and discovered that the " tanks " were all dummies.

Shortly after the Armistice, Major Wells-Smythe went off to Paris on a few days' leave. Hepworth was to fetch him back by aeroplane. And so one morning three Bristols left Bersée, Hepworth flew with sand ballast, Fraser and I went together, and Gale flew Alec Trent in the third. There was a following wind and we covered the 140 miles in an hour and five minutes. It was an intensely cold day and we were nearly frozen when we landed at Le Bourget. We met the C.O. at Maxim's for lunch and he introduced us to a potent cocktail, called a " President Wilson," with the kick of a horse behind it. After lunch, Ian, Alec and I went to see the exhibition of War trophies, big guns, field-guns, tanks—but what interested us most were the captured aircraft. We recognised many old friends among them, D.F.W.s, L.V.G.s, Pfalz Scouts and Fokkers, both triplanes and biplanes.

Paris, after the long strain, was in holiday mood. The hotels were crowded and it was only after an effort that we all managed to get into the same hotel. The skipper and Gale were to share one room, and Fraser, Trent and I the other.

When the three of us returned to the hotel shortly before dinner, Alec suggested a drink. Our small Scotsman had an aggressive manner. " Here ! " he called out peremptorily to a man in evening clothes who had been pacing slowly up and down the lounge, " bring us three whiskies and sodas ! "

The man swung round, stared at Alec, and exploded, " I'm not a waiter, *damn* you ! "

Alec coloured up to the roots of his hair, twitched his shoulders and muttered some apology. His sudden collapse was so comical that Fraser and I burst out laughing. The stranger, after glaring wrathfully at us for a second or two, suddenly grinned and walked off.

We got back to the Squadron on the following day, before midday, and had to move that same afternoon to Aulnoye, just east of the Forêt de Mormal. It was bitter weather. There was snow on the ground and a biting wind blowing. Instead of flying with an observer, I had half a dozen kit-bags and some haversacks in my rear cockpit. Three Bristol squadrons were on the aerodrome at Aulnoye when we arrived.

The village was in ruins, but we found an empty house which still had a roof over it and this we commandeered as our mess. An order had been posted prohibiting anyone from removing wood from any of the houses, but this order we ignored. Soon we had a roaring blaze in the open fireplace in our mess. After dinner, which consisted of bully-beef, hard-tack and wine, all of which we had carried in our Bristols, most of the pilots and observers left for their sleeping quarters excepting five of us who decided to stay where we were.

From time to time during the night as our store of firewood got less one of us would go out and replenish it from the shattered houses nearby. At ten o'clock Conway, Bobby Westcott and Fowler came back to the fire. They had been billeted with some of the few remaining inhabitants, but had been nearly frozen as they had only their Sidcot suits and no blankets with them. Still more of the fellows came back as the night wore on, and, long before morning, most of the Squadron was back in the room. When Bobby Westcott, who was sleeping in his Sidcot on the floor, opened his eyes in the morning, he glanced round, and exclaimed :

WHEN 2ND-LIEUT. DAWSON GLIDED DOWN INTO THE MIST.

TRAIN WRECKAGE AT ENGHIEN, PHOTOGRAPHED AFTER THE ARMISTICE.

"Why, here we all are, ready for breakfast. Mine's plenty of bacon and four fried eggs, done lightly on one side only, please."

Just before the Armistice, an ammunition train had been blown up outside Aulnoye and all the inhabitants of the village were firmly convinced that this had ended the war.

From Aulnoye we were scheduled to move to Dour, but for four days we could not budge on account of the heavy fog which had settled down over everything. Food was scarce, cigarettes were scarcer, and we were rapidly running out of drink. On the afternoon of the fourth day the fog showed signs of breaking and we determined at all costs to get away. Jimmy Gale's observer, Marriott, came with me. Jack Marriott was a Canadian, tall and thin, and his bosom-friend was "Tiny" Jefferson, also a Canadian, but short and fat. They were always known in the Squadron as Mutt and Jeff, after well-known characters in the "Comics" of those days. In the back cockpit of my Bristol were four valises, with Mutt perched on top of them. Six of us left the ground, Hepworth leading, and directly we got up we realised that the fog was not breaking, but that we had merely come up through an air-hole in it. A few more of the gaps were visible here and there below us, but it was impossible to pick up landmarks through them, and before long even the skipper, with his uncanny sense of direction, was lost. We nosed round the air-holes and then a new pilot, Dawson, flying one of the Bristols, glided down into the mist, and we saw him no more.

In flying over one of the larger air-holes, we saw a clear field below and Hepworth decided to go down into it. We were not flying in close formation and I had overshot the hole before I realised Hepworth's intention. At once I turned, and after making a circuit, saw the machines just landing, and began gliding down. The fog had closed over the other four Bristols before Mutt and I reached the ground, and we just managed to come down along an edge of the field before it closed over that, too. In my hurry to get down I landed the machine too fast, but the heavy load in the back seat saved our Bristol from going up on its nose.

Mutt and I set off towards the other machines and soon could make out their blurred shapes ahead of us.

For an hour we sat together smoking and then the fog began to thin. As we were discussing what to do, an old woman and a younger one came towards us, from a large, neglected-looking house at the edge of the field, bearing a tray of coffee. Supplies were exceedingly scarce among the civil population at this time, and this act of hospitality must have entailed some sacrifice.

We gathered from them that there was a Balloon Wing nearby, and after drinking the coffee we set off for this. Here Hepworth obtained a guard for our machines, and they also lent him a motor-cyclist and side-car to take him back to the Squadron. A very amiable Brigadier-General invited the remainder of us to tea, and then we returned to the Bristols.

The women at the farmhouse offered us shelter for the night but regretted that they had no beds or bedding of any sort to give us. We accepted their offer gratefully and carried over the valises from our machines. None of us had any provisions in his Bristol so we went hungry to bed that night, for knowing the scarcity there was of food we would not accept any from our hostesses. The valises we spread next to each other on the floor in a large room upstairs.

The next morning we walked in to Maubeuge, where we were lucky enough to find an Officers' Club. After a wash, a shave and a huge breakfast, we returned to our machines, to find a tender from the Squadron waiting for us. The mist was still too thick to allow of flying, so we went by tender to Dour.

Here we learned that when Dawson went down into the mist he had glided into a house, and had been very

APRÈS LA GUERRE

badly injured. Fortunately he had been flying with ballast instead of an observer. The mist cleared the following day and we returned to the field for our Bristols.

(ii)

Dour was a small village about eight miles south-west of Mons.

Word went round that Albert, King of the Belgians, was to address his people in Mons, on a certain day.

After breakfast on that morning, two tenders left the Squadron for Mons. A dozen of us from one tender, by some judicious " wangling," obtained a good view of the proceedings from the windows of an hotel facing the main square. The town was *en fête* for the occasion. Crowds of excited Belgians thronged the streets and the enthusiasm on all sides was tremendous.

After listening to the speeches we went off for lunch. There was to be a further ceremony in the afternoon, but the twelve of us decided not to stay for that. After lunch, we sought out our tender and instructed " Lightning," the driver, to get back to Dour. The street we were in came to a dead end and we had to turn off into a street which lay in the path of the procession. Crowds lined the sides of the street and some distance down a dense mass of people across the road marked the corner round which the King was to come. As we neared the corner, officials shouted and waved excitedly to us to get back. Lightning jammed on his brakes, they broke, and the tender took the bit between its teeth and bolted down the street, heading straight for the mass of people at the corner. We yelled and waved to the people to get out of the way, shouting that our brakes were gone, and at the last moment they parted and we shot down the lane between them. As we passed the corner we saw the royal car drawn up, waiting for us to go by! The King's loyal subjects must have been justly incensed at our behaviour, but we did not stop to argue with them.

One by one pilots and observers went off, in rotation, on leave and returned again after an all-too-short fortnight. My turn came round once more, about the middle of December. The train service was deplorable, and Ian Fraser offered to fly me to our old aerodrome at Ascq, just outside Lille. Eastwood was flying a V.C. infantry Colonel across, who was also going on leave. The two Bristols left immediately after lunch. On landing at Ascq, Fraser and Eastwood had their sandbags filled, and returned to Dour. The Colonel and I set off lorry-hopping to Lille. As we turned away I glanced up and saw a flight of Fokker biplanes overhead, and an involuntary shiver went down my spine.

Colonels were not always very affable with junior officers, but there was no snobbishness at all about this man. He was natural and unassuming, and he had a genial, kindly manner. On his breast he was wearing the ribbons of the V.C., D.S.O., M.C. and bar. After a few minutes' walking a car came along, going towards Lille, and the driver took us right into the city. The Colonel invited me to go to the Officers' Club with him, and it was a proud youth who drank tea that afternoon with the much-decorated and friendly veteran.

After tea I made my way to the Railway Station and heard from some officers there that a fast civilian train was leaving almost immediately for Calais.

In the compartment were two disgruntled infantry officers who told me that it had taken them twenty-four hours to get from Tournai to Lille.

After spending a few days with cousins in London I went across to Ireland, and in the train from Dublin to Belfast got into conversation with an officer who had seen service in destroyers, cruisers and submarines. He had then joined the R.N.A.S. as an observer and he showed me some extraordinarily interesting photographs. He had relieved the boredom of long patrols by snapshotting Archie-bursts, and had obtained some unique results.

APRÈS LA GUERRE

Three days before Christmas I had to begin my return journey. I spent a night in London and in the Trocadero Bar ran across an old Canadian friend, Lt. A. A. Leisk, the club-footed man, whom I had first met at Camp Mohawk. He was wearing the ribbons of the D.F.C. and the M.C. He had just come out of hospital. He told me that he had been asked to test the first Sopwith Salamander that had been sent out to his Squadron. After flying it round for a while he had intended to side-slip the all-metal machine down preparatory to landing. After pushing the stick over he remembered nothing more till he came-to in the C.C.S. The heavy machine had side-slipped straight into the ground.

After a tedious journey of twenty hours from Calais to Valenciennes, I found out at the R.A.F. Headquarters in the latter place that M Squadron had moved from Dour to Nivelles, near Brussels. Then began another wearisome journey. It took the train nine hours to get from Valenciennes to Charleroi, a distance of under fifty miles. From Charleroi I could get no farther and went to an hotel for the night. The following day was Christmas Day. After breakfast I set about finding transport to Nivelles, and was lucky enough to spot my fat friend Griffith in a tender.

" 'Ullo, Vee, ol' man," he said. " Yes, we're going back to Nivelles as soon as I can find some whisky. I've got everythink but the whisky. We 'adn't enough left this morning to see us through the day, let alone the night."

When we reached Nivelles in the late afternoon, most of the members of the Squadron were already " tight " and the rest were rapidly becoming so. Hepworth told me that the Ack Emmas had all been given the day off and were to have their Christmas dinner and celebrations that night. " The officers," he added, " will have their spread to-morrow."

" It seems a good idea, Hep, though I can't see how any of the officers are going to celebrate any more to-morrow than they appear to be doing to-day."

"By the way, the C.O. is driving his car into Brussels to-night. He told me he could take four of us with him. Will you come?"

"Thanks. Should like to. Who are the other two?"

"Simmy and Gambrell."

It was nearly dark when we started. At the best of times the C.O. was a reckless driver, but now he drove like a madman. Hepworth sat in front with him. It was intensely cold and as the car tore along the road it passed over several patches coated with ice. On these the car skidded alarmingly but the C.O. never lifted his foot from the accelerator. Once we came to a long stretch on either side of which great trees had been felled. The surface was particularly treacherous here and the car slithered from side to side, missing the fallen trunks by inches.

"God!" whispered Simkins, "this is worse than a low-show!"

The climax came near Brussels, when the light had gone. The road was narrow with a sharp kerbing on the right. Along the centre of the road ran a railway track, and up the track, round a bend, came an electric train. There simply did not seem to be room for the car to squeeze between the train and the kerbing. The C.O. pressed the accelerator right down and the car shot forward like an arrow for the narrow opening. It was impossible to miss both the train and the kerbing. As the train flashed past the right wheel of the car hit the kerbing. It was little short of a miracle that the car did not capsize.

The tyre had vanished completely. On either side of the road the ground fell away steeply, and somewhere in the black hollow was our missing tyre, but we never found it. By the time we had fitted the spare wheel, the C.O. was nearly sober, but in no way did this lessen his outrageous speed after we had started once more for the city. The broad streets were crowded with people, and they scattered like hens in front of us.

THREE BRISTOL FIGHTERS OF "A" FLIGHT TAKING OFF IN FORMATION.

APRÈS LA GUERRE

"We must have a drink," said the C.O., as the car skidded to a standstill in front of the Palace Hotel.

(iii)

The aerodrome at Nivelles was a large one. Usually machines would all take off in the same direction, into the wind. This direction was shown by the "sausage" hanging from a tall mast on one of the hangars. One morning the sausage hung limply against the mast. After running up my engine outside the hangars I waved my hand, the mechanics kicked away the chocks, and I opened the throttle. The Bristol sped away from the line of hangars towards the centre of the aerodrome.

Along the lower edge of the aerodrome were some more hangars, at right-angles to ours, housing the machines of another squadron. My tail-skid had left the ground and the Bristol was speeding along on its wheels when I noticed a machine from the other squadron taking off at right-angles to me. I realised at once that there was every likelihood of a collision, but I was going much too fast now to turn till I got into the air. Our machines were racing nearer each other and were very close before I dared pull the Bristol off the ground. Directly I did so I pushed the stick over to the left and kicked on left rudder, swinging the machine round in a sharp turn to the left. It was so low that the left wing actually scraped the ground. The pilot of the other machine banked over and turned equally sharply to the right. For an instant our wheels were pointing towards each other, with only a couple of feet between them!

People watching from the hangars had given us up for lost.

Contour chasing is an exhilarating sport. If a pilot flies at 115 miles per hour at a height of 1,000 feet he is not conscious of his speed relative to the earth. But let him descend to within a few feet and skim like a swallow, following the contours of the ground ! When he approaches a line of trees bordering a road, he keeps well down to the last split-second and then suddenly zooms up over them and down again on the other side, in a glorious switch-back motion.

Between Nivelles and Brussels is the famous Mound of Waterloo, and " Bristol merchants " would frequently make the field in which it stood a resting-perch. Two or three of us would meet there, get out to light cigarettes and stretch our legs a bit, and then fly off again.

We made several trips by tender, too, to neighbouring towns. A tender could usually be obtained when wanted. The drive to Namur was a particularly pretty one. We paid several visits, too, to Brussels and to Charleroi.

In Brussels, Fraser and I bought Hepworth a meerschaum with an amber stem. He had recently taken to smoking a pipe, but had no taste whatsoever in tobacco. All brands were alike to him. However, he always insisted on *blending* three popular *mixtures*, declaring that every pipe-smoker must have his own mixture. Hepworth was pleased with our gift, but after smoking it once or twice, he tapped it sharply on his heel and broke it.

Several new pilots had come out after the Armistice to fill gaps in the Squadron. Among them was a Canadian, Kerran, who had arrived shortly after Christmas. He had been with us for about a week before he was sent up with sandbags on his first flight. Half a dozen of us watched him take off. Kerran opened the throttle, shot away across the aerodrome, and directly he got the machine off the ground, pulled her up in a climbing turn. He had not sufficient speed for this. The Bristol stalled, flopped over, and spun straight into the ground with the engine full on. Kerran was killed instantly.

(iv)

One morning we heard that H.R.H. Prince Albert was to visit the Squadron. About midday the officers were assembled in front of the hangars. As H.R.H., accompanied by Major Wells-Smythe, came down the line he shook hands with each officer in turn. Standing next to me was a shy, self-conscious fellow who was a pilot in B Flight. When they reached us the C.O. said :

" Lieutenant Dilley, sir."

" How d'you do," said the Prince, shaking hands with him.

Dilley goggled, swallowed, and blurted forth :

" Quite well, thank you ! "

It was many a day before Dilley heard the last of this.

A present arrived for the Squadron one day in the form of a Fokker biplane. Only two of us took it up as our mechanics discovered that there was some defect in it, which I understood to be a leak between the petrol and oil tanks. Hepworth was the first to fly it, and he was surprised at its sensitiveness to the controls. When he landed I went up. The single-seater was very small and light after our heavier machines. I got in, ran up the engine, and waved the chocks away. Just before I left, the Flight-Sergeant advised me to open the throttle slowly as the engine choked easily. The pitot-tube and other instruments had been removed, so as I began pushing forward the throttle I intended to take good care to get up sufficient speed before taking the Fokker off the ground. When the throttle was about half-open I glanced over the side and, to my surprise, found that we were already in the air. Immediately I opened the engine fully and eased forward the stick. The little Fokker answered beautifully to her controls, but was very, very sensitive to them. I realised then why the Fokkers moved so jerkily compared to our own more graceful machines.

After flying round for half an hour I brought her down safely. A few days later some of us decided to visit Cologne, on the Rhine. We had no difficulty in obtaining permission for the trip. Hepworth was to fly a D.H.9 A, with a 400 Liberty engine, the pilot of this bus being a visitor at our aerodrome at the time. Hepworth's observer, Dillon, was away on leave and the skipper had promised Marriott that he would take him. Fraser and I were to fly our own Bristols, with Redfern and Trent in the back seats. The day before we were to leave, Dillon got back to the Squadron.

" Dash it all, Mutt," he said when he heard of the trip, "I'm Hep's observer and I'm damned well going with him."

" You back up, Dillon," said Mutt solemnly, " and take a running jump at yourself."

The dispute was settled by dealing them three poker hands. Mutt won all three, and the following morning was in the back cockpit of Hepworth's bus when it left for Cologne.

Alec and I had to turn back with engine trouble, but borrowed Simkins' machine and set off after the others. We were lucky in again having a following wind with us and covered the 130 miles in under an hour.

We all met on the aerodrome outside Cologne and got a tender to take us into the city. The driver took us to the Billeting Officer in Cologne, and he gave us rooms in the Kronprinz Hotel. We had not to pay anything for the rooms, but could obtain no food in the hotel, and so we had meals at the Officers' Club.

Two days passed rapidly in Cologne and we met with great politeness from the Germans, politeness which sometimes bordered on servility. In the picture gallery a well-educated old man acted as our guide. He had evidently fallen on hard days, for he was very shabbily dressed, but he preserved a quiet dignity of manner that commanded respect. His English was perfect. In one room he pointed to a large portrait and said reverently, " That is our Kaiser." Before leaving we bought some etchings from the old man.

We also spent a day in Bonn, fifteen miles down the river. On the return journey to Cologne the electric train

"WE WOULD FREQUENTLY MAKE THE FIELD IN WHICH IT STOOD A RESTING-PERCH."

ANOTHER VIEW OF THE MOUND AT WATERLOO.

APRÈS LA GUERRE

was crowded. Every seat was taken and many people were standing. Once after it had stopped to let more people in, a German woman was standing next to me and I got up and offered her my seat. There was bitter hatred in her eyes as she glared at me, but she accepted the seat.

Before we returned to our aerodromes we saw some extraordinarily good flying by pilots of an American squadron. Several of them in small scout machines, flew one after the other under a bridge over the Rhine. This feat requires a very nice judgment. A South African whom I had known in A Squadron had been killed a few days before in trying to fly under the same bridge in a Bristol.

It was freezing when we flew back to Nivelles. On the way back I turned my head once to shout something to Trent, and saw him hanging more than half out of his cockpit, warming his hands on the long exhaust pipe that ran below it. All of us were numbed with the cold when we landed once more on our aerodrome.

" All Colonials," said Hepworth one day, as he took his seat at lunch, " are to be in readiness to leave at any time for the Pilots' Pool at Setques. I've got this from the C.O. He's going to give us a lorry to take us down."

We pestered Hepworth for particulars but he knew nothing beyond the bare fact. Just after lunch our popular Wing-Commander, Colonel Napier, walked into the mess and dropped a bombshell among us. There was every likelihood, he declared, of the war breaking out again, and of Holland coming in on the side of Germany. " I've flown down straight from Brigade," he said, " and when I left, Brigade was spinning ! "

We had clustered round the Wing C.O. while he was telling this exciting news, but now Hepworth drew Fraser and me to one side.

" If we have to leave before this comes off," he said, " we may not get back to M Squadron." There and then the three of us sat down and wrote formal letters requesting that we be allowed to remain in M Squadron as we understood there was a possibility of hostilities breaking out again. These letters we handed to Colonel Napier who took them gravely from us and dropped them into his pocket. Then he grinned. "I shall keep these as mementoes of my best lie. The drinks are on me."

At last the day arrived when the Colonials got their marching orders. There were nine of us in the Squadron. We were to start the following day, after lunch, by lorry, and travel by easy stages to Setques, near St. Omer.

Of the pilots among the nine of us, everyone decided that on the following morning he would go up and put his Bristol through every conceivable stunt, for the last time. Hepworth suggested that we should start off with a race from the aerodrome to the Mound at Waterloo, and back again. This suggestion was adopted with enthusiasm and each of us at once went along to his two Ack Emmas and told them to strip his Bristol of every gadget that was not absolutely necessary, and which by offering resistance to the air might lower his speed.

We celebrated in princely fashion, that night, our last with the Squadron. The early hours of the morning had arrived before we crawled, or were carried, to bed.

The race was to commence at nine-thirty ack emma. One or two of the observers had been hesitant about the race, so it was decided to call for volunteers. My batman was a nervous youngster who stammered badly. He had told me once that before the war he had been a stable-boy on Lord ——'s estate. As far as I knew he had never been up in a machine so I asked him that morning, when he called me, if he would care to come with me. Jenkins' face flushed with pleasure and he stuttered out, "I sh-sh-should just l-l-l-love to, sir."

"All right then, Jenkins. Nine-thirty. I'm going to stunt a bit. Do you mind?"

APRÈS LA GUERRE 305

" N-n-n-no, sir. I'd l-l-l-l——"

" You'd like it ? "

" Y-y-y-yes, sir."

At a quarter-past nine the five pilots with their voluntary observers assembled on the aerodrome. A breeze was blowing in over the hangars so after running up our engines we taxied out half-way across the aerodrome and turned, facing the hangars and the line of trees behind them. When the five Bristols were in line, fat old Griffith, standing to one side of them, fired a Very pistol and the five throttles were opened and the Bristols roared over the ground towards the hangars. After leaving the ground we had to clear not only the hangars, but the tall trees behind them. Directly in front of me were three or four particularly high ones and I could not swerve to one side of them because of the Bristols on either side of me. For a fleeting instant I glimpsed, through the wrong end of the telescope of Time, a tiny, clear-cut picture of a wooded hill in Canada and a tiny Buffalo-Curtiss straining to get over it.

Our undercarriage flicked the topmost leaves, and the danger was past.

Then we made a bee-line for the Mound. When we left the trees all of the Bristols were ahead of me but I was higher than they were, and by pushing forward the stick was able to dive past all of them excepting Hepworth's machine with the Rising Sun of Australia painted on its side.

We had to fly round the Mound and as we neared it we zoomed up in climbing-turns round it, then back towards the hangars again, and Hepworth's Bristol led the field by a short head all the way back, sweeping over the hangars an instant before mine. After this we separated, and for over an hour, five Bristols could be seen looping, rolling, stalling and spinning, over the aerodrome and town.

I glanced round once or twice to see how Jenkins was

taking it, and each time he grinned back cheerfully. Then we set off on a long contour-chase, over hill and dale, switchbacking over hedges, trees and houses, and landing eventually at midday, for the last time, on the aerodrome at Nivelles.

Jenkins was beaming when he climbed out.

"Oh, sir, th-th-thank you ever so m-m-m-much. It was *g-g-g-gorgeous!*"

Valises had to be rolled up then, and odds and ends pushed into great-coat pockets and haversacks. Ian Fraser and I gave small presents to our landlord and his wife, and we also handed him a tin of South African tobacco, which pleased him hugely. Then we had to rush off to lunch. The C.O. made a short farewell speech, and Hepworth replied. Home addresses were being exchanged across the tables, and everyone was drinking everyone else's health when the lorry drew up outside the mess.

"Colonials, fall in!" shouted the Adjutant attempting to rise, and being pulled back sharply into his seat by Fraser.

"Time for a last drink!" yelled the latter.

"Cheerio, Daddy! Drop us a line now and then—good-bye, old fellow, good luck—good-bye, Major, till the next war!"

Farewells were being exchanged all over the mess. I caught a glimpse of Griffith, wringing our Flight Commander's hand. "Goo'-bye, 'Eppy, goo'-bye, ol' boy! I'm *damn* sorry you're going," then he trumpeted loudly into a large silk handkerchief.

We climbed aboard the lorry, the driver let in his clutch, and we moved off down the street.

Looking back, I saw a crowd of the best fellows in the world waving after us. Prominent among them was the fat figure of our P.M.C., napkin tucked under his chin, waving a large silk handkerchief.

A FOKKER-BIPLANE AT NIVELLES.

APPENDIX

EXTRACTS FROM THE R.A.F. COMMUNIQUÉS

"*May 15th.* The weather was fine all day."

There was a great deal of activity in the air on this day and many engagements took place. Among others:

"Lts. J. S. C—— and E. C. G——, No. 11 Squadron, dived on one E.A. and opened fire at 100 yards' range. A burst of flame was seen in the E.A. observer's cockpit, followed by clouds of smoke. Immediately afterwards Very lights of many colours were seen to explode and the E.A. went down in flames."

"Major A. D. C——, No. 19 Squadron, got on the tail of an E.A. triplane which was attacking another Dolphin; he fired a long burst into the E.A., which dived. Pieces of material were seen flying from the E.A. and the right-hand plane then fell off and the E.A. went spinning to the ground."

"A patrol of No. 201 Squadron engaged a formation of E.A. scouts which were attacking a patrol of Bristol fighters. All the pilots of No. 201 Squadron's patrol remarked on the fine performance put up by the Bristol fighters (No. 11 Squadron) against at least thirty enemy machines which were in the vicinity at the time."

On *May 16th.* "Lt. E. B. C——, No. 87 Squadron, dived on one E.A. which was attacking another of our machines, and fired a burst of about twenty rounds into it. The E.A. pilot was seen to fall forward and the machine went down in a nose-dive and crashed into the sea."

On *May 17th*. " Enemy aircraft were by no means so active as on the previous days, but several large formations were encountered well east of the lines."

" Captain E. Mannock, No. 74 Squadron, attacked the rear machine of a formation of E.A. scouts and fired a long burst from both guns into it, and the E.A. spun down out of control. Captain Mannock was then attacked by another E.A. and forced to spin away, but No. 210 Squadron confirm the first E.A. attacked by Captain Mannock as having crashed in flames. Later in the day Captain Mannock observed an E.A. two-seater crossing the lines near Ypres. He climbed north and then east and approached the E.A. at which he fired approximately 200 rounds at close range during a fight which lasted about one minute, the E.A. going down alternately diving and spinning. At about 4,000 feet the E.A. burst into flames and was seen to crash and to burn itself out on the ground."

" Captain H. P. S——, No. 84 Squadron, while escorting back a formation of D.H.4's (bombing machines) observed several E.A. scouts about to attack. He dived on the nearest E.A. and fired 400 rounds, chasing it down to 6,000 feet. He followed it down and saw it crash near Rosières. He then zoomed up and started back to our lines alone. While returning, he suddenly felt a blow in the right ankle and found that he was wounded by a bullet from an E.A. triplane which was attacking from behind ; almost at the same moment his petrol tank was hit and his engine stopped. He at once dived for our lines, kicking his rudder as he went, eventually crossing the enemy's trenches at Villers Brettoneaux at a height of 100 feet and crashing in ' No-man's-land.' While extricating himself from his machine he was hit in the left ankle, and his left arm was broken badly by a machine-gun bullet. He, however, managed to roll over into a slight depression in the ground and was finally pulled into a sap-head by some Australians, one of whom was badly wounded while attempting to rescue Captain S——."

" Lt. W. J. A. D——, No. 60 Squadron, observed fifteen E.A. scouts attacking an R.E.8. He attacked the E.A. and fired at one which was diving vertically and a wing of the E.A. came off as it disappeared through the clouds. Lt. D—— then fired at several machines of the E.A. formation which had followed the R.E.8 down, and was eventually forced to break off the combat as the whole enemy formation started to attack. The R.E.8 got back safely to our lines."

On *May* 18*th*. " The weather was fine—Enemy aircraft activity was slight on the front, but several large formations were met well east of the lines."

" Major R. S. Dallas,* No. 40 Squadron, observed an E.A. getting height over its own lines. Major Dallas was unable to get to the E.A.'s height, so he followed under its tail for an hour. A Camel passed below the E.A., which it is thought the E.A. mistook for Major Dallas breaking off the combat, and the E.A. then started to lose height over Lille. Major Dallas then fired a drum of Lewis into the E.A. which went down emitting volumes of smoke and flame."

" Lt. J. I. T. Jones,* No. 74 Squadron, attacked one E.A. two-seater, which was being engaged by A.A. fire. He got into position under the E.A.'s tail and fired 250 rounds into it, causing an explosion, and the E.A. burst into flames and was seen to crash. Shortly afterwards Lt. Jones observed another E.A. which was being engaged by our A.A. fire. He attacked this E.A. from under its tail, but was fired at by the enemy observer, who was firing through a hole in the fuselage. Lt. Jones then attacked the E.A. from directly underneath, and fired up. The

E.A. banked steeply, and after a few rounds had been fired into it, the observer was seen to fall overboard. Lt. Jones was then forced to break off the combat owing to lack of ammunition and gun-jam."

"Lt. P——, No. 42 Squadron, carried out a good shoot on the evening of the 17th instant, with the 44th Siege Battery on a bridge. Two explosions were caused in the south end of the bridge and the position generally damaged. Lt. F——, No. 42 Squadron, registered the same battery on to the same bridge on the morning of the 18th. As a result, both north and south ends of the bridge and the railway in proximity were badly torn up, and a fire broke out, which was probably caused in an ammunition dump as large flames arose at intervals."

On *May* 19*th*. "Captain H. G. W——, No. 29 Squadron, dived on a Pfalz scout. After firing fifty rounds he zoomed up and collided with the E.A. which rolled over and went down vertically, followed by Captain W——, who, after firing another 100 rounds into it, saw the wings fall off in the air. Captain W——'s engine stopped and he crashed on attempting to land as his machine was more or less out of control."

May 21*st*. "A patrol of No. 74 Squadron encountered six Pfalz scouts, upon whom they dived, shooting down five of them—of which Major K. L. C—— destroyed one, Captain E. Mannock three, and Captain W. E. Y—— one. Captain Mannock also destroyed another E.A. earlier in the day."

June 5*th*. "Lt. E. C. B—— and Second Lt. C. G. G——, while leading a patrol of No. 22 Squadron, sighted a Halberstadt two-seater, which on their approach fired a green light. Lt. B——, suspecting a trap, waited, and in a short time some Albatros scouts appeared and joined

APPENDIX

the Halberstadt. Almost at once, six Albatros scouts dived out of the sun on to the others, apparently mistaking them for one of our patrols. Lt. B—— then led the patrol into the mêlée and shot down the Halberstadt. Lt. S. F. H. T—— and Sergeant R. M. F—— shot down two of the Albatros scouts while the E.A. continued to fight among themselves, several of them being seen to go down out of control. Lt. B——'s good leadership thus led the Huns into their own trap."

June 9th. "Lts. R. C. A—— and F. J. H——, 3rd Squadron, A.F.C., on returning from the line had their attention attracted by anti-aircraft bursts to an E.A. two-seater which was making for the line. Lt. A—— cut the E.A. off and by skilful manœuvring forced it to land intact on his own aerodrome."

"The following information was obtained from a German prisoner:— 'On May 28th a British single-seater was forced to land near Morcourt. The Germans who took him prisoner questioned him, but he refused to answer. Thereupon they threatened to shoot him; but as he still refused to reply to their questions he was taken to the rear. Subsequently the Battalion Commander told the men to imitate his example, if captured.'"

June 13th. "Lt. H. A. G——, No. 60 Squadron, in company with Lt. R. G. L—— and Captain J. D. B——, dived on an E.A. two-seater which went down out of control, closely followed by Captain B—— into the mist. Lt. G—— then followed Lt. L——, who was losing height, and landed beside him between Ablaincourt and Chaulnes, Lt. L—— smashing his undercarriage. Some soldiers soon appeared, who opened fire on them. Lt. G—— ran to his machine, calling to Lt. L—— to get in with him, but the latter, apparently mistaking the soldiers for friends, walked towards them. As they were still firing, Lt. G——

took off and then circled back over the body of men, intending to fire on them, but seeing Lt. L—— in their midst, refrained from doing so, as he was afraid of hitting him. Lt. G——then returned home, having had one wire of his rudder-control shot through and a longeron practically shot away."

June 19th. " Major W. A. Bishop, No. 85 Squadron, while flying alone attacked three Pfalz scouts which were immediately joined by two others. After firing a short burst into one of them it went down vertically and crashed near Ploegsteert. Two of the other E.A., while circling round, collided and fell together. Major Bishop then attacked one of the remaining two E.A. which had started to dive east and shot it down. The last escaped in the clouds. Ten minutes later Major Bishop attacked an enemy two-seater and shot it down in flames."

June 30th. " Major A. W. K——, No. 40 Squadron, dived on one of three Fokker triplanes, which turned very sharply to the left in an attempt to get on the S.E.'s tail. Major K—— looped, coming out 100 feet above the E.A., and fired a burst of ten rounds before he overshot it. The E.A. went into a flat spin and, after several bursts had been fired at it, broke up in the air, both its wings being seen to fall off."

July 2nd. " Captain P. J. C——, No. 1 Squadron, attacked a Hanoveraner over Armentières. On opening fire the E.A. machine suddenly went into a steep dive, the observer's map fell overboard quickly followed by the observer himself, who caught hold of the gun-mounting and lay along the top of the fuselage. The machine caught fire and finally crashed."

July 5th. " In the middle of a low reconnaissance, Lts. D—— and S——, No. 53 Squadron, had their petrol tank pierced by machine-gun fire from the ground. Lt. S—— (observer) climbed out on to the wing of the machine to investigate the extent of the damage. He then climbed back into his seat, removed his cloche, stepped out on to the wing again and blocked the rent with his stick and leather cap. The reconnaissance was then completed and messages dropped at Divisional Headquarters on the return journey."

" Whilst on night reconnaissance, Lts. A. J. E. B—— and G. B. N——, No. 102 Squadron, observed two trains moving west near Hermies. A flare was dropped from a height of 800 feet which showed that the one train was loaded with carts or artillery and that the other was a goods train with about fifty trucks. Four bombs were dropped on the first train, one of which was an O.K., another bomb hitting the line immediately in front of the engine. They then dived on the second train and dropped four twenty-five pound bombs from 500 feet. The truck next the engine was knocked off the line and also one in the centre of the train."

July 13th. " The following is an extract from Intelligence Summary of the 1st Australian Division, dated 12th instant : ' Several prisoners stated they were unable to offer any resistance owing to one of our aeroplanes, which by machine-gun fire forced them to keep their heads down in their shell-hole position.' "

July 25th " Captain J. S. R——, No. 84 Squadron, attacked and set on fire a hostile balloon near Warvillers. He was heavily fired at from the ground and was hit in the buttock. At 2,000 feet, near Villers Brettoneaux, Captain R—— fainted and came to at 900 feet over Warfusee-Abancourt, still flying east and being shot at. He then turned west, and, his vision becoming blurred a second time, landed on our side of the lines and crashed, having fainted just as he was flattening out."

August 2nd. " Two machines of No. 151 Squadron carried out offensive patrols over Estrees and Guizancourt aerodromes during the night. Major C. J. Q. B—— was the first to arrive over Guizancourt where he dropped two bombs on hangars. He then fired into a large two-seater machine which was landing and observed his bullets ricochet from cockpit and engine. Seeing white lights being placed round the machine on the ground he fired 100 more rounds into it, and all lights were put out. A little later he dropped two more bombs in the path of another machine which was landing. After having fired at hangars and searchlights, he attacked another E.A. but was himself attacked from behind by an enemy scout. He then returned home, having been over the aerodromes for forty minutes.

"Captain S. C—— dropped four bombs on the hangars at Guizancourt which were lit up by searchlights, and then attacked each searchlight in turn till they were extinguished. A little later he attacked a Gotha which was preparing to land, all lights being extinguished at once. The Gotha landed or crashed about two miles from the aerodrome."

August 6th. " Captain J. I. T. Jones, No. 74 Squadron, observed a formation of nine E.A. climbing from their aerodrome and, closing up behind the rear machine, joined the enemy formation with whom he remained for five minutes without being observed. Soon after, two of the enemy machines left the formation to attack an R.E.8. Captain Jones dived at one of these, firing a short burst, whereupon one E.A. side-slipped into the other and they became interlocked. After a long burst had been fired at them, Captain Jones saw them go down together in flames." (On August 25th, the D.S.O. was awarded to Captain J. I. T. Jones, M.C., D.F.C., M.M.)

August 8th. " Lt. N. W. R. M——, No. 84 Squadron, attacked two enemy balloons which were being towed by a team of horses. Having fired at the first without result, in spite of heavy machine-gun fire he successfully attacked the second, which was at a height of twenty-five feet, and set it on fire. Having again attacked the first one unsuccessfully, he turned his attention to an anti-tank gun, which was hastily limbered up, but the horses scattered and the gun was observed to upset into a ditch. After having attacked various parties of infantry on the ground, Lt. M—— returned to his aerodrome, having been wounded in the stomach and the arm by fire from the ground."

August 9th. The popular corruption of "Communiqués" to "Comic Cuts" was not without its justification, as the following extract will show :

" Lt. M——, No. 201 Squadron, while firing at enemy infantry, was shot down by four Fokker biplanes 300 yards behind the enemy's lines. He made a dash for one of our tanks and got into it, but on learning that it was about to go into action got out again and escaped to our lines under heavy machine-gun fire."

August 12th. " Captain W—— and Lt. H——, No. 8 Squadron, were attacked by seven E.A. who fired explosive bullets, hitting Captain W——five times in the left leg, which was almost severed and fell among the controls. He lifted his leg out of the controls and landed his machine close behind our lines, fainting shortly afterwards. Lt. H—— was wounded in the ankle."

August 13th. " A raid was carried out by No. 17 American Squadron on Varssenaere Aerodrome, in conjunction with squadrons of the 5th Group. After the first two squadrons had dropped their bombs from a low height, machines of No. 17 American Squadron dived to within 200 feet of the ground and released their bombs, then proceeded to shoot at hangars and huts on the aerodrome, and a château on the N.E. corner of the aerodrome was also attacked with machine-gun fire. The following damage was observed to be caused by this combined operation : A dump of petrol and oil was set on fire, which appeared to set fire to an ammunition dump ; six Fokker biplanes were set on fire on the ground, and two destroyed by direct hits from bombs ; one large Gotha hangar was set on fire and another one half-demolished ; a living hut was set on fire and several hangars were seen to be smouldering as the result of phosphorous bombs having fallen on them. In spite of most of the machines taking part being hit at one time or another, all returned safely, favourable ground targets being attacked on the way home. No. 211 Squadron bombed the aerodrome after the low-flying attack was over, and demolished the château previously referred to."

August 15th. " An E.A. two-seater approached by a patrol of No. 56 Squadron started to dive, eventually going straight into the ground and crashing without any shots having been fired into it. "

August 21st. " A patrol of No. 62 Squadron while on escort duty engaged a large number of hostile scouts. Captain E. T. M—— and Second Lt. L. M. T—— attacked one machine, which went down emitting smoke. Captain M—— then fired at a second, which collapsed in the air ; he was then hit in the leg and the petrol tank was pierced, the fuselage of the machine catching fire. Second Lt. T— kept the fire under control with the Pyrene extinguisher until the machine landed, when it blazed up. He, however, managed to lift Captain M—— clear."

August 23rd. " Lt. A. R. S—— and Sergeant F. W. B——, No. 49 Squadron, became separated from their formation by clouds, and after flying west for some time came down. Seeing an aerodrome which they believed to be one of ours they prepared to land, when they were attacked by a Fokker biplane. Lieut. S—— then noticed about thirty Fokker biplanes below him, and dived into the centre of the formation firing continuously. One of the hostile machines went down in flames and two went down in spins, one of which was seen to crash. Four Fokkers then got on their tail, one of which Sergeant B—— shot down in flames and another, which attacked from the side, was also shot down in flames by the observer. The three enemy machines were seen burning on the ground as the D.H.9 started for the lines, climbing, followed by three of the E.A. which, however, did not attack. On the way home they were again attacked by an E.A. two-seater which turned away on being fired at."

" Lt. M—— and Corporal H——, No. 39 Balloon Section, were engaged by two guns and their balloon badly holed. They, however, remained in the basket and observed for a six-inch gun on one of the hostile guns, although their balloon was fast losing height. The balloon dropped the last few hundred feet from the ground, both observers climbing into the rigging to avoid the shock on landing."

August 26th. " Lt. W. H——, No. 3 Squadron, after a combat with two enemy two-seaters—the second of which went down spinning after its observer had been killed— had engine failure and was compelled to spin down to avoid another E.A. As his machine touched the ground he was fired at by a German from about fifteen yards, with a revolver, which burst his petrol tank. At this moment his engine picked up sufficiently to carry him just behind our lines. Although under fire, Lt. H—— removed the locks of his gun, Aldis sight, and all his instruments before leaving his machine, which was obviously unsalvable."

" A hostile kite balloon, which was guarded by eight enemy scouts, was attacked and shot down in flames by

Captain A. W. Beauchamp-Proctor, No. 84 Squadron. His patrol were chased back to the lines by the E.A. As soon as another balloon appeared on the front he lured the enemy machines away and then dived into a cloud and steered by compass to the balloon, coming out just over it. This balloon he also shot down in flames. His engine was hit by A.A. fire, the lines being crossed at 500 feet."

September 1st. "Captain W—— and Lt. P——, No. 59 Squadron, had their starboard top and bottom planes broken by A.A. fire. Lt. P—— balanced the machine by leaning over the fuselage with the Lewis gun in his hands and enabling the pilot to land the machine, in spite of all the controls except the elevator being useless."

September 2nd. "Lts. I—— and C——, No. 59 Squadron, while on counter-attack patrol, saw 65 of the enemy in a trench and a sunken road, who fired at them. Lt. I—— dived and fired back, killing one and wounding three of the party, whereupon they waved a white flag. The machine then decended to fifty feet and ordered the enemy to go to our lines, where they were seen to be taken over by our troops."

September 5th. "Major A. C——, No. 92 Squadron, attacked the leader of a patrol of Fokker biplanes which, after zooming vertically, stopped on its back long enough to dislodge its pilot, who hung by one arm for a few seconds, and then fell, hitting the ground near Cambrai."

September 7th. "Lt. G. W. W——, No. 29 Squadron, attacked a hostile balloon which went down in flames. He then saw about fifteen people rush out from what looked like the officers' mess, one of whom started firing at him with a rifle. Lt. W—— turned his machine-gun on him and he collapsed on the ground. Meanwhile, Captain L—— silenced two machine-guns near the balloon."

APPENDIX

September 18th. "Major C. J. Q. B—— saw one E.A. held in our searchlights, which he attacked at close range. This machine started to fall in flames when one of its bombs exploded and blew it to pieces."

September 27th. "Lt. R. E. B—— and Second Lt. B. H——, No. 13 Squadron, were attacked by eight Fokker biplanes. Second Lt. H—— was wounded early in the fight but succeeded in shooting one E.A. down out of control. Lt. B—— was then also wounded, and in trying to avoid the E.A. spun to the ground and landed in the German lines. The Fokkers then withdrew and Lt. B—— took off again, returning safely to his aerodrome where he crashed owing to faintness."

October 4th. "Second Lt. W. H. B——, No. 65 Squadron, in an engagement with several Fokker biplanes, dived to within 100 feet of the ground after one of them, firing continuously, when he saw it crash a complete wreck. He was now so close to the ground that enemy infantry threw stones at him."

"Lt. A. F. C—— and Second Lt. G. B. N——, No. 102 Squadron, attacked a moving train during the night between Bertry and Caudry. After dropping a flare from 1,500 feet they descended to 700 feet and dropped three 112-pound bombs, making two direct hits. A second flare revealed the train to be a complete wreck, but before leaving they fired 100 rounds and four Very lights into it."

October 7th. "Annappes and Lille Stations were attacked from a height of 200 feet by 2nd Squadron, A.F.C., who dropped seventy-one twenty-five pound bombs. Several trains were hit, one of which was full of troops, who rushed out and were then attacked with machine-gun fire, many casualties being caused. In the course of their flight some of them took shelter in a house, which was bombed and destroyed."

October 8th. "Low-flying scouts of the 3rd Brigade consistently bombed and shot up enemy transport and troops throughout the day to a depth of twelve miles beyond the line, causing considerable confusion and greatly hampering the enemy's movement both in bringing up local reinforcements and in the general trend of guns and transport eastwards."

October 29th. "Lts. L—— and S——, No. 29 Squadron, after a fight, were compelled to land east of the Scheldt in the enemy's lines, the latter being seriously wounded and pinned under his machine. Lt. L——, having succeeded in extricating him, and finding that he was unconscious, carried him across the swamps to the river-bank, where he met a British officer. They succeeded between them in swimming the river, both supporting Lt. S——, whom they carried safely under cover, in spite of being under machine-gun fire during the crossing."

www.ingramcontent.com/pod-product-compliance
Lightning Source LLC
Chambersburg PA
CBHW070959160426
43193CB00012B/1840